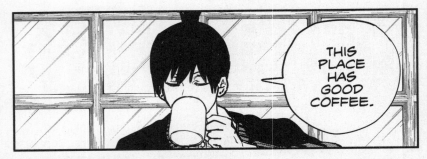

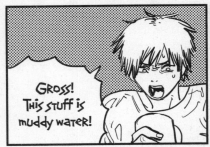

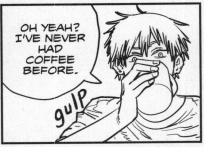

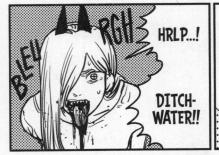

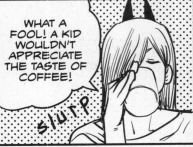

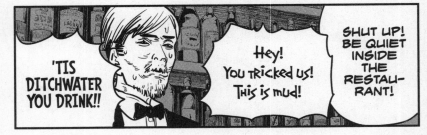

# YOU'RE READING THE WRONG WAY!

# CHAINSAW MAN

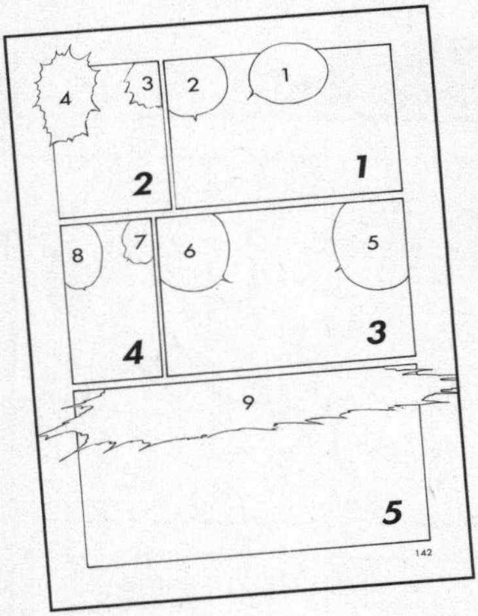
1
2
3
4
1
2
5
6
7
8
3
4
9
5
142

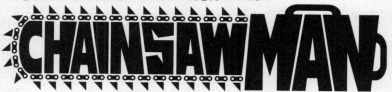

*Chainsaw Man* reads from right to left, starting in the upper-right corner. Japanese is read from right to left, meaning that action, sound effects and word-balloon order are completely reversed from English order.

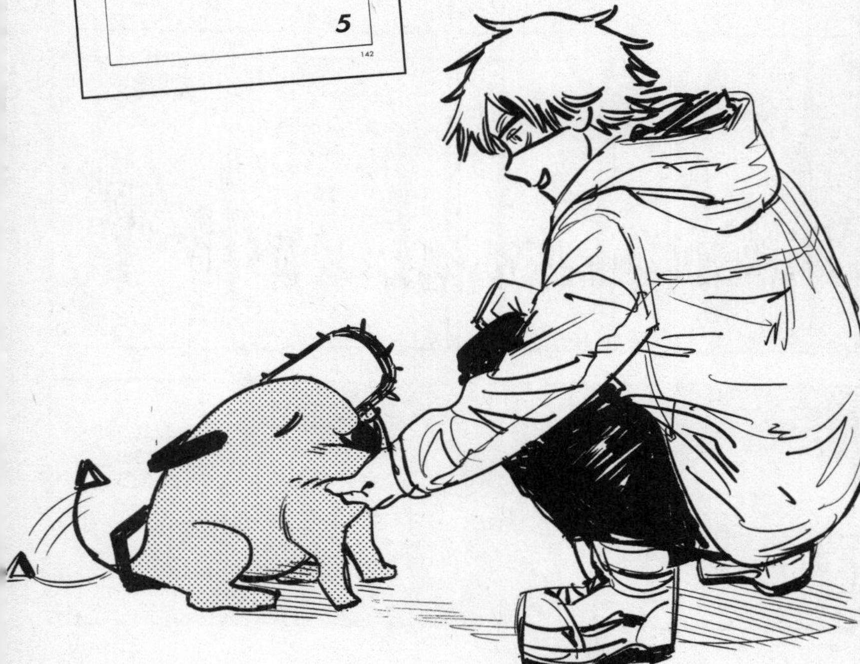

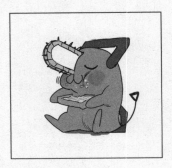

# Tatsuki Fujimoto

*I love The Texas
Chainsaw Massacre!*

Tatsuki Fujimoto won Honorable Mention in the
November 2013 Shueisha Crown Newcomers' Awards for
his debut one-shot story *Love Is Blind*. His first series,
*Fire Punch*, ran for eight volumes. *Chainsaw Man* began
serialization in 2019 in *Weekly Shonen Jump*.

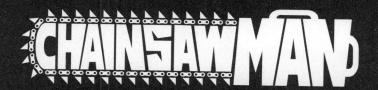

# 2

## SHONEN JUMP Manga Edition

### Story & Art TATSUKI FUJIMOTO

Translation/AMANDA HALEY
Touch-Up Art & Lettering/SABRINA HEEP
Design/JULIAN [JR] ROBINSON
Editor/ALEXIS KIRSCH

CHAINSAW MAN © 2018 by Tatsuki Fujimoto
All rights reserved.
First published in Japan in 2018 by SHUEISHA Inc., Tokyo.
English translation rights arranged by SHUEISHA Inc.

The stories, characters and incidents mentioned in this publication are
entirely fictional.

Printed in the U.S.A.

Published by VIZ Media, LLC
P.O. Box 77010
San Francisco, CA 94107

10 9 8 7 6 5
First printing, December 2020
Fifth printing, June 2021

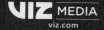

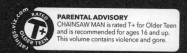

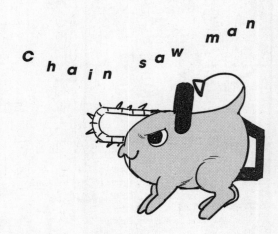

Chain saw man

# Denji & Pochita's Staple Dish

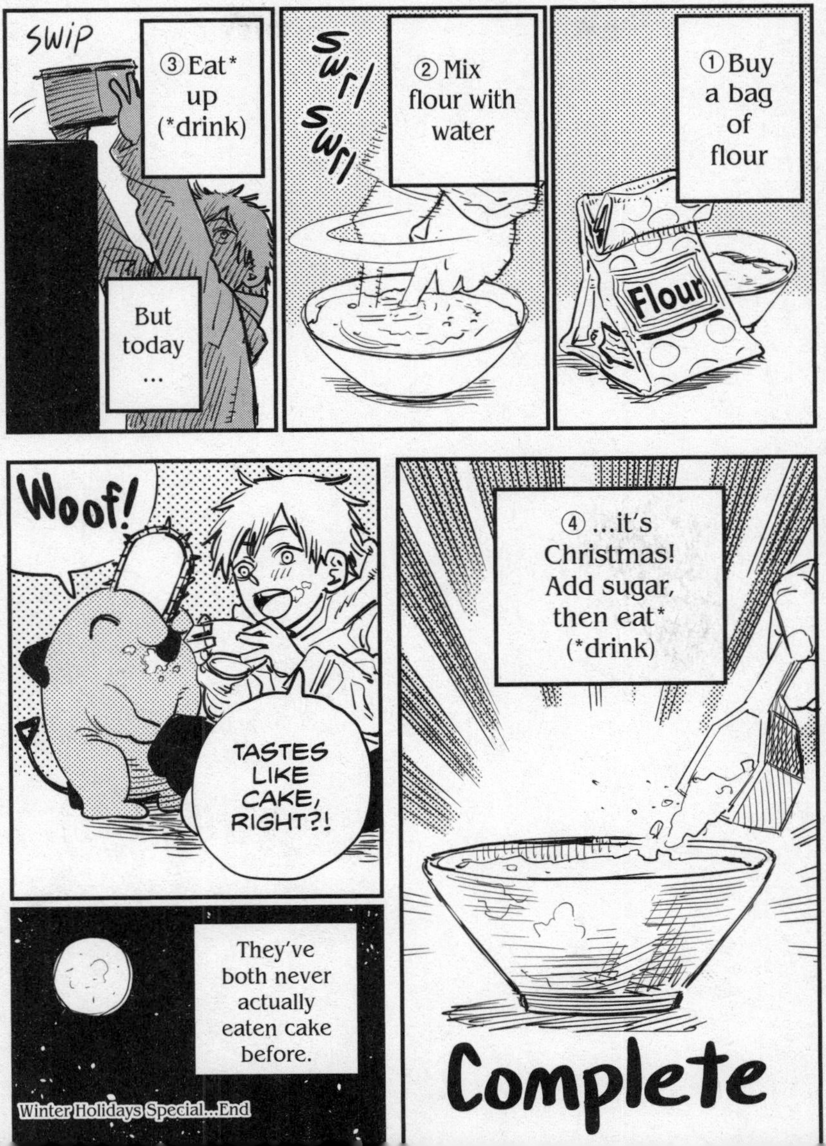
①Buy a bag of flour
②Mix flour with water
SWIP
③Eat* up (*drink)
But today ...
④ ...it's Christmas! Add sugar, then eat* (*drink)
Complete
Woof!
TASTES LIKE CAKE, RIGHT?!
They've both never actually eaten cake before.
Winter Holidays Special...End

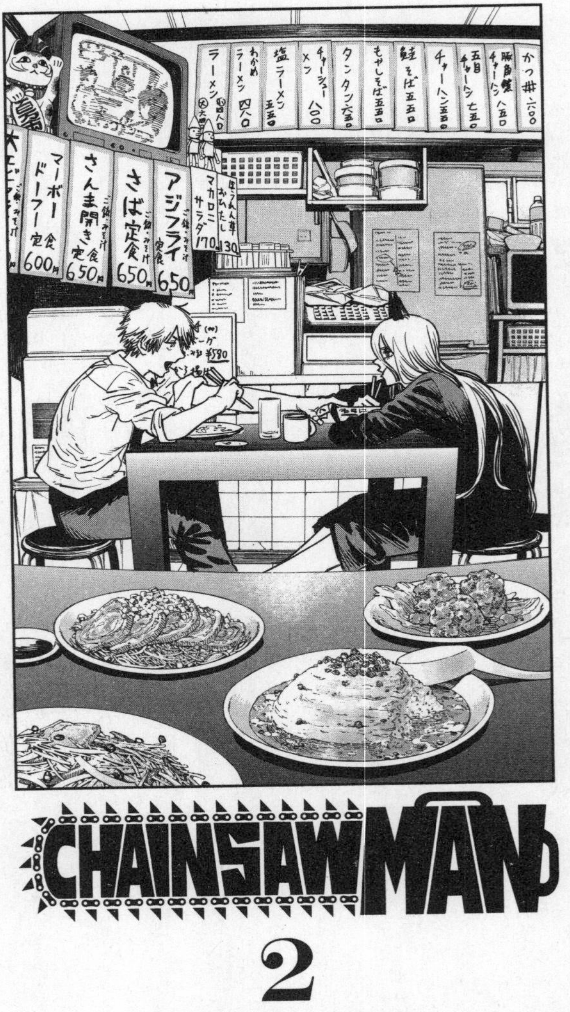
かつ丼 六〇〇
チャーハン 五五〇
鮭そば 五五〇
もやしそば 五五〇
塩ラーメン 五五〇
わかめラーメン 四八〇
アジフライ定食 650
さば定食 650
さんま開き定食 650
マーボードーフー定食 600
マカロニサラダ 170

# CHAINSAW MAN

## 2

### CHAINSAW vs. BAT

Tatsuki Fujimoto

# CHARACTERS

## Denji

A young man-slash-Chainsaw Devil who carries his partner Pochita inside him. He's always true to his desires. Likes Makima, the first person to ever treat him like a human being.

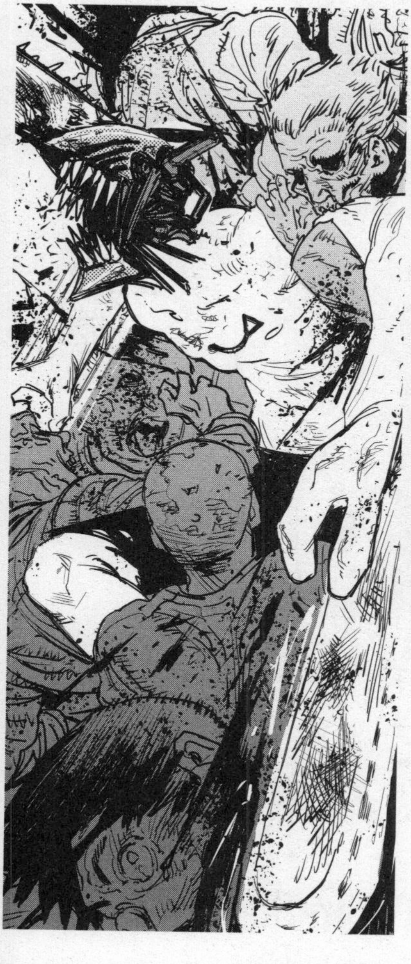

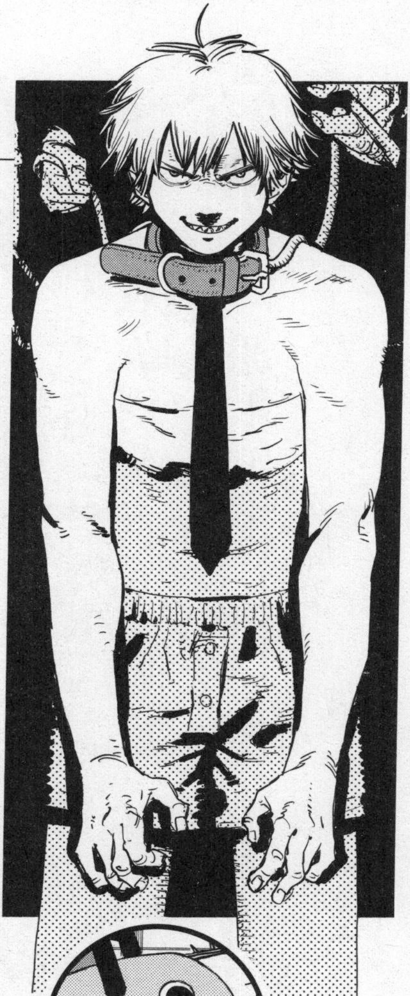

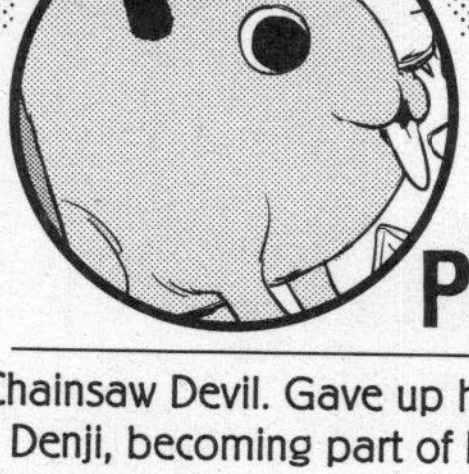

## Pochita

Chainsaw Devil. Gave up his heart to Denji, becoming part of his body.

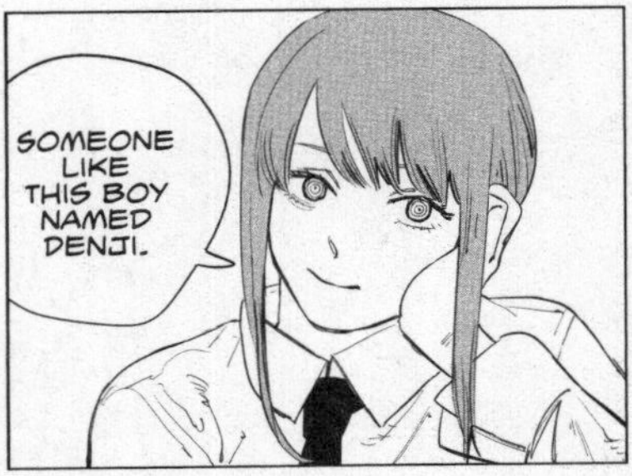
SOMEONE LIKE THIS BOY NAMED DENJI.

## Makima

The mysterious woman in charge of Public Safety Devil Extermination Special Division 4. Can smell Devil scents.

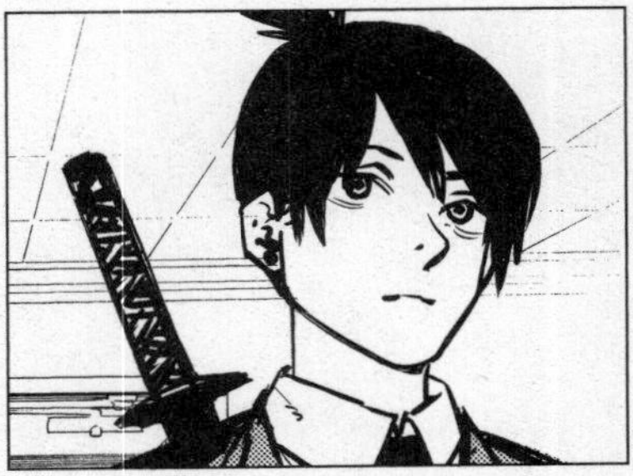

## Aki Hayakawa

Makima's loyal subordinate. Denji's senior at Public Safety by three years, he's assigned to keep an eye on him.

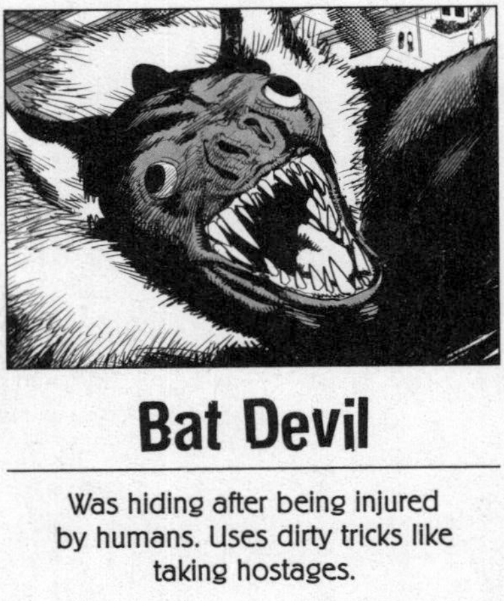

## Bat Devil

Was hiding after being injured by humans. Uses dirty tricks like taking hostages.

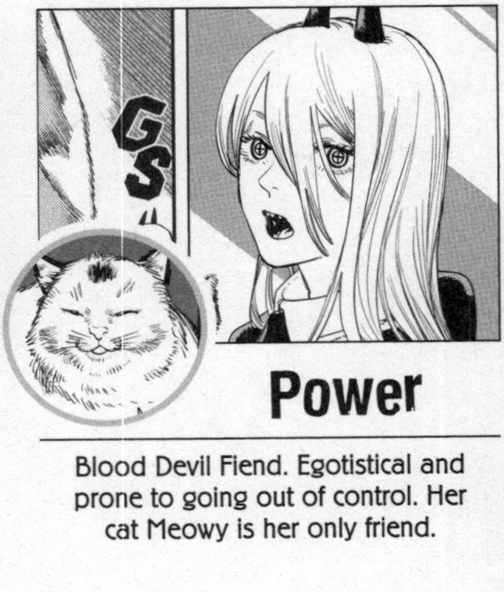
GS

## Power

Blood Devil Fiend. Egotistical and prone to going out of control. Her cat Meowy is her only friend.

# STORY

Denji is a young man who hunts Devils with his pet Devil-dog Pochita. To pay off his debts, Denji is forced to live in extreme poverty and worked like a dog, only to be betrayed and killed on the job without ever getting to live a decent life. But Pochita, at the cost of the pooch's own life, brings Denji back—as Chainsaw Man! After Denji buzzes through all their attackers, he's taken in by the mysterious Makima, and begins a new life as a Public Safety Devil Hunter.

At Public Safety HQ, Denji is assigned to the squad of Makima's subordinate Hayakawa, but they clash from day one. While Hayakawa has a strong conviction to kill Devils, Denji, who never had anything but simple dreams, has only just discovered a new life goal—to touch some boobs. As Denji deliberates how to achieve his dream, he's paired up with a buddy—the Blood Devil Fiend Power. Denji is none too happy to be jerked around by this arrogant new partner. When Power offers to let him touch her chest if he saves her pet cat Meowy from another Devil, though, he jumps right on board! The duo heads straight for the spot where the Bat Devil awaits, but it's a trap, and Power was in on it. Once the Bat Devil regenerates by drinking Denji's blood, he eats not only Meowy, but Power too. Relating to Power's sadness over losing her precious pet, Denji faces off against the Bat Devil!

# CONTENTS

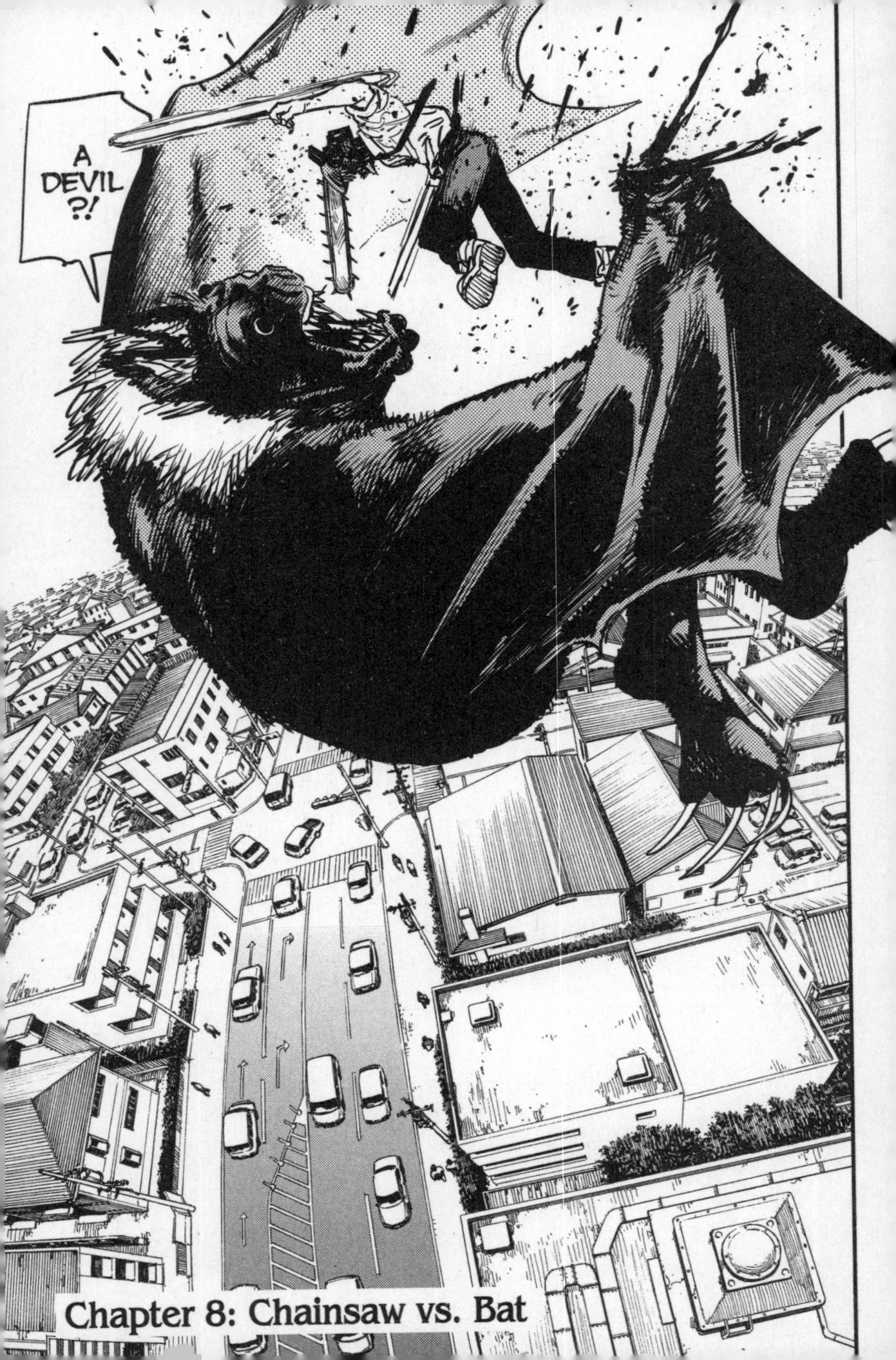
A DEVIL ?!
Chapter 8: Chainsaw vs. Bat

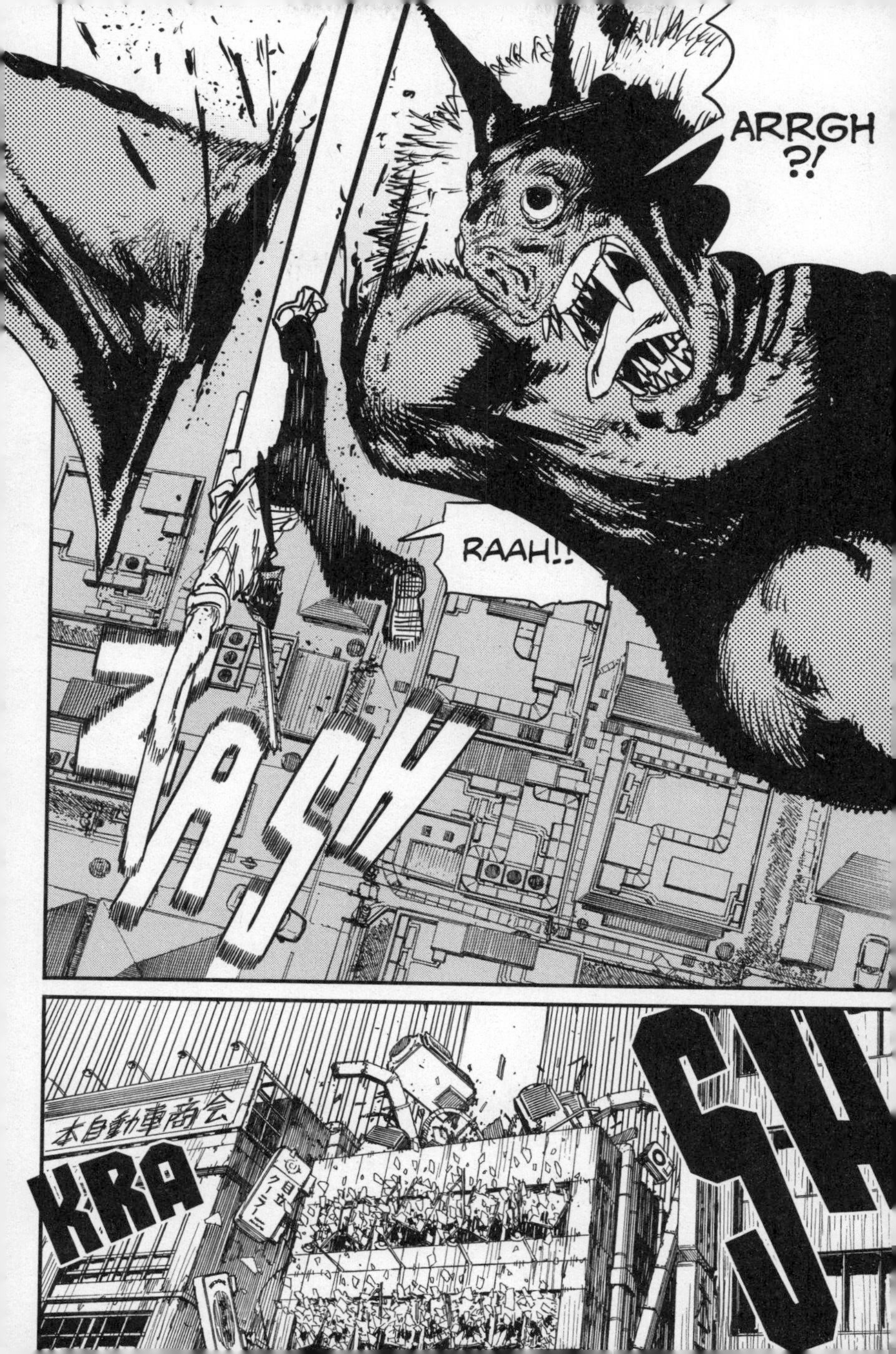
ARRGH ?!
RAAH!!
ZASH
本自動車商会
KRA
SH

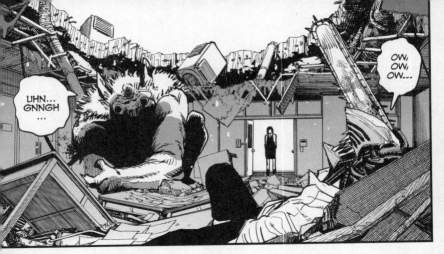

OW, OW, OW....

UHN... GNNGH...

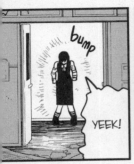

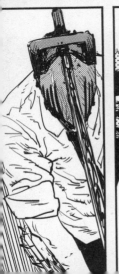

bump

YEEK!

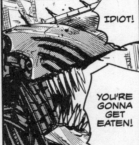

IDIOT!

YOU'RE GONNA GET EATEN!

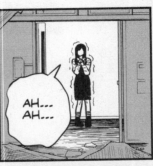

AH... AH...

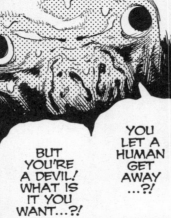

BUT YOU'RE A DEVIL! WHAT IS IT YOU WANT...?!

YOU LET A HUMAN GET AWAY ...?!

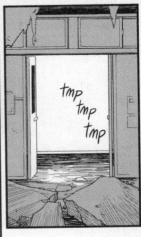

tmp tmp tmp

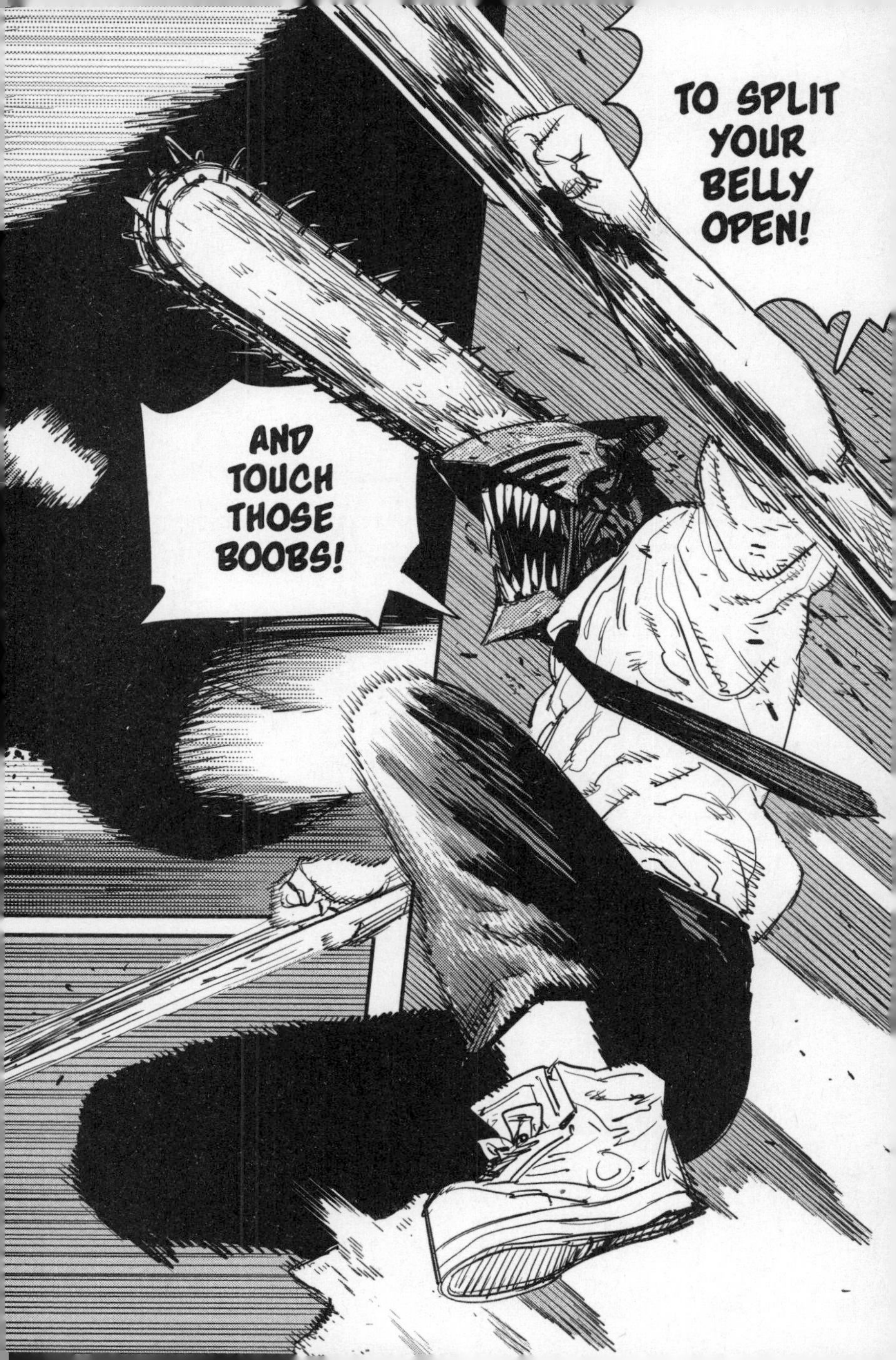
TO SPLIT YOUR BELLY OPEN!
AND TOUCH THOSE BOOBS!

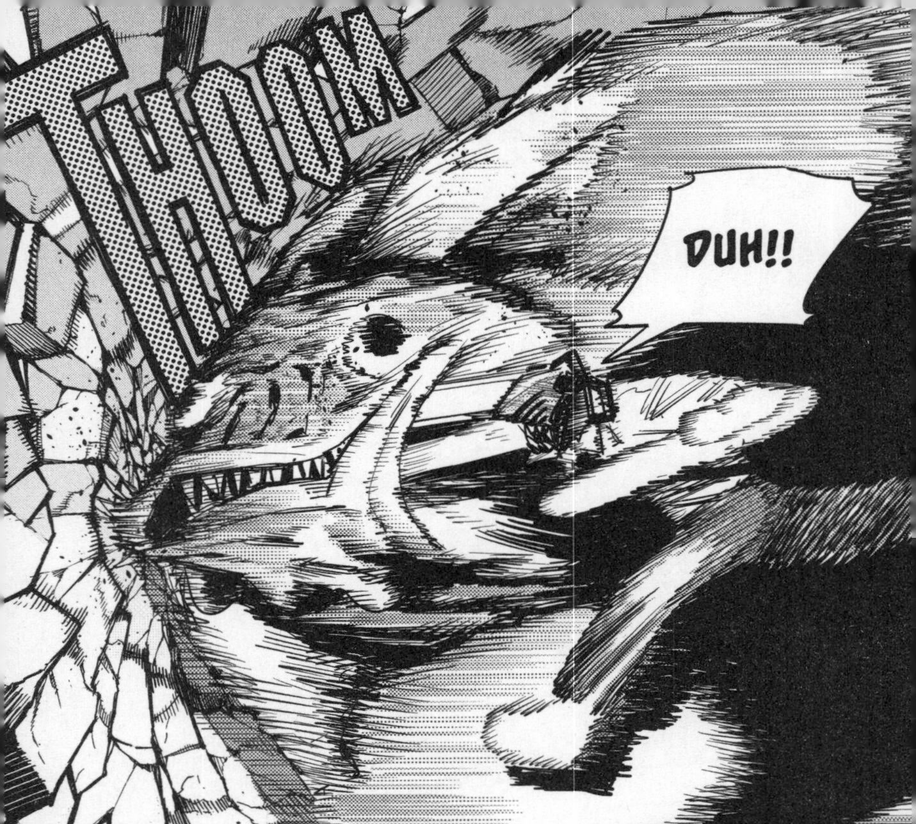
THOOM
DUH!!
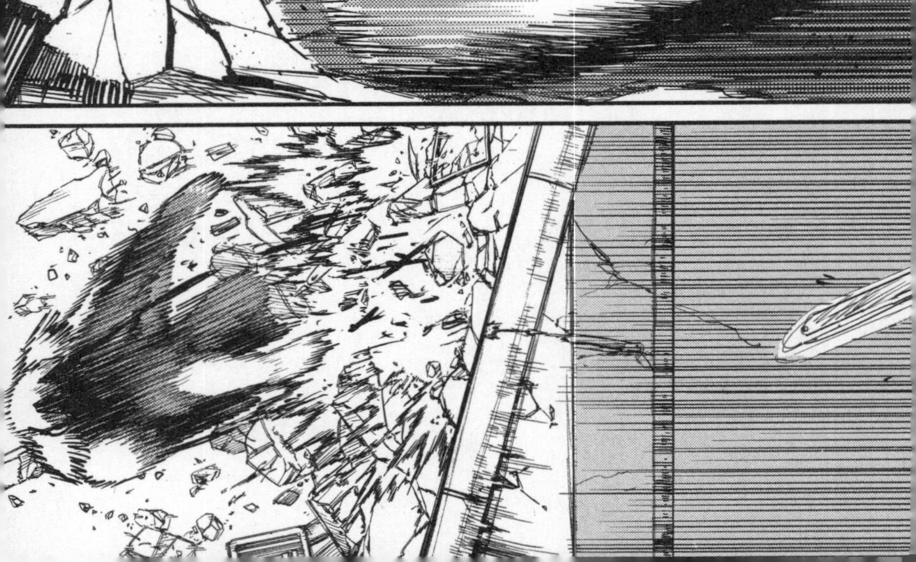

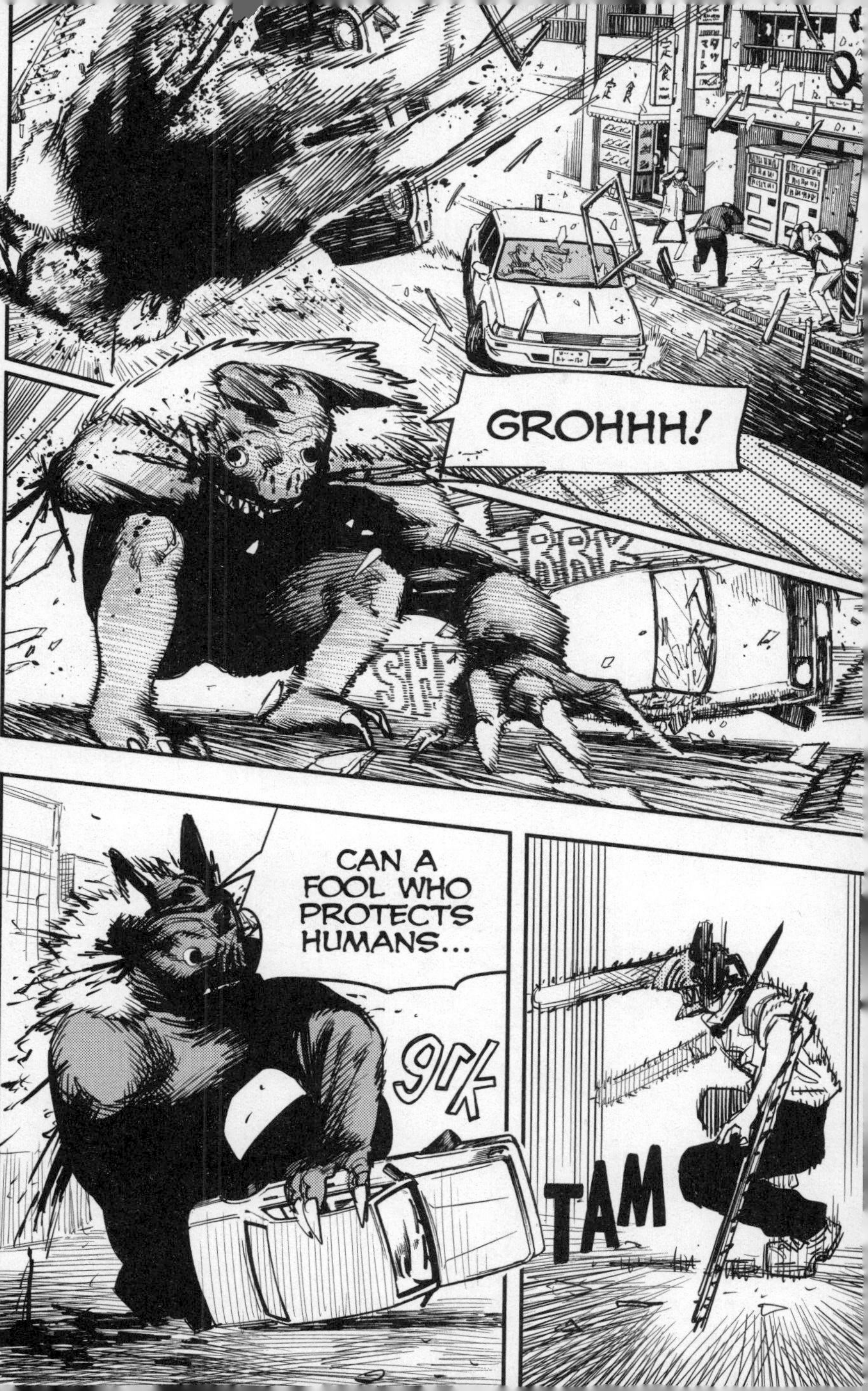
GROHHH!
TAM
CAN A FOOL WHO PROTECTS HUMANS...
grk

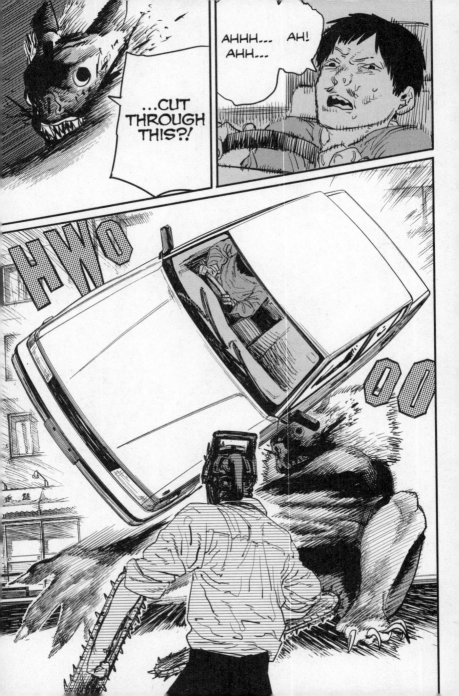

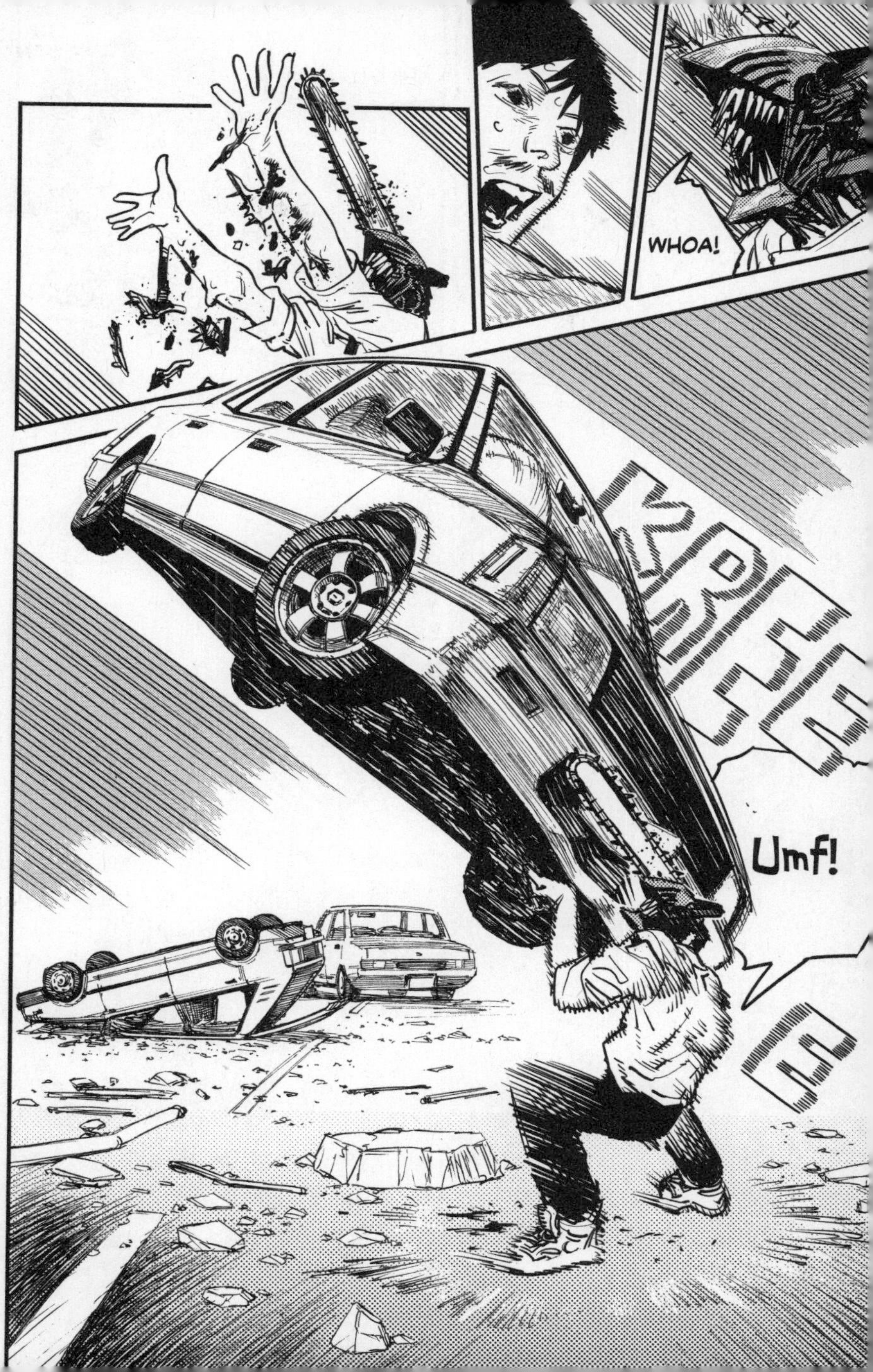
WHOA!
KREEEE
Umf!

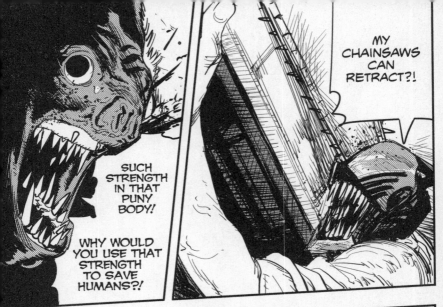

MY CHAINSAWS CAN RETRACT?!

SUCH STRENGTH IN THAT PUNY BODY!

WHY WOULD YOU USE THAT STRENGTH TO SAVE HUMANS?!

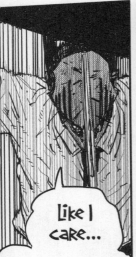

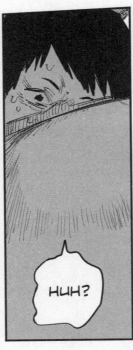

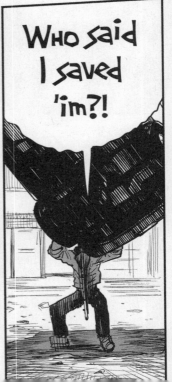

WHO said I saved 'im?!

LiKE I care...

...about some GUY'S...

HUH?

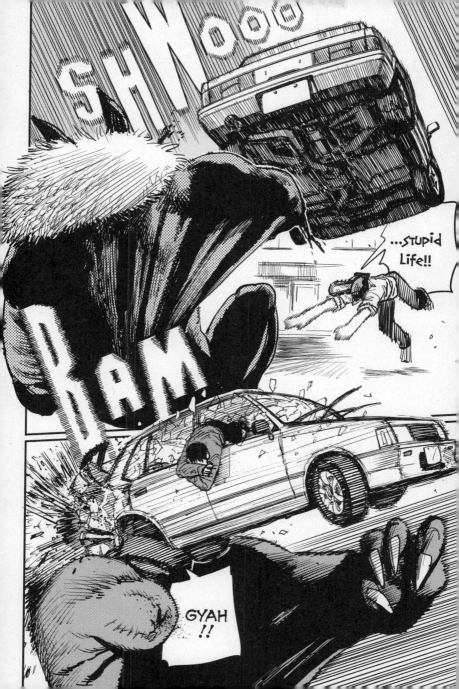

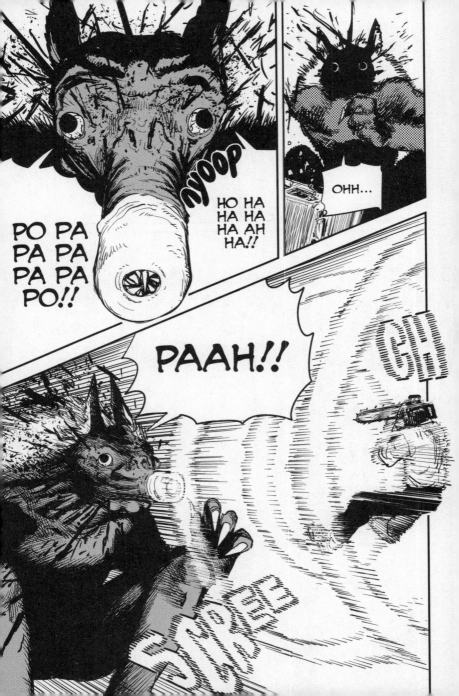

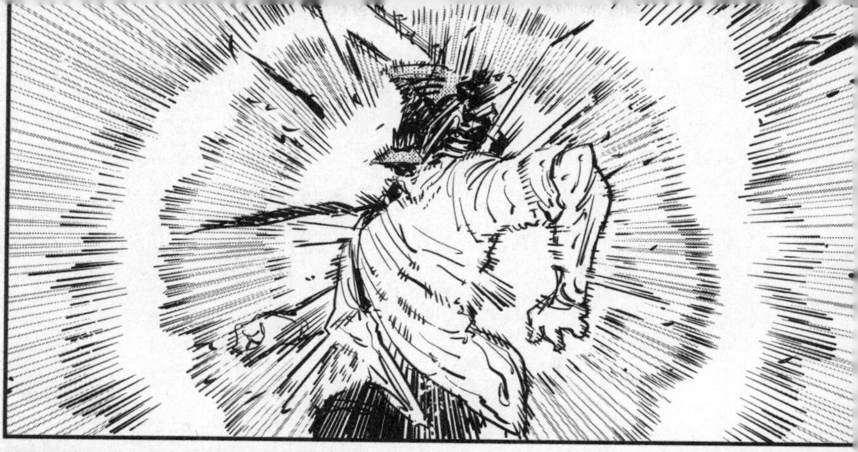

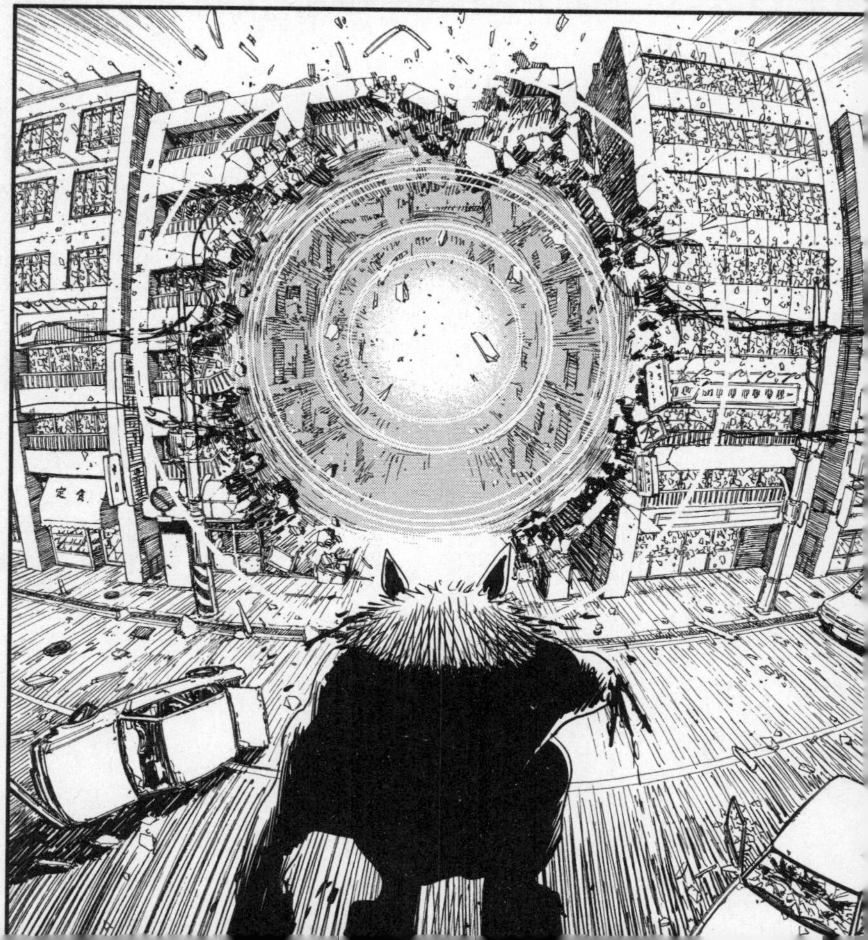
定食

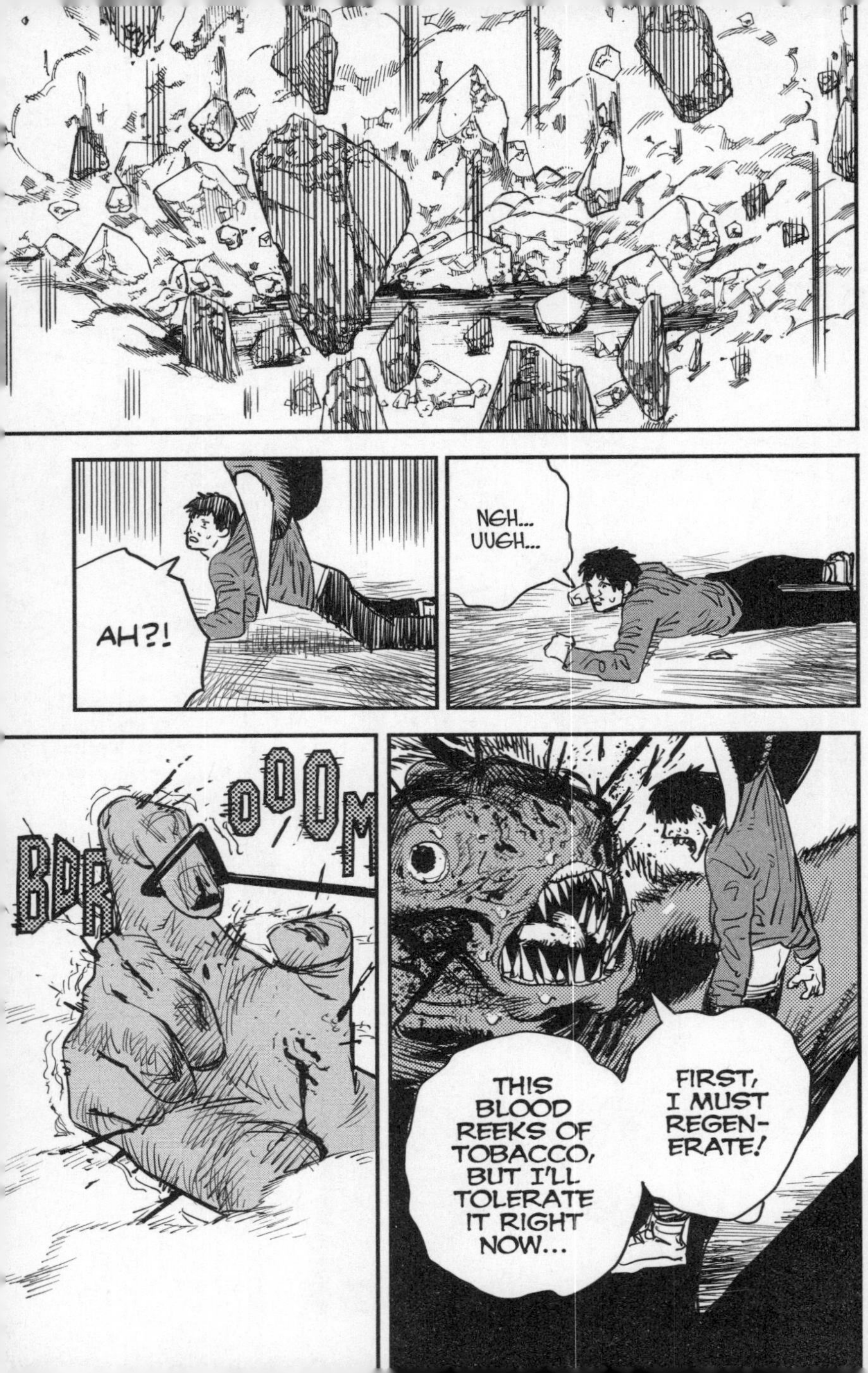
NGH... UUGH...
AH?!
FIRST, I MUST REGENERATE!
THIS BLOOD REEKS OF TOBACCO, BUT I'LL TOLERATE IT RIGHT NOW...
BDROOOM

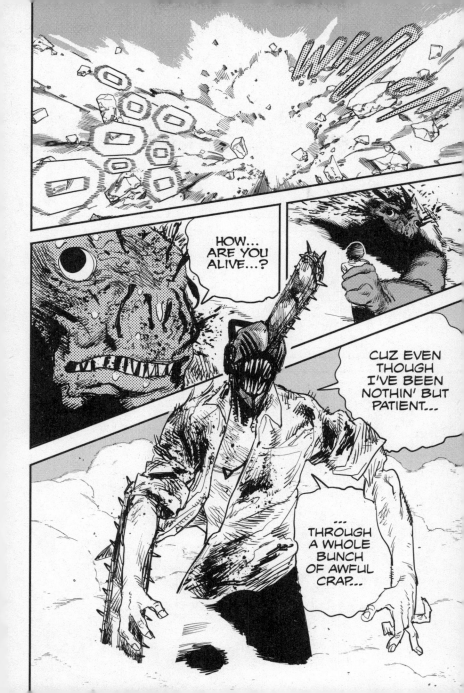

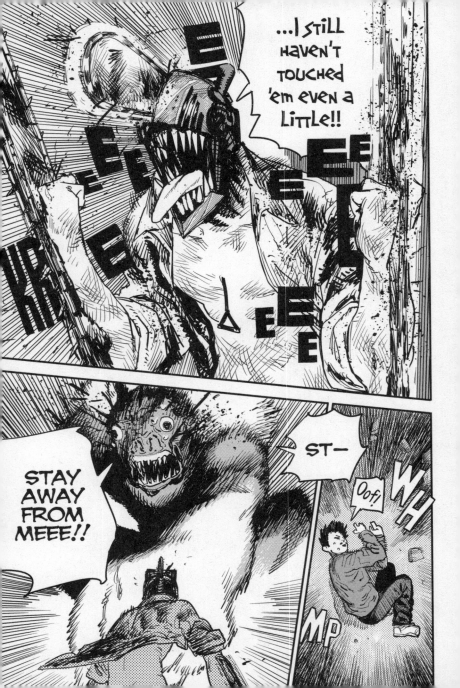

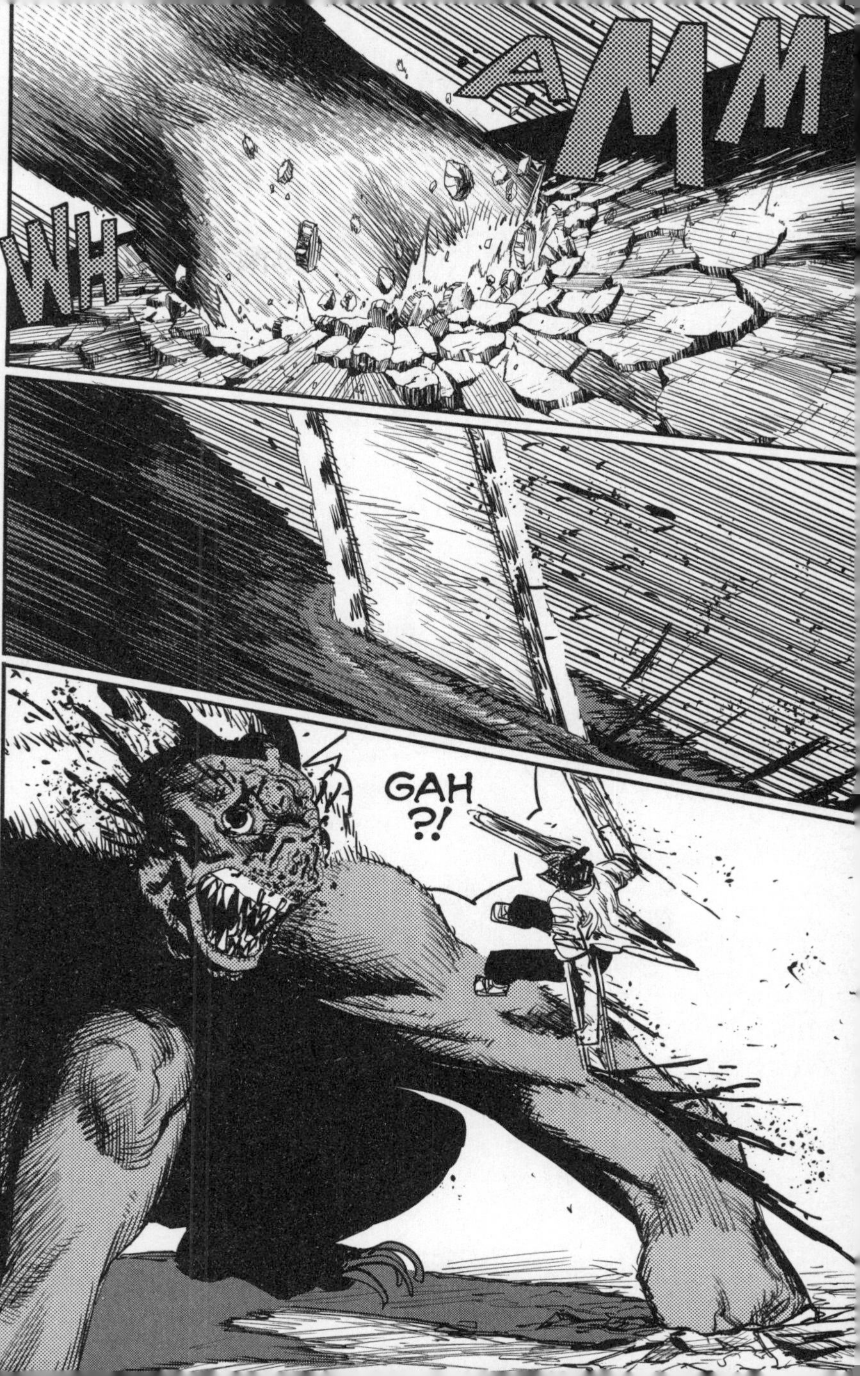
WH
AMM
GAH ?!

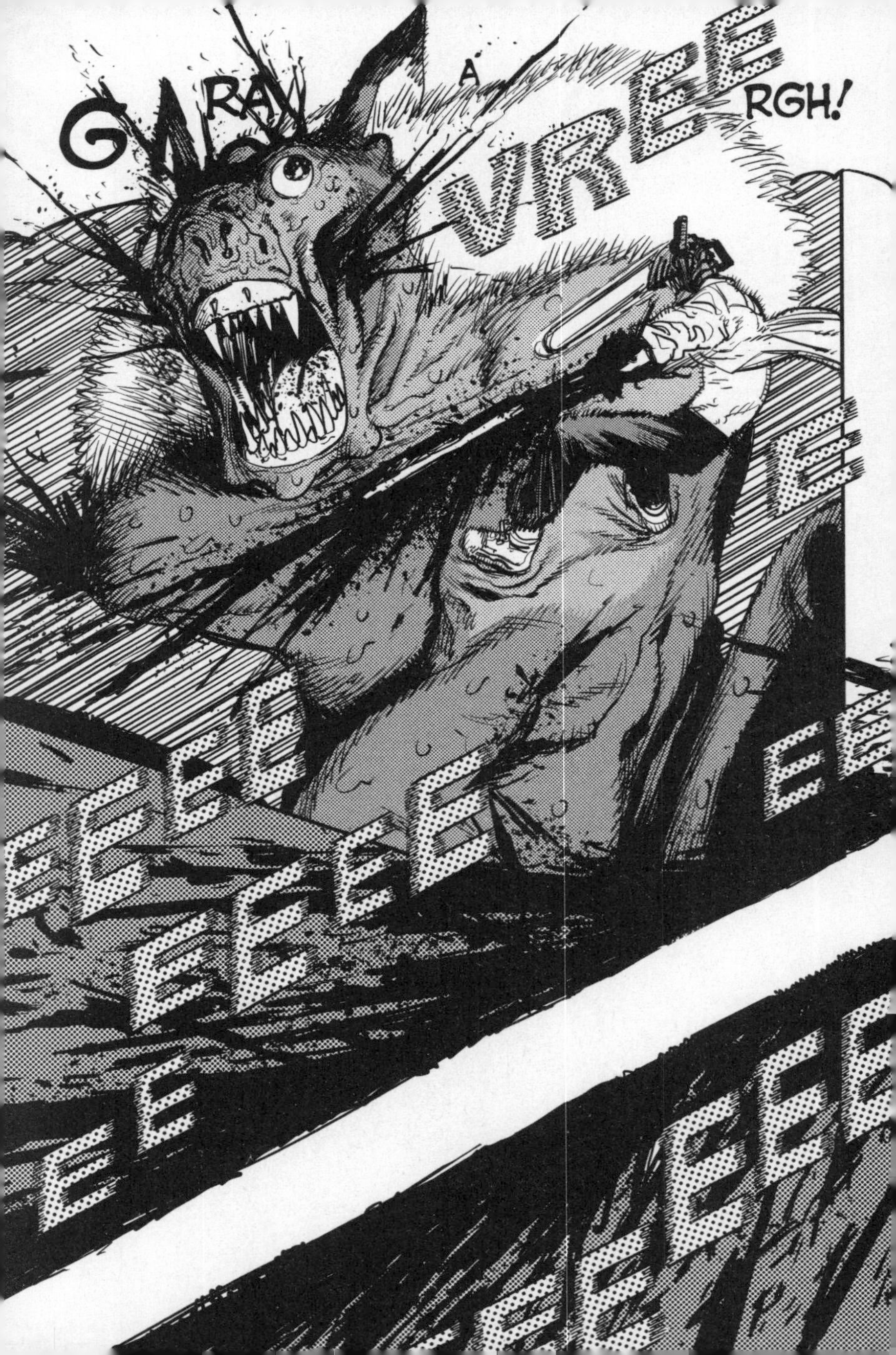
GARAARGH!
VREEEEEEEEEEEE

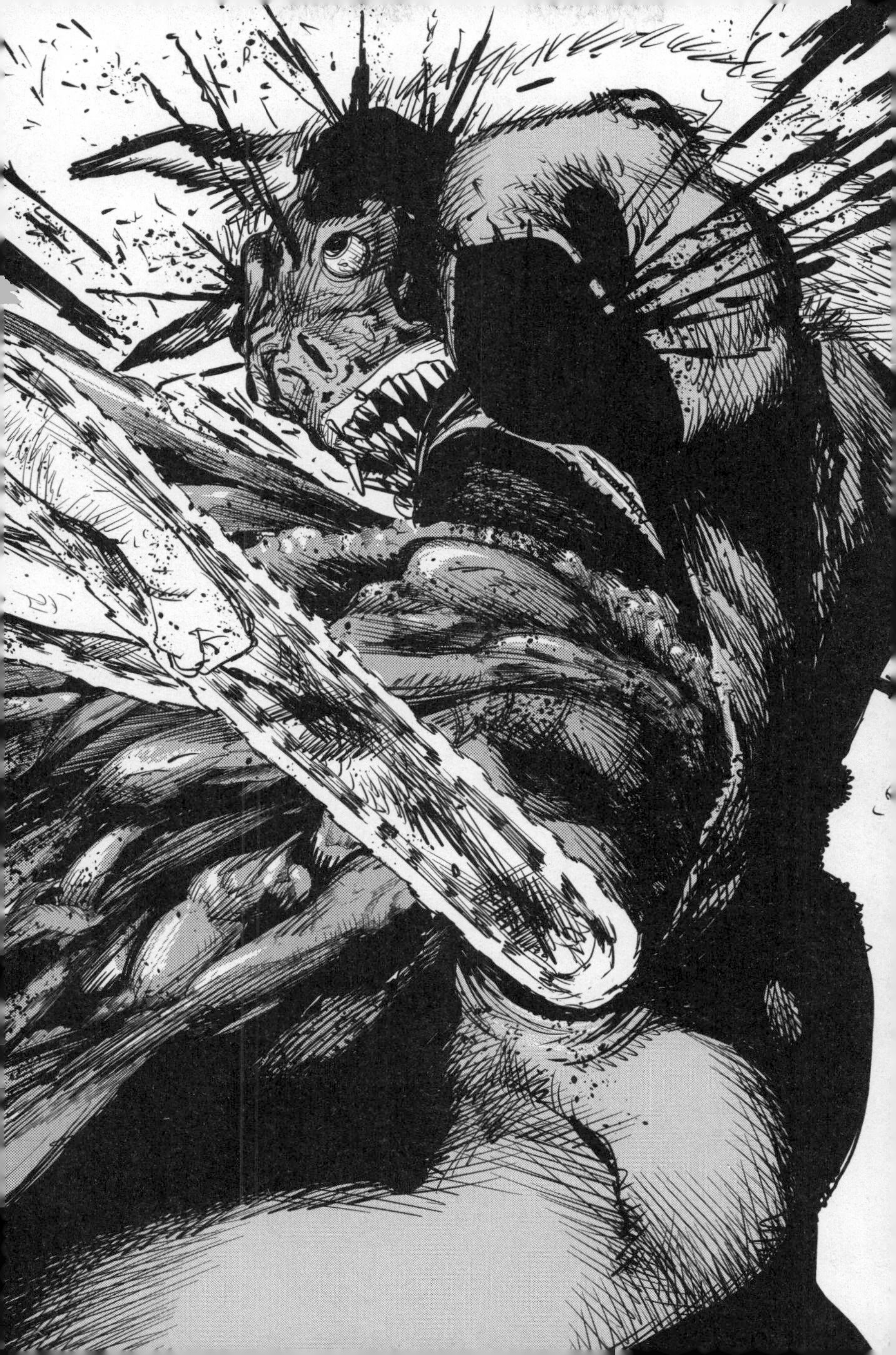

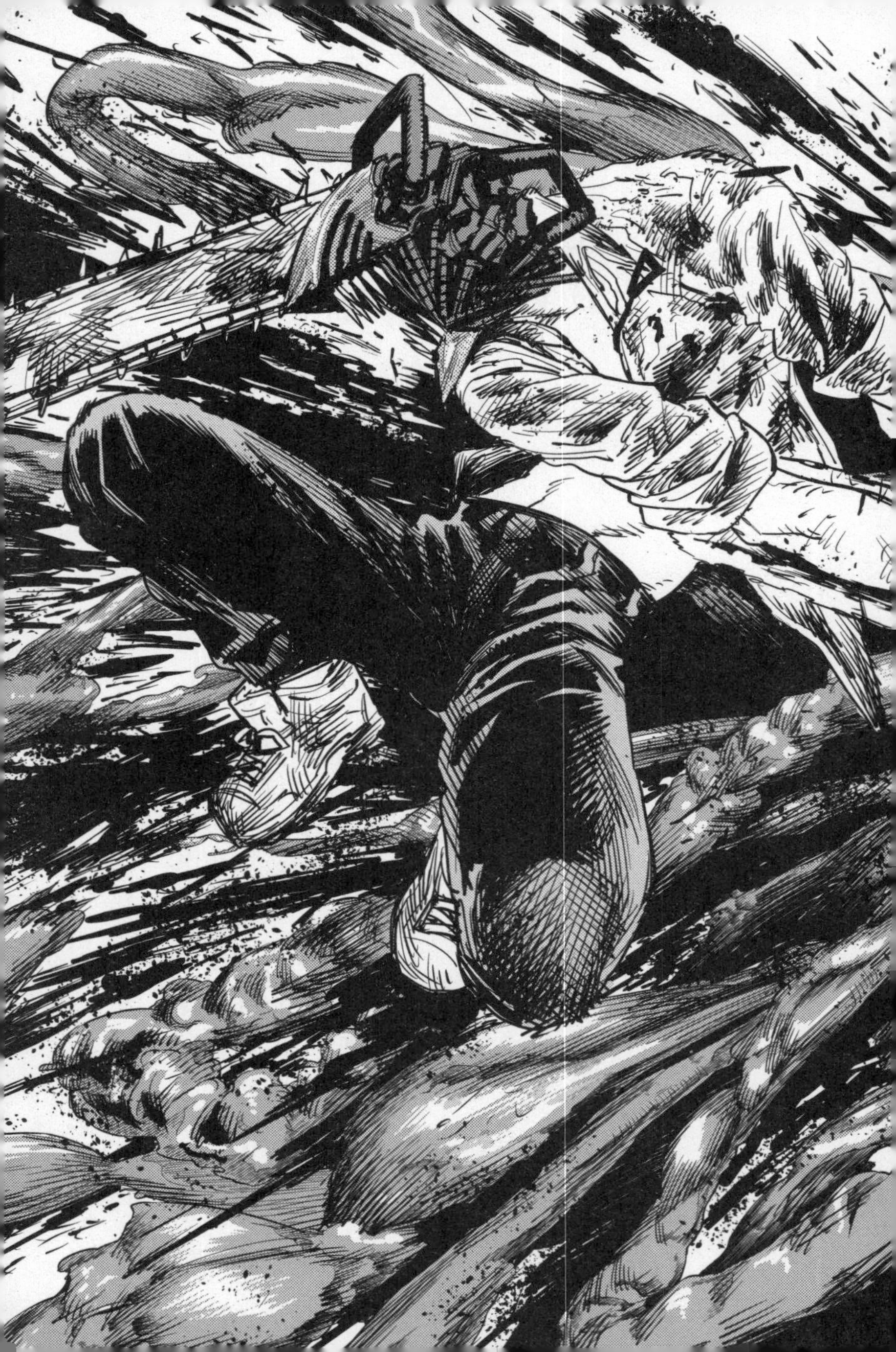

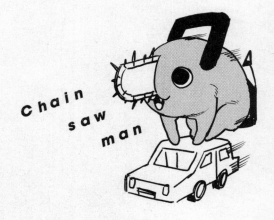

Chain saw man

# Chapter 9: Rescue

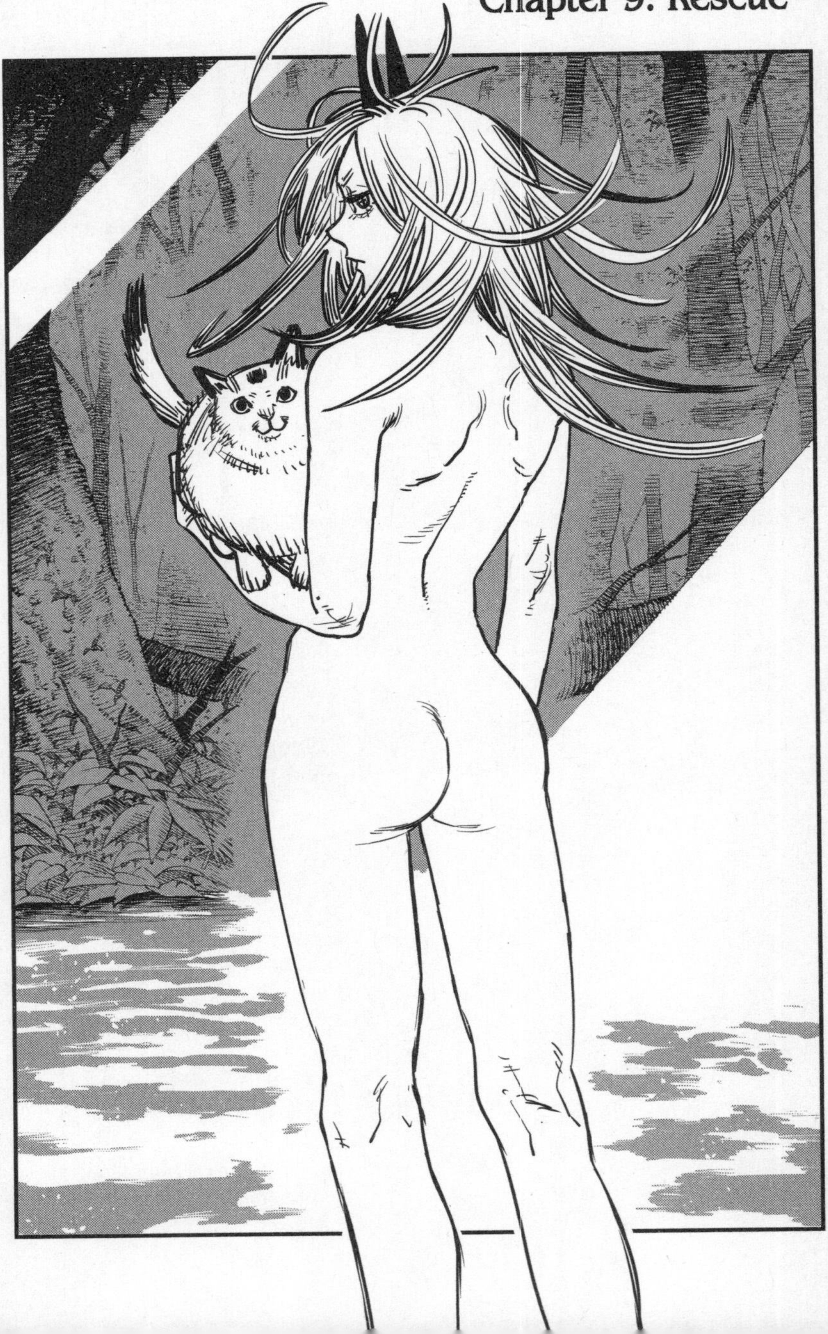

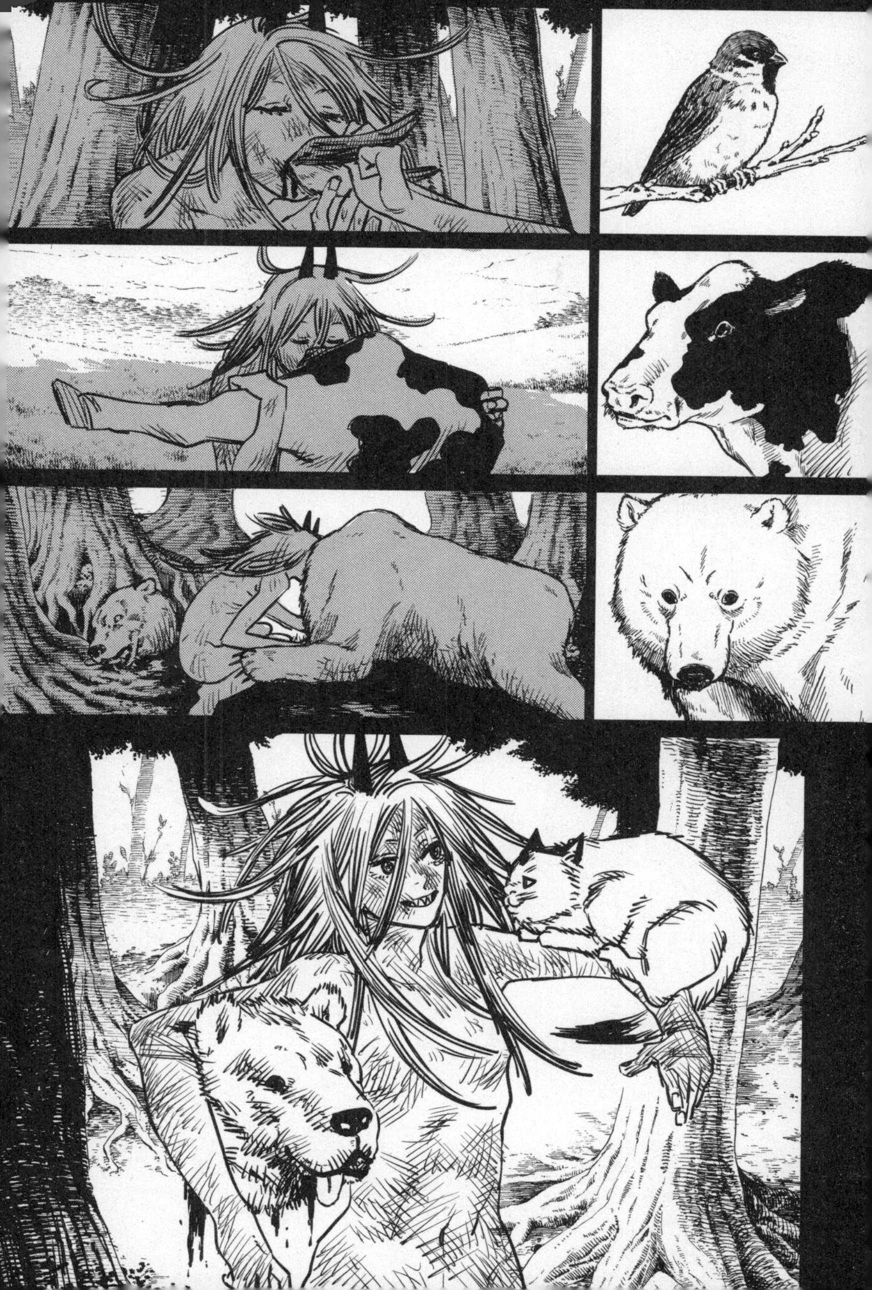

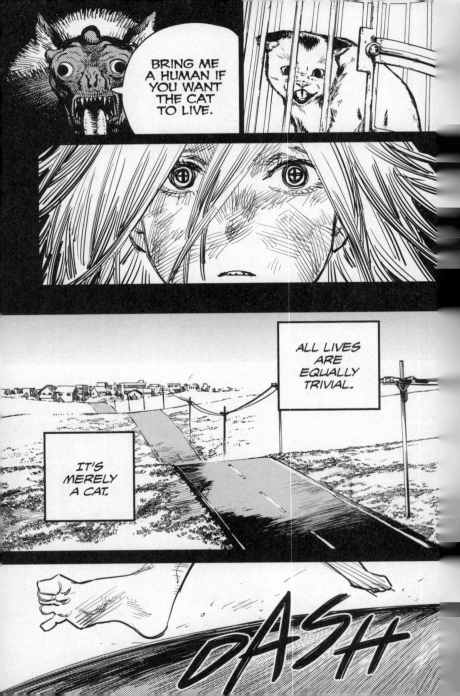

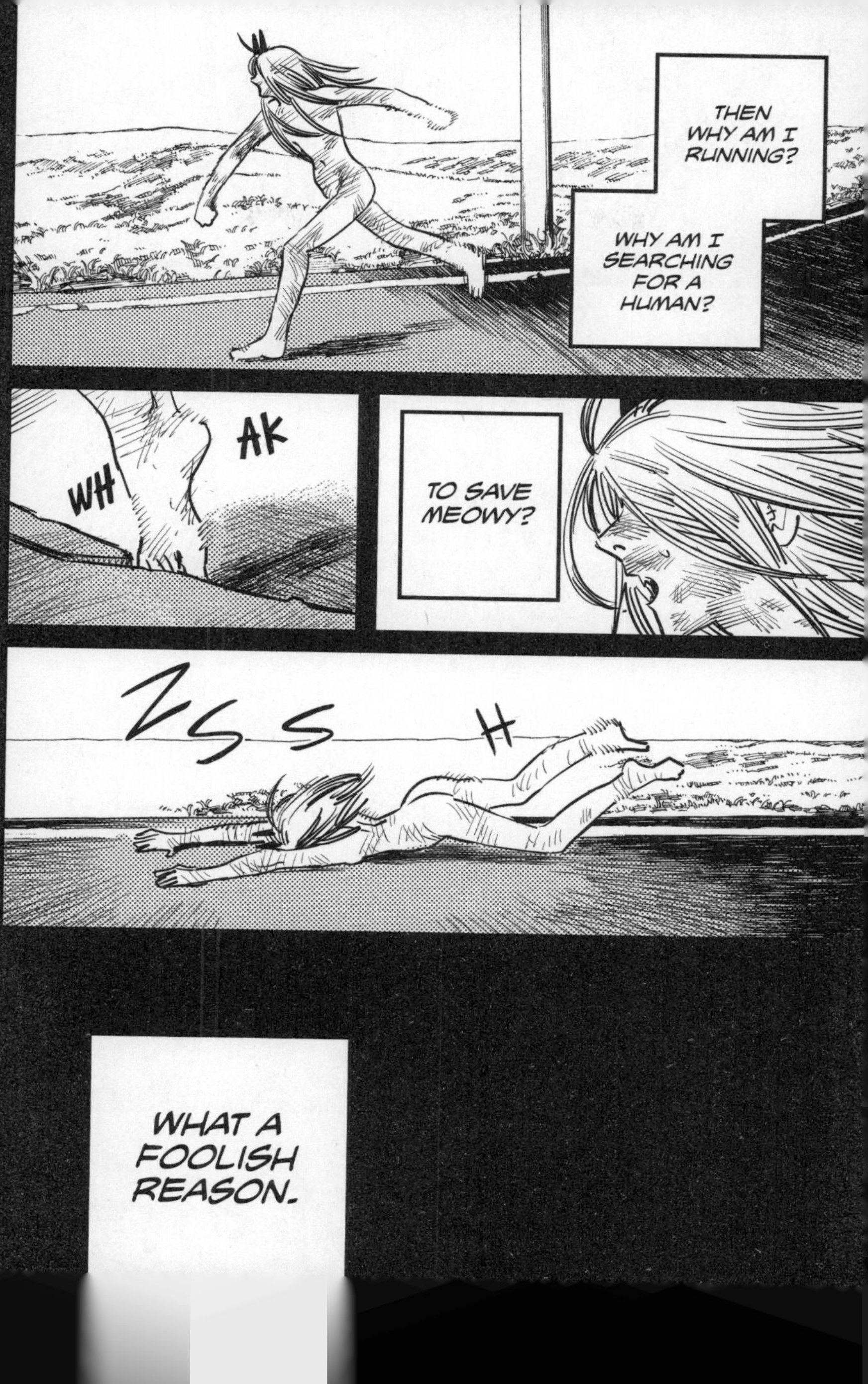
THEN WHY AM I RUNNING?
WHY AM I SEARCHING FOR A HUMAN?
TO SAVE MEOWY?
WH AK
ZSSSH
WHAT A FOOLISH REASON.

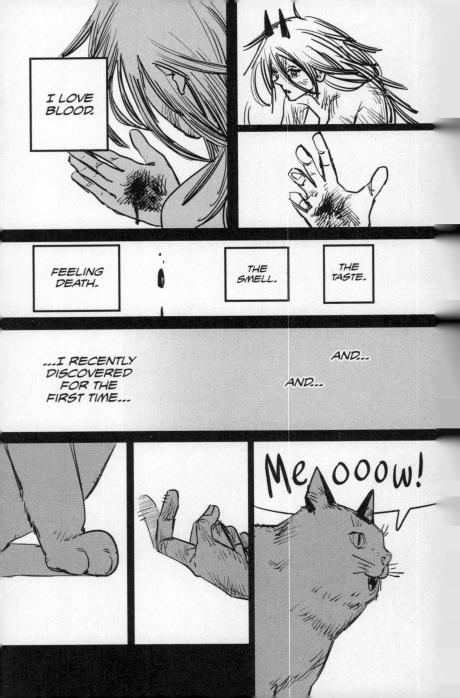

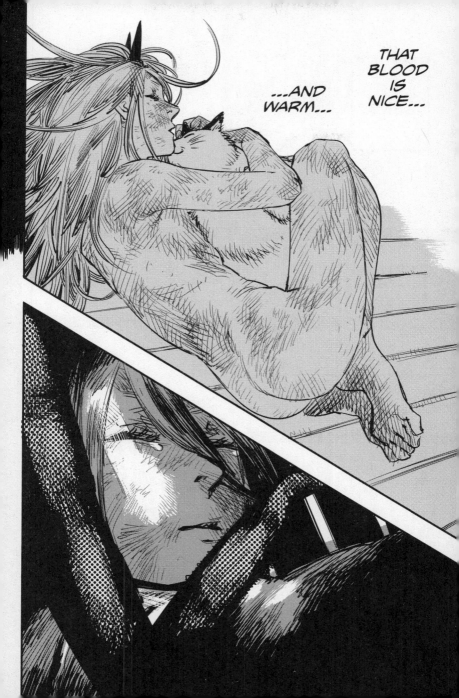

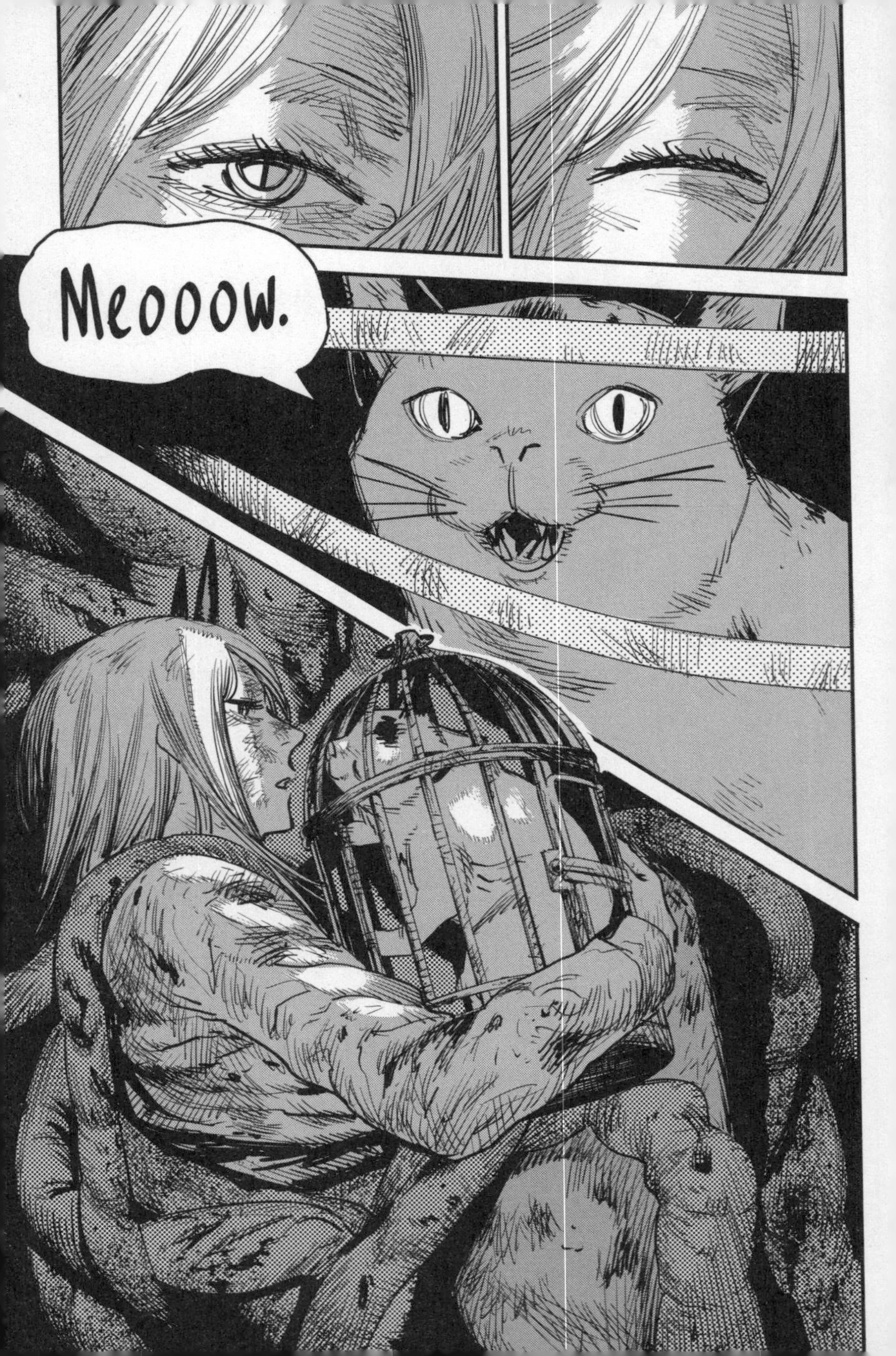
Meooow.

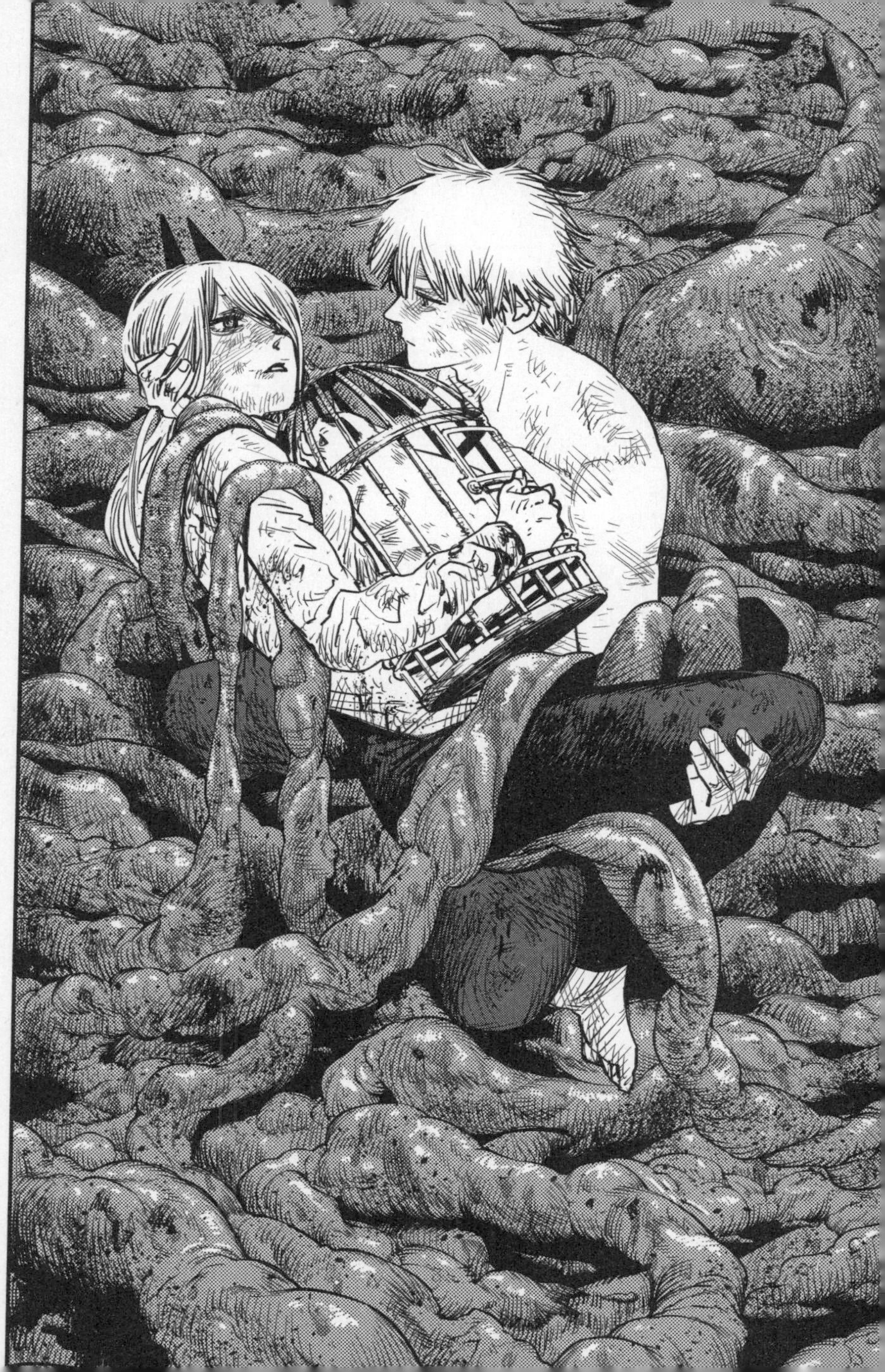

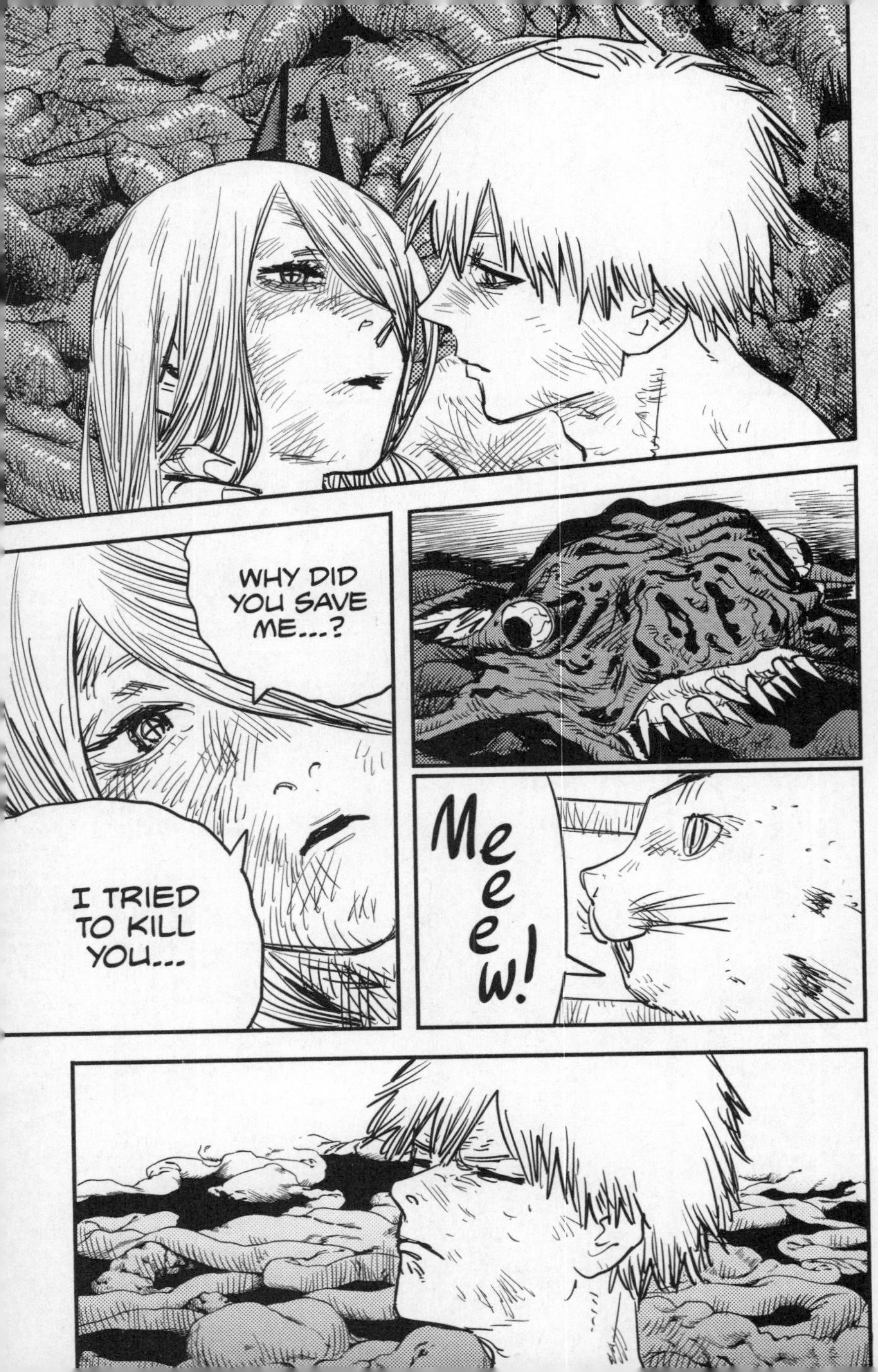
Meeew!
WHY DID YOU SAVE ME...?
I TRIED TO KILL YOU...

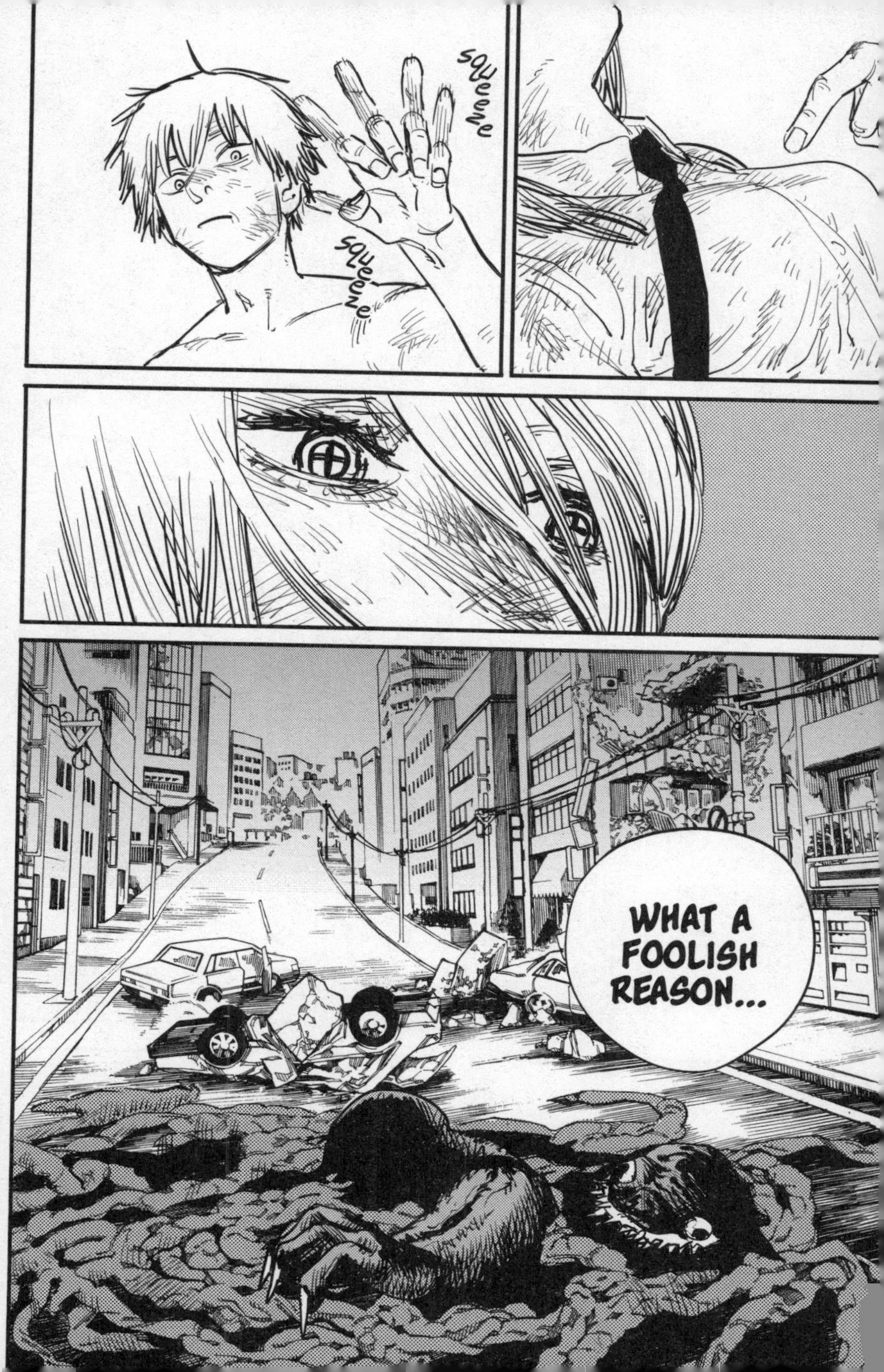
SQUEEZE
SQUEEZE
WHAT A FOOLISH REASON...

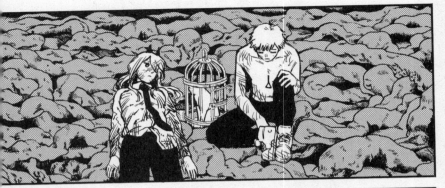

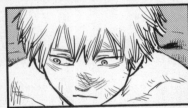

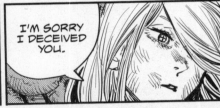

I'M SORRY
I DECEIVED
YOU.

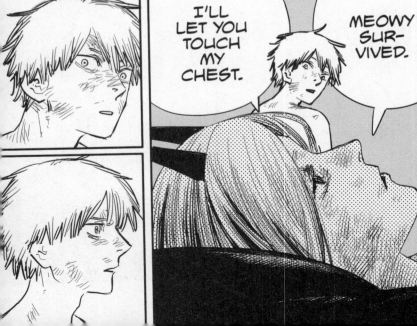

I'LL
LET YOU
TOUCH
MY
CHEST.

MEOWY
SUR-
VIVED.

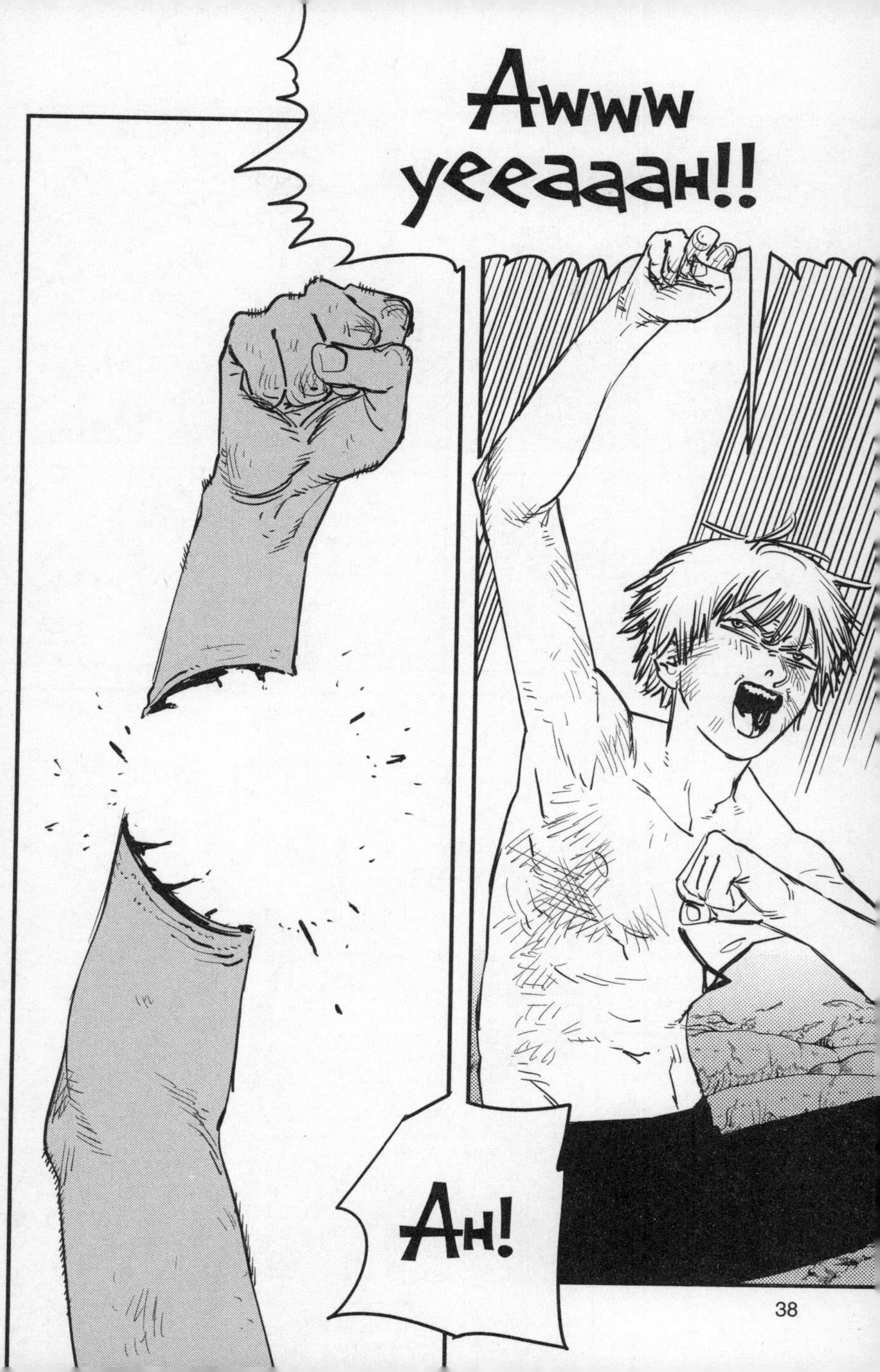
Awww yeeaaah!!
Ah!

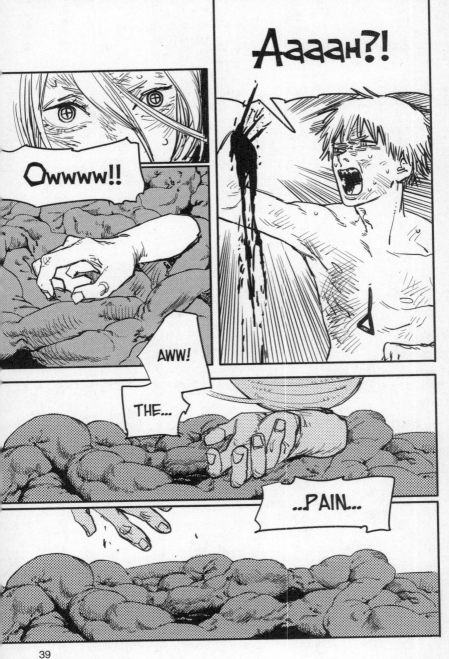

39

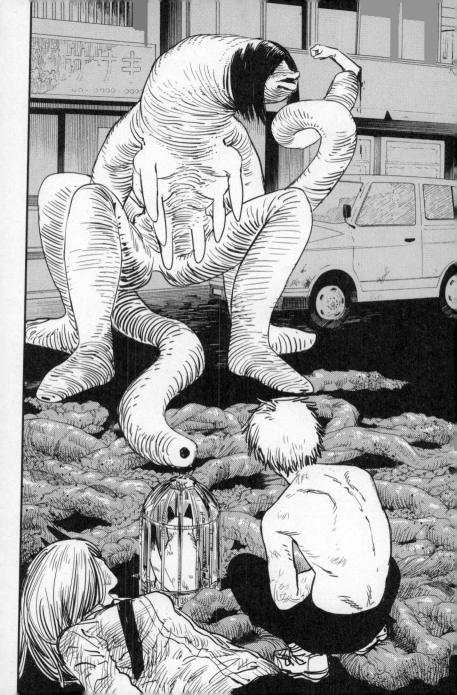

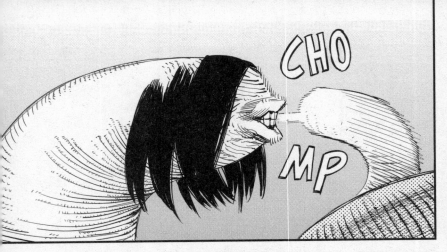

CHO

MP

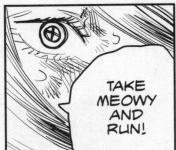

TAKE MEOWY AND RUN!

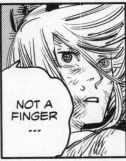

NOT A FINGER ---

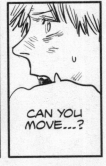

CAN YOU MOVE...?

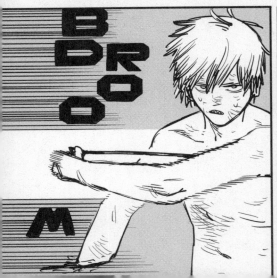

BROOM

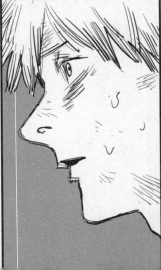

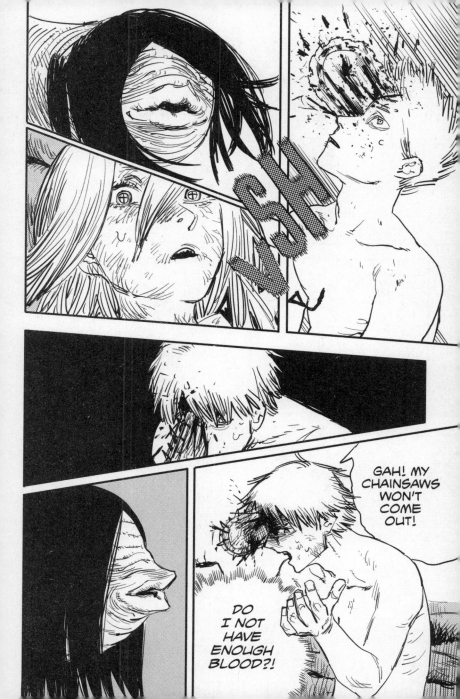

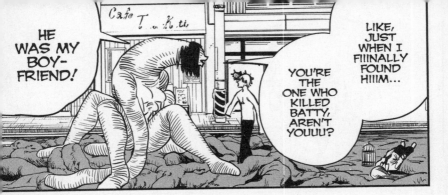

HE WAS MY BOY-FRIEND!

YOU'RE THE ONE WHO KILLED BATTY, AREN'T YOUUU?

LIKE, JUST WHEN I FIIINALLY FOUND HIIIM...

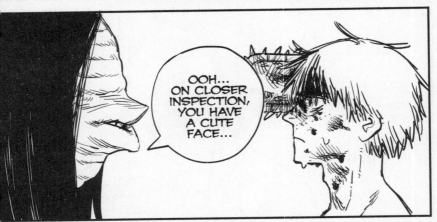

OOH... ON CLOSER INSPECTION, YOU HAVE A CUTE FACE...

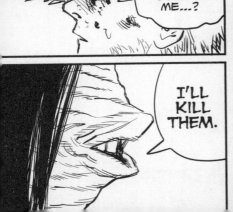

AND THOSE TWO BEHIND ME...?

I'LL KILL THEM.

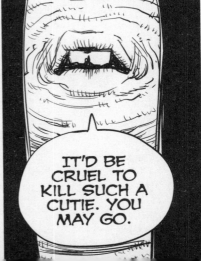

IT'D BE CRUEL TO KILL SUCH A CUTIE. YOU MAY GO.

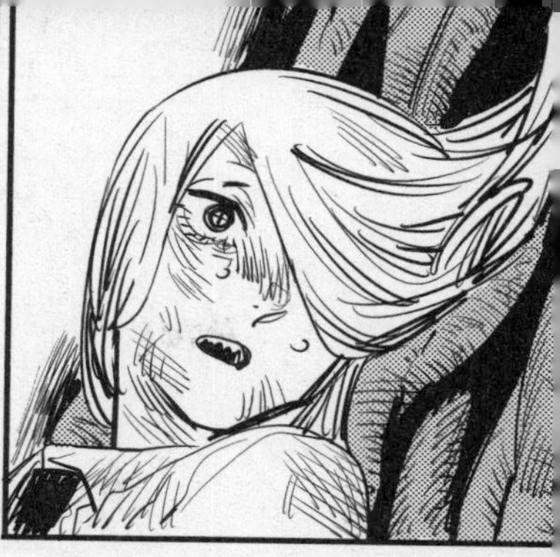
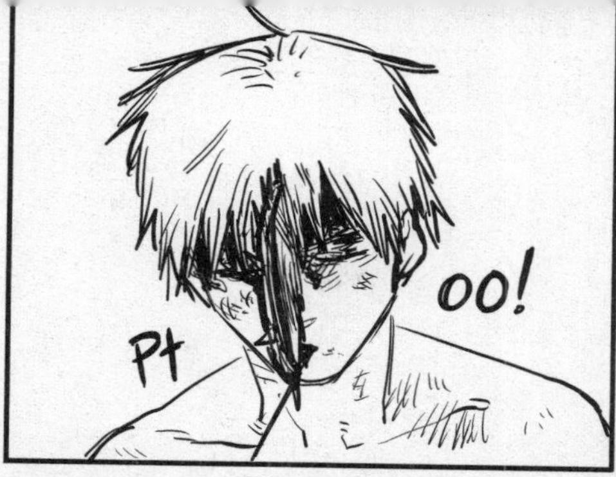
OO!
Pt
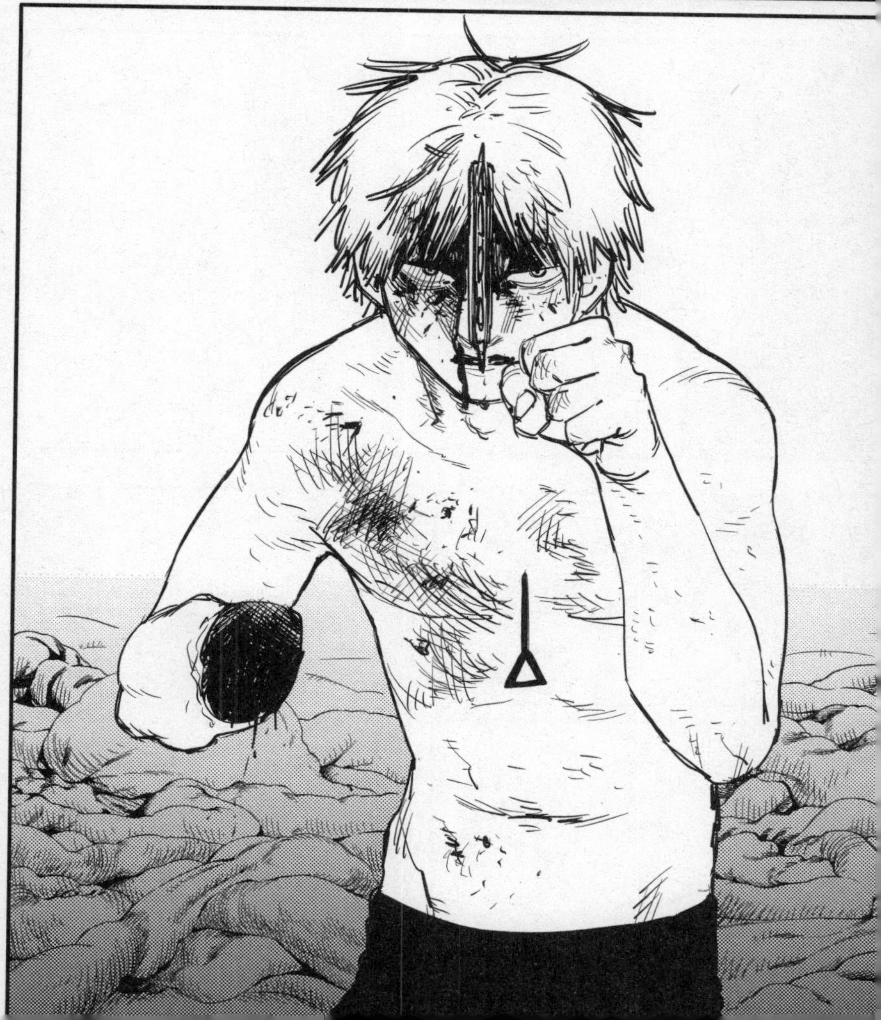

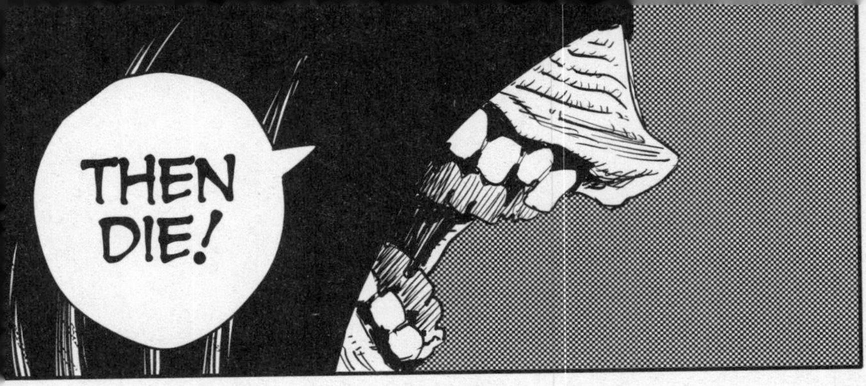
THEN DIE!
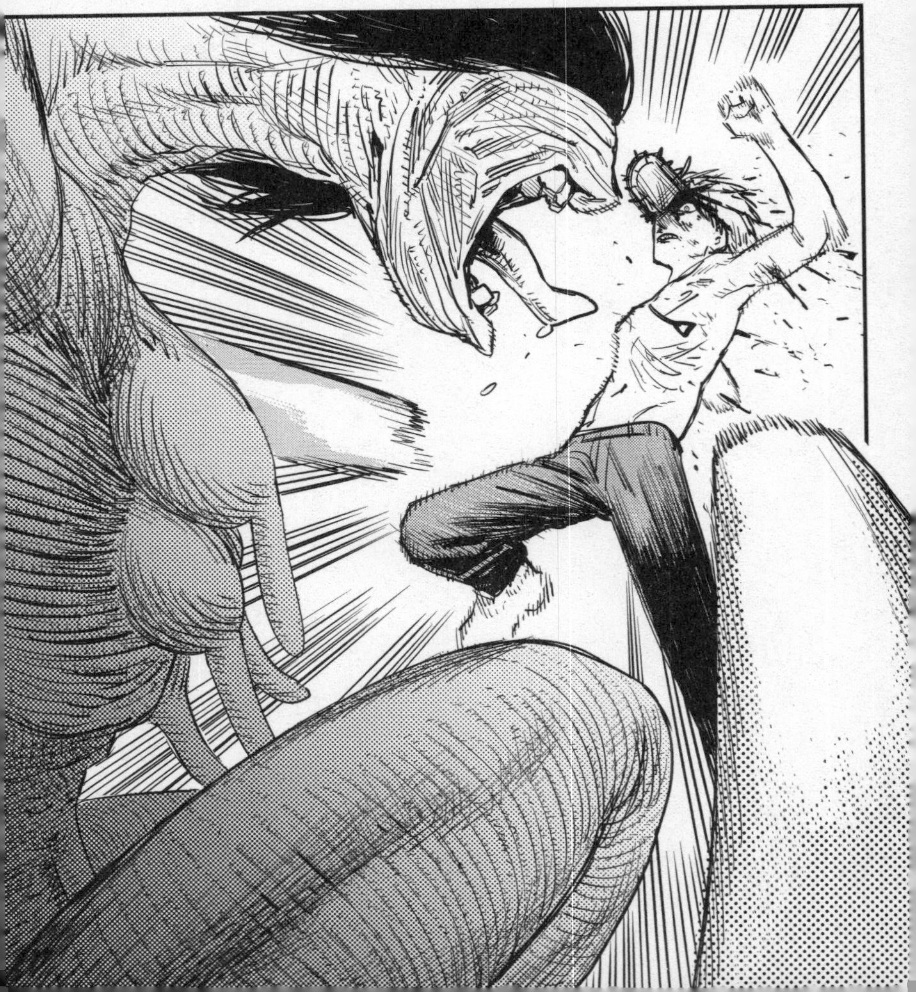

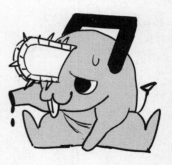

Chain
saw
man

# Chapter 10: Kon

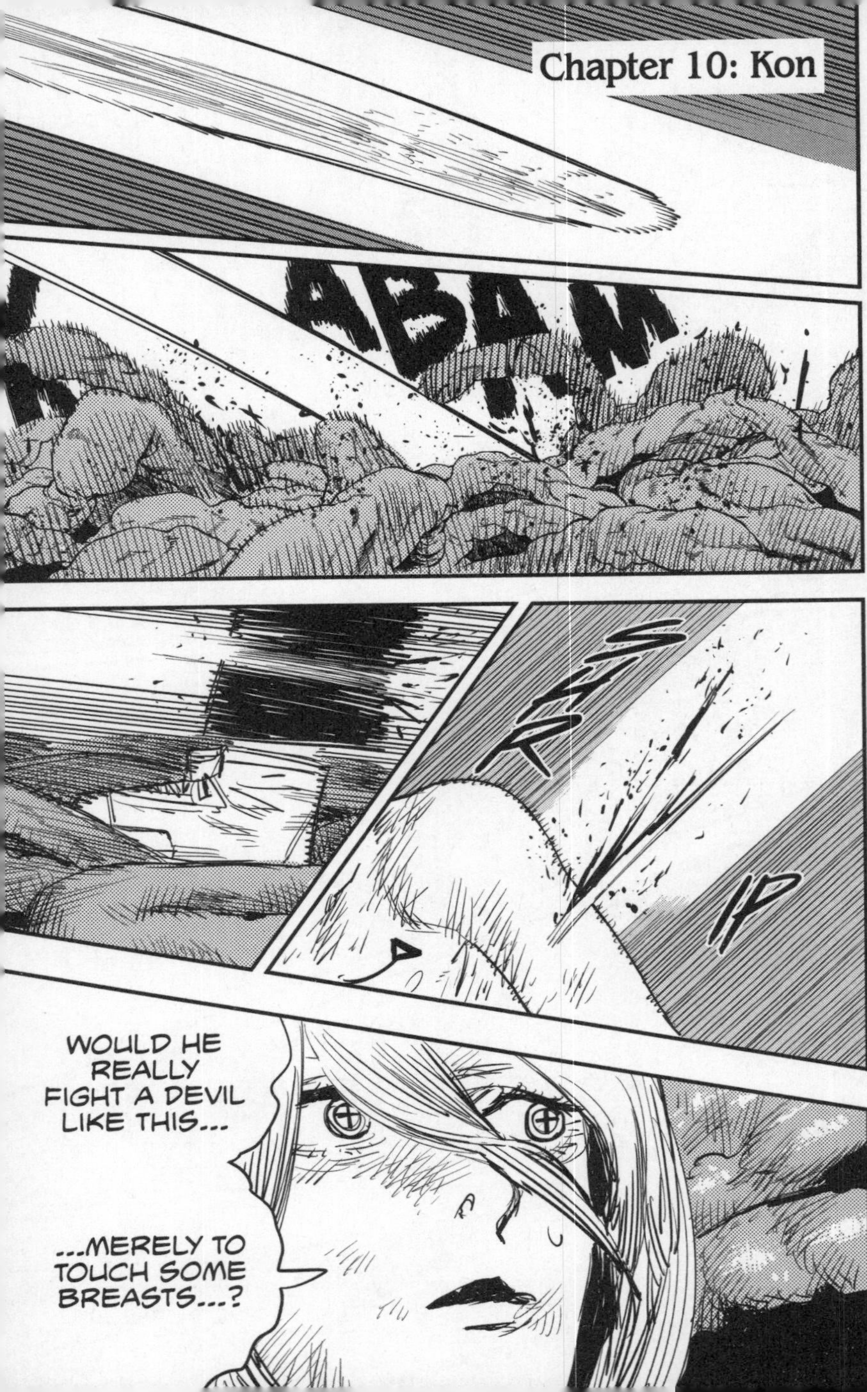
WOULD HE REALLY FIGHT A DEVIL LIKE THIS...
...MERELY TO TOUCH SOME BREASTS...?

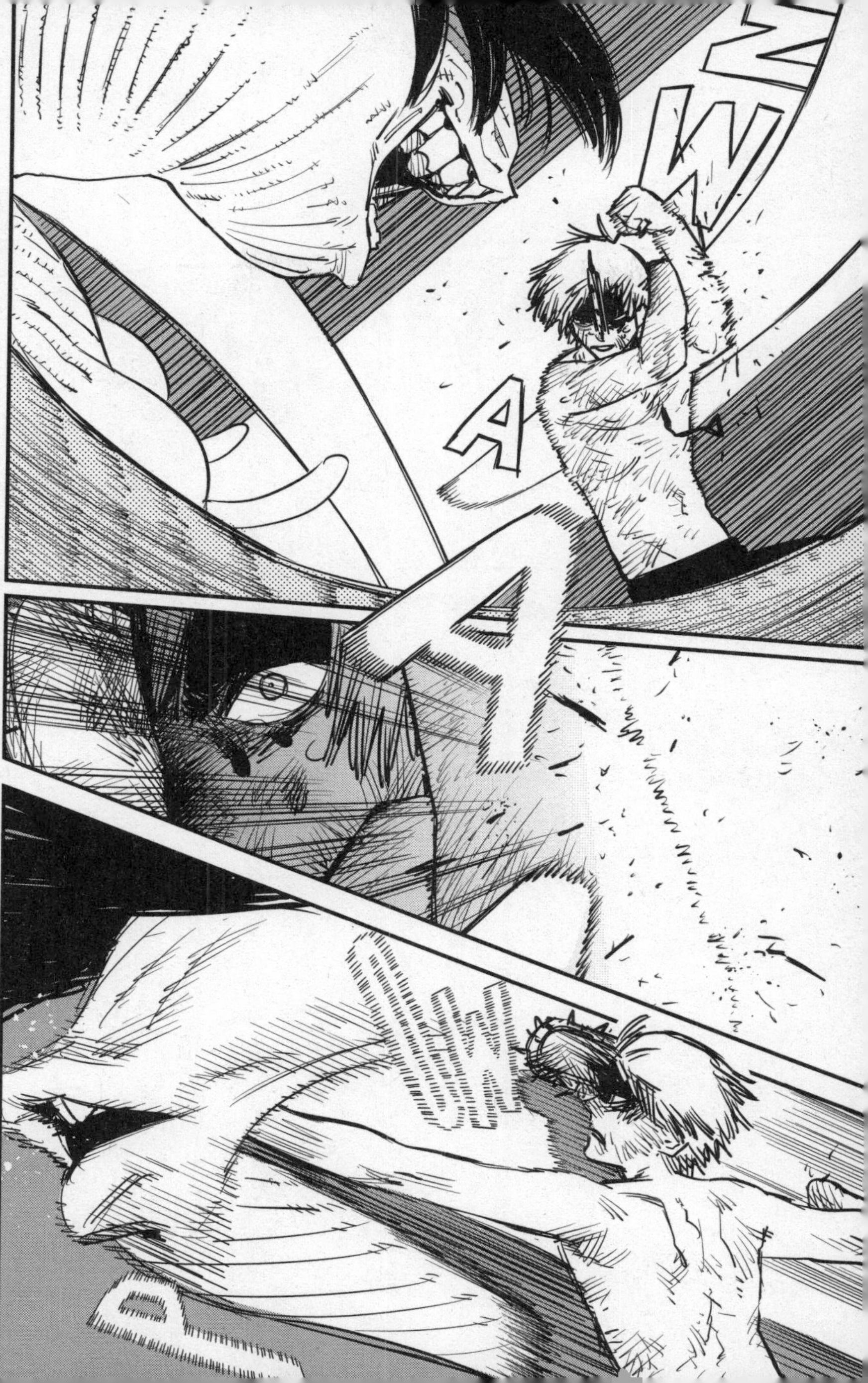

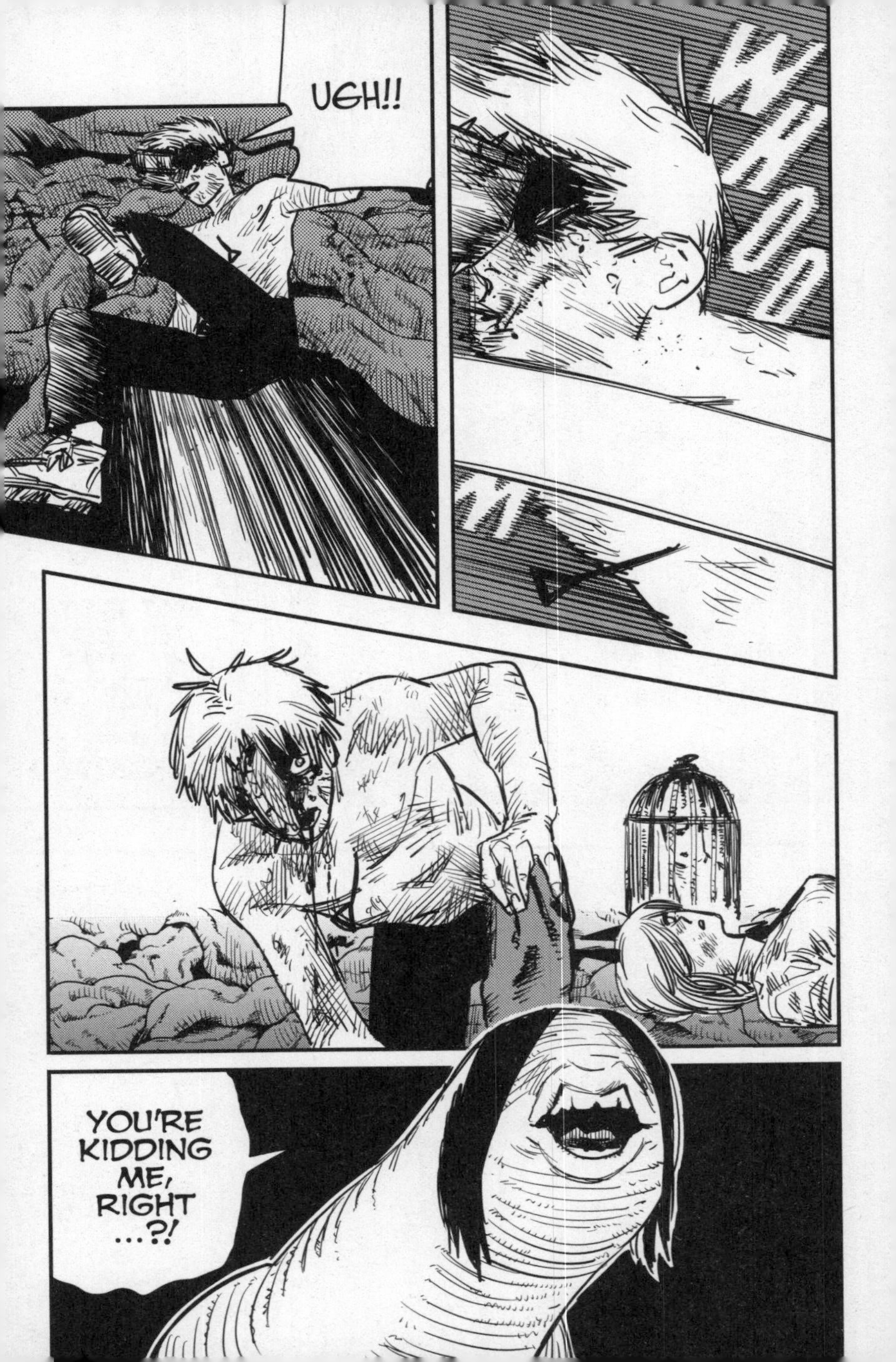
UGH!!
YOU'RE KIDDING ME, RIGHT ...?!

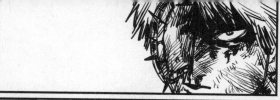

BAT AND I DREAMED OF EATING ALL THE HUMANS TOGETHER...

AN IMPOSSIBLE DREAM, BUT SUBLIME AND BEAUTIFUL...

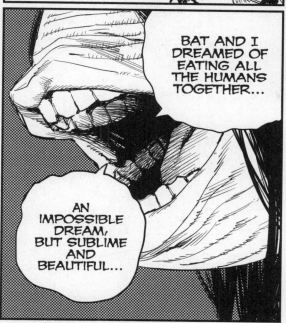

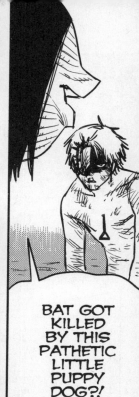

BAT GOT KILLED BY THIS PATHETIC LITTLE PUPPY DOG?!

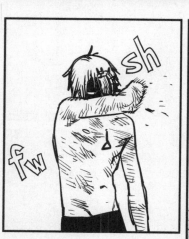

sh

fw

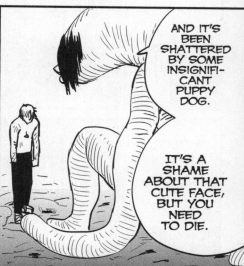

AND IT'S BEEN SHATTERED BY SOME INSIGNIFI-CANT PUPPY DOG.

IT'S A SHAME ABOUT THAT CUTE FACE, BUT YOU NEED TO DIE.

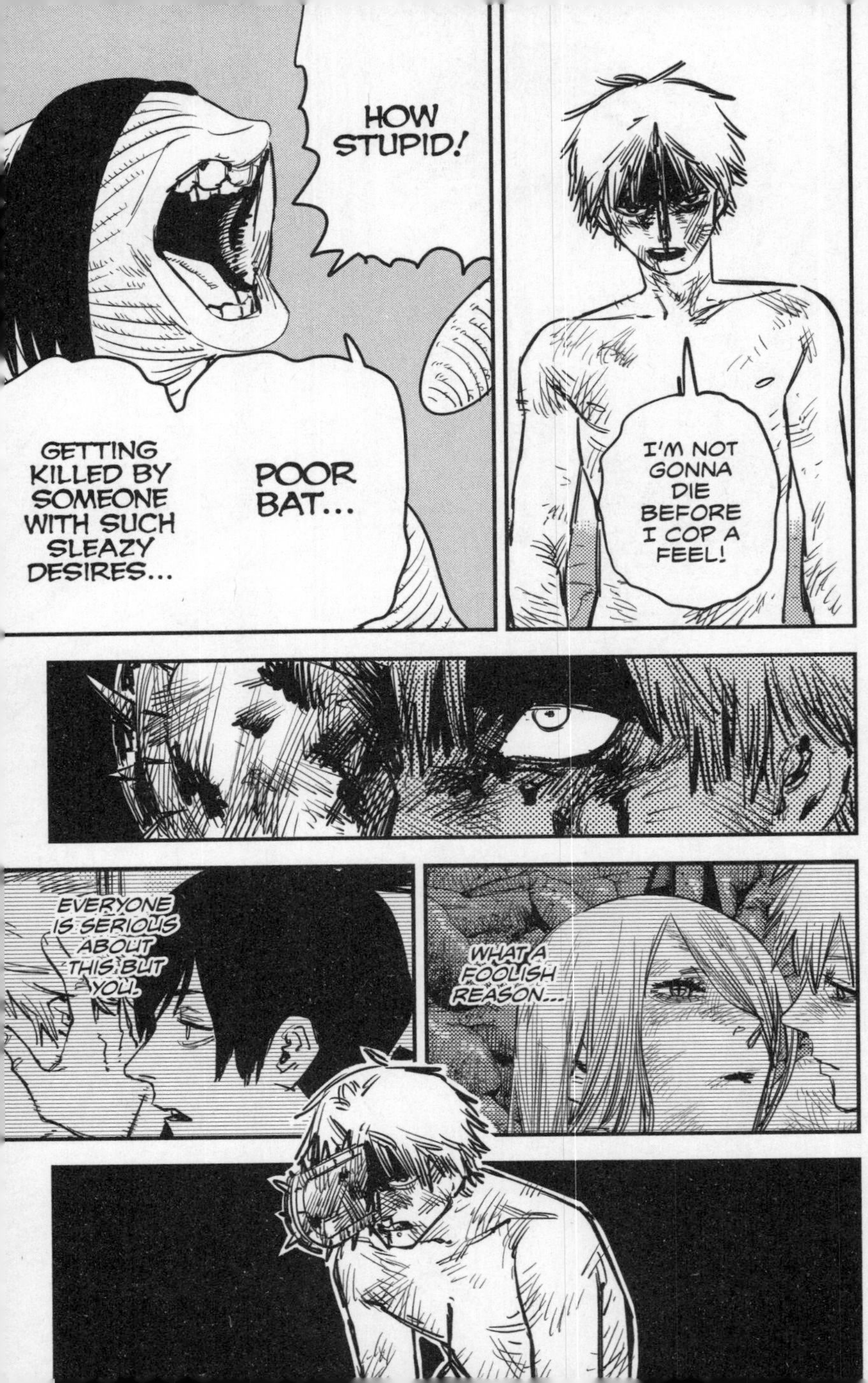
I'M NOT GONNA DIE BEFORE I COP A FEEL!
HOW STUPID!
POOR BAT...
GETTING KILLED BY SOMEONE WITH SUCH SLEAZY DESIRES...
WHAT A FOOLISH REASON...
EVERYONE IS SERIOUS ABOUT THIS BUT YOU.

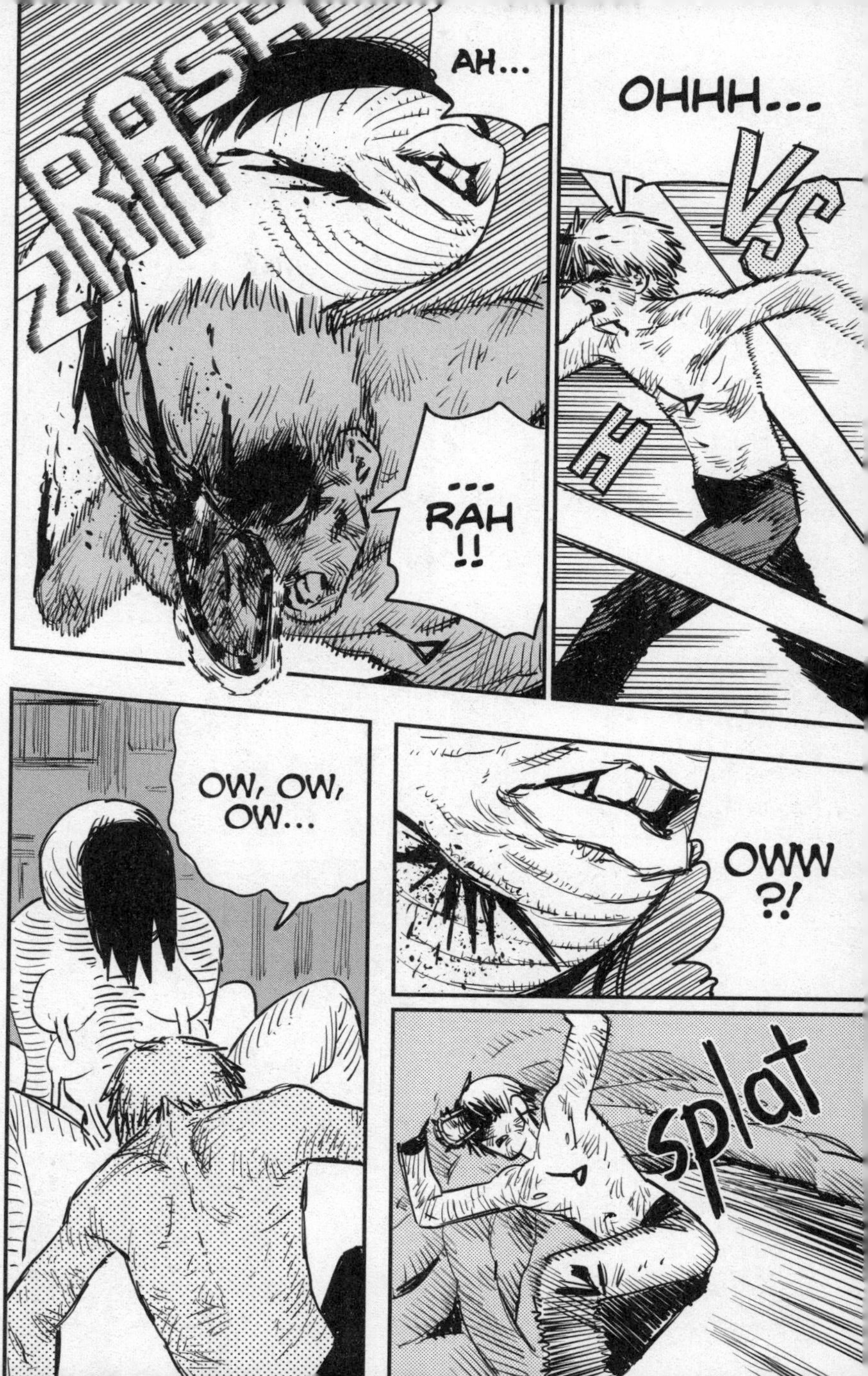
OHHH...
AH...
...RAH!!
OWW?!
splat
OW, OW, OW...

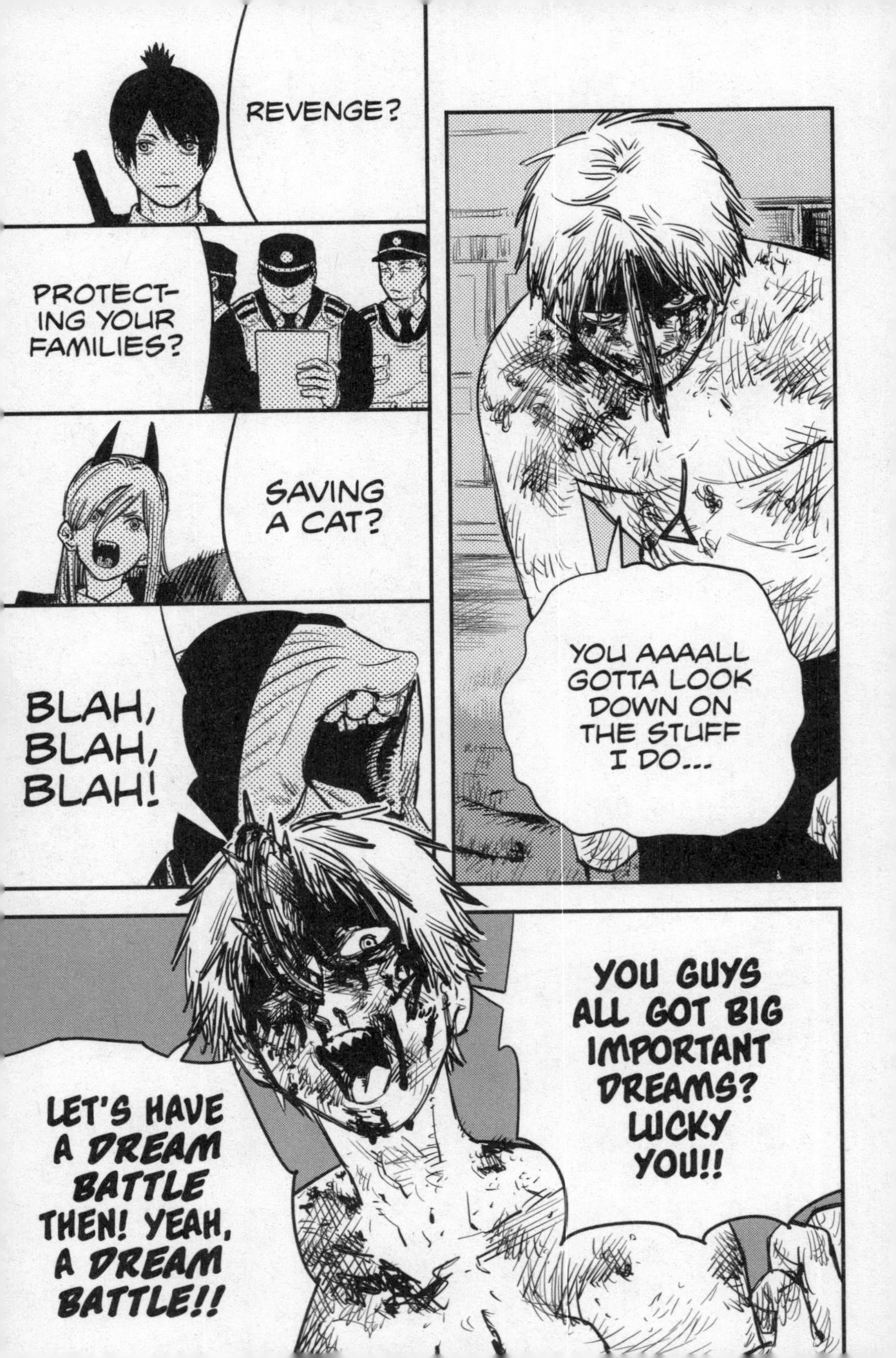
REVENGE?
PROTECTING YOUR FAMILIES?
SAVING A CAT?
BLAH, BLAH, BLAH!
YOU AAAALL GOTTA LOOK DOWN ON THE STUFF I DO...
YOU GUYS ALL GOT BIG IMPORTANT DREAMS? LUCKY YOU!!
LET'S HAVE A DREAM BATTLE THEN! YEAH, A DREAM BATTLE!!

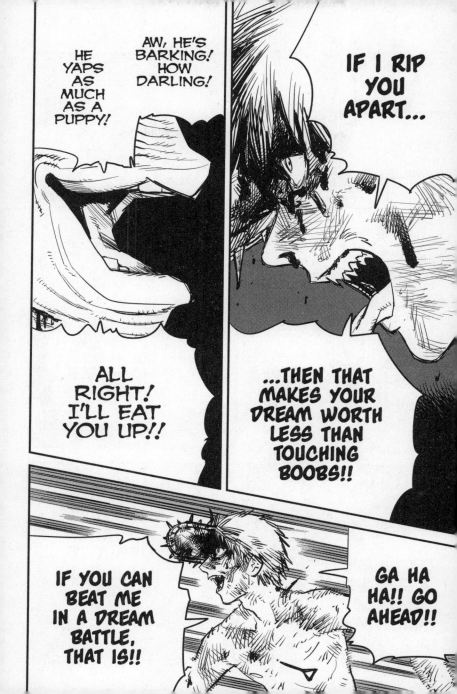

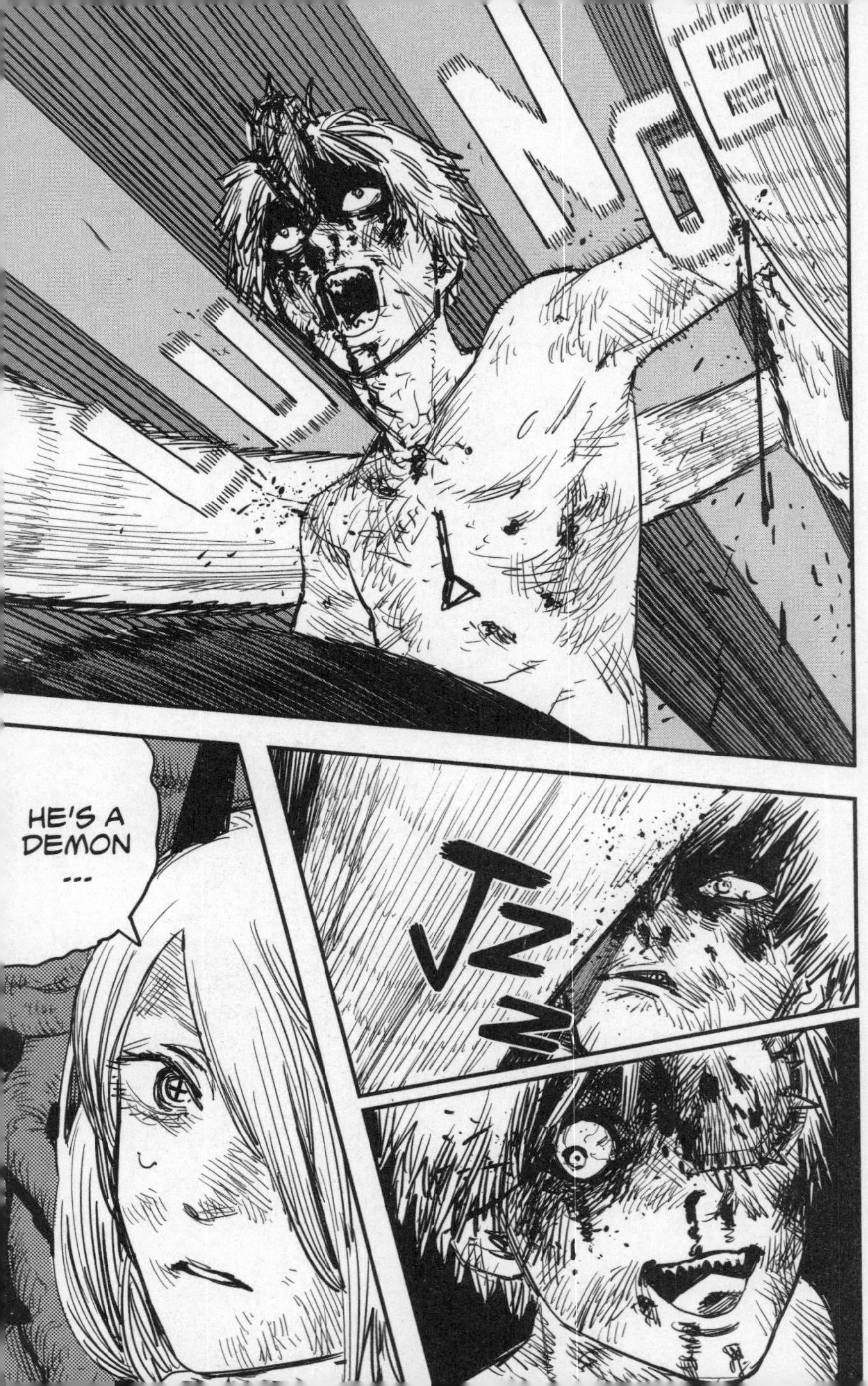
HE'S A DEMON ...

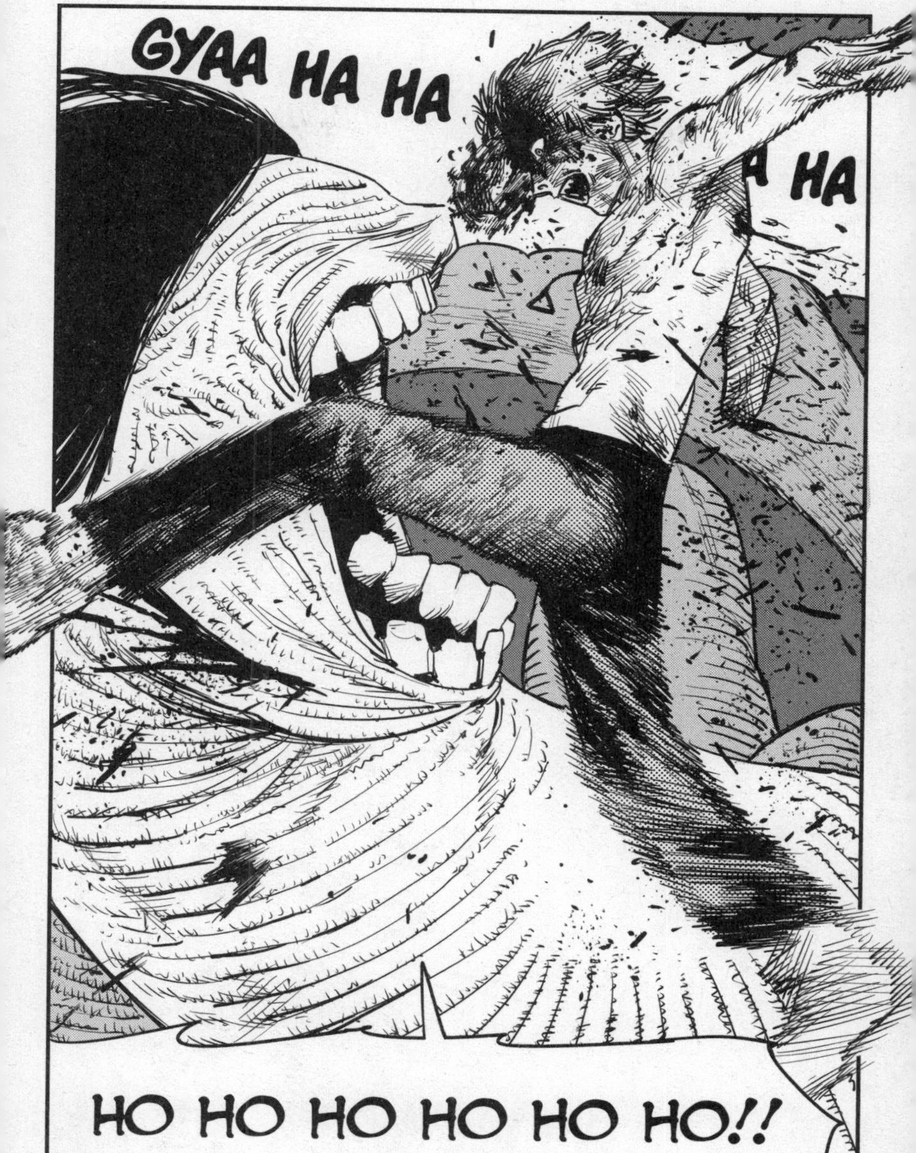
GYAA HA HA
HA HA
HO HO HO HO HO HO!!

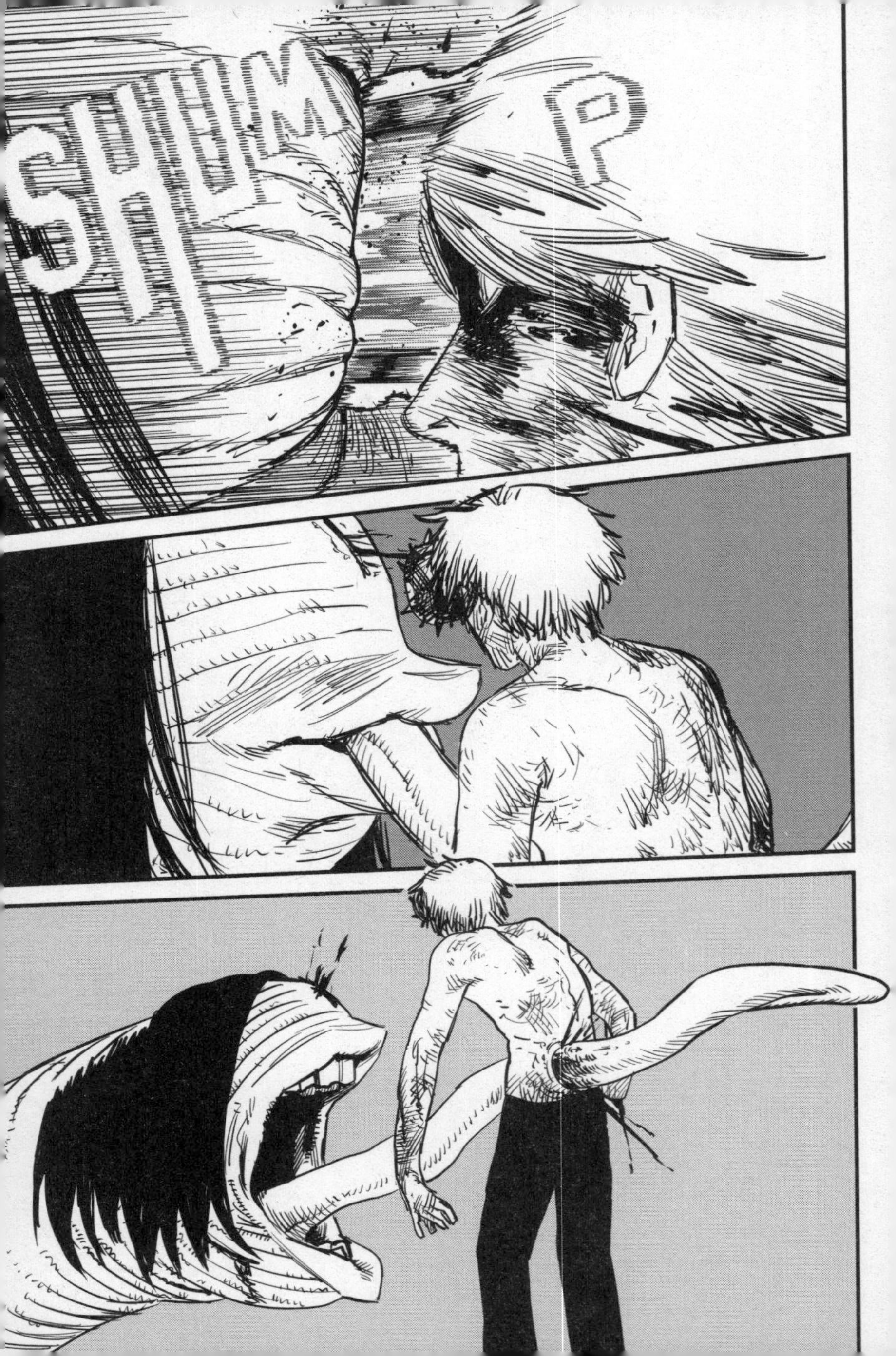
SHHHMP

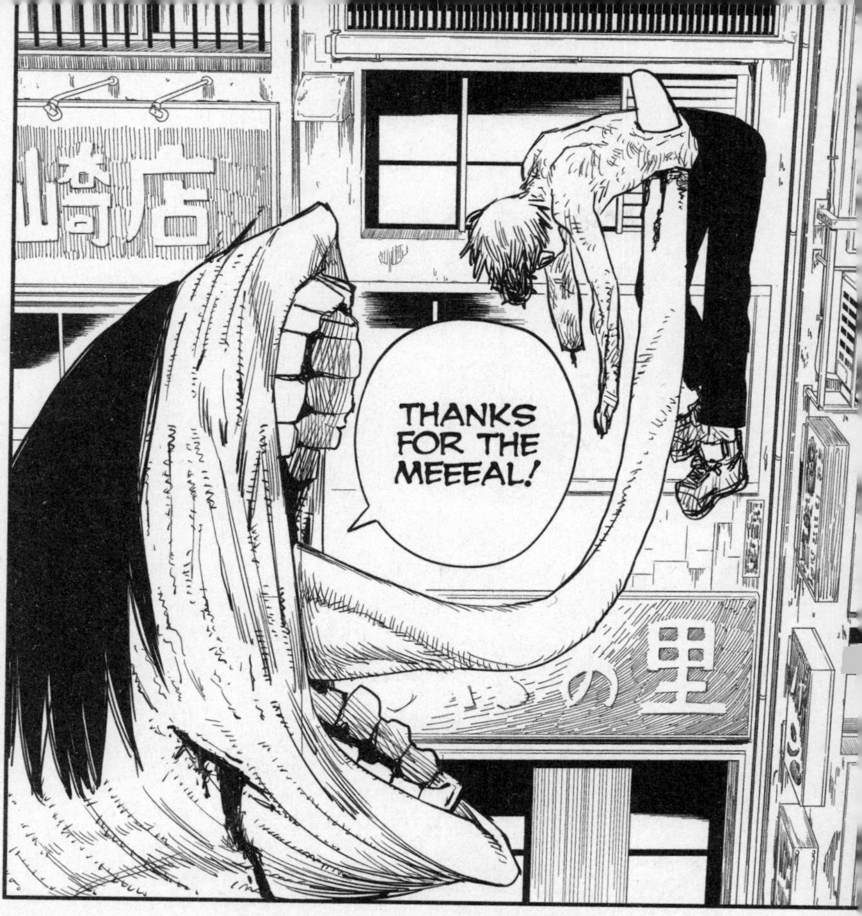
崎店
THANKS FOR THE MEEEAL!
の里
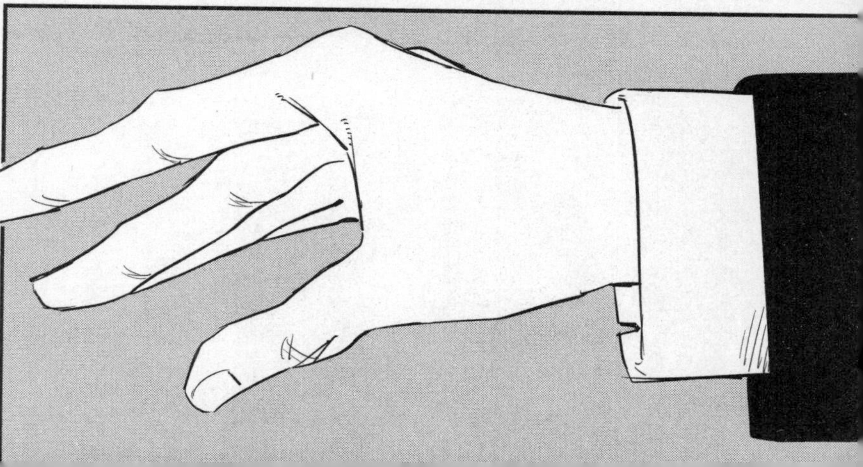

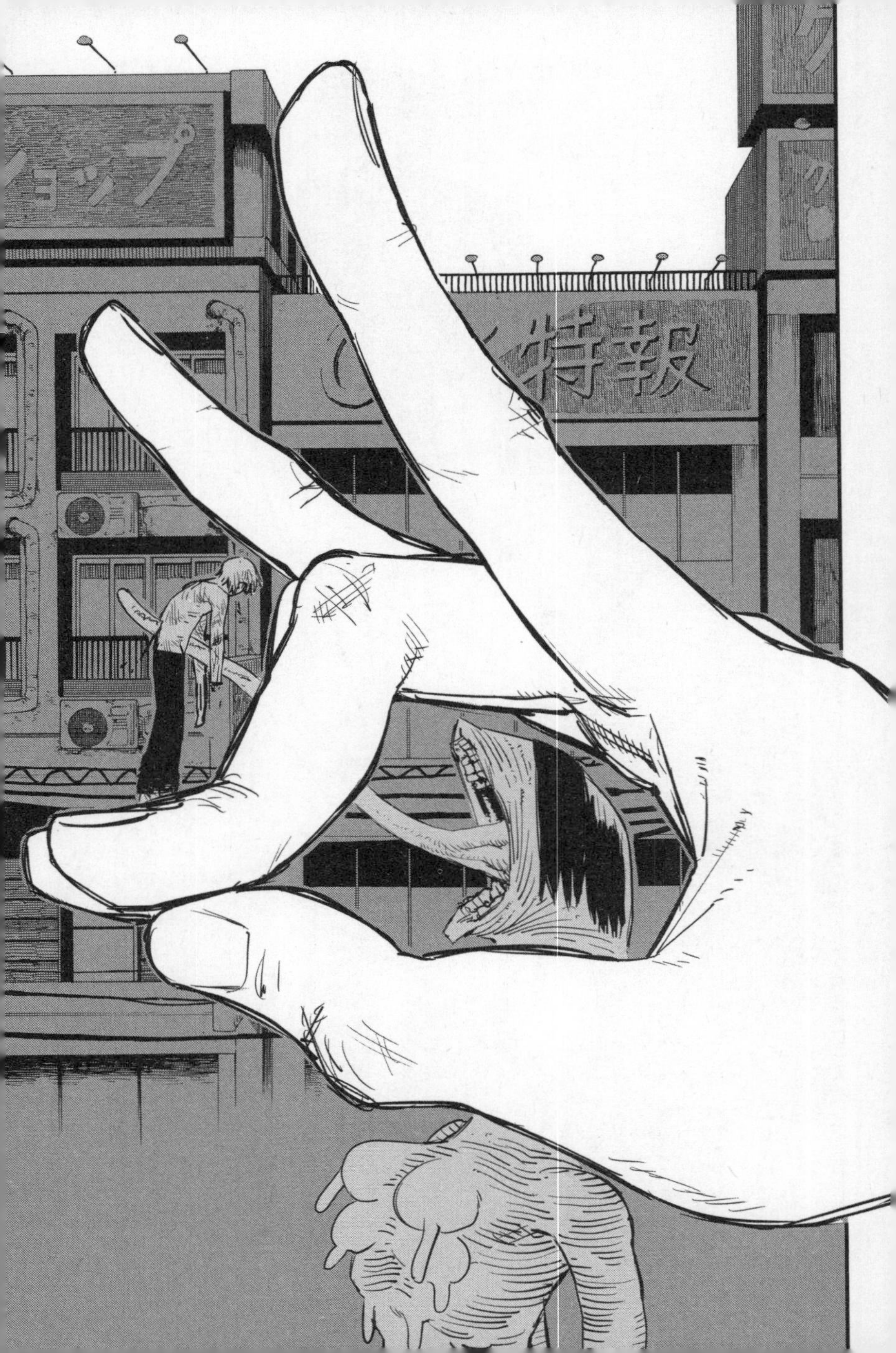
特報

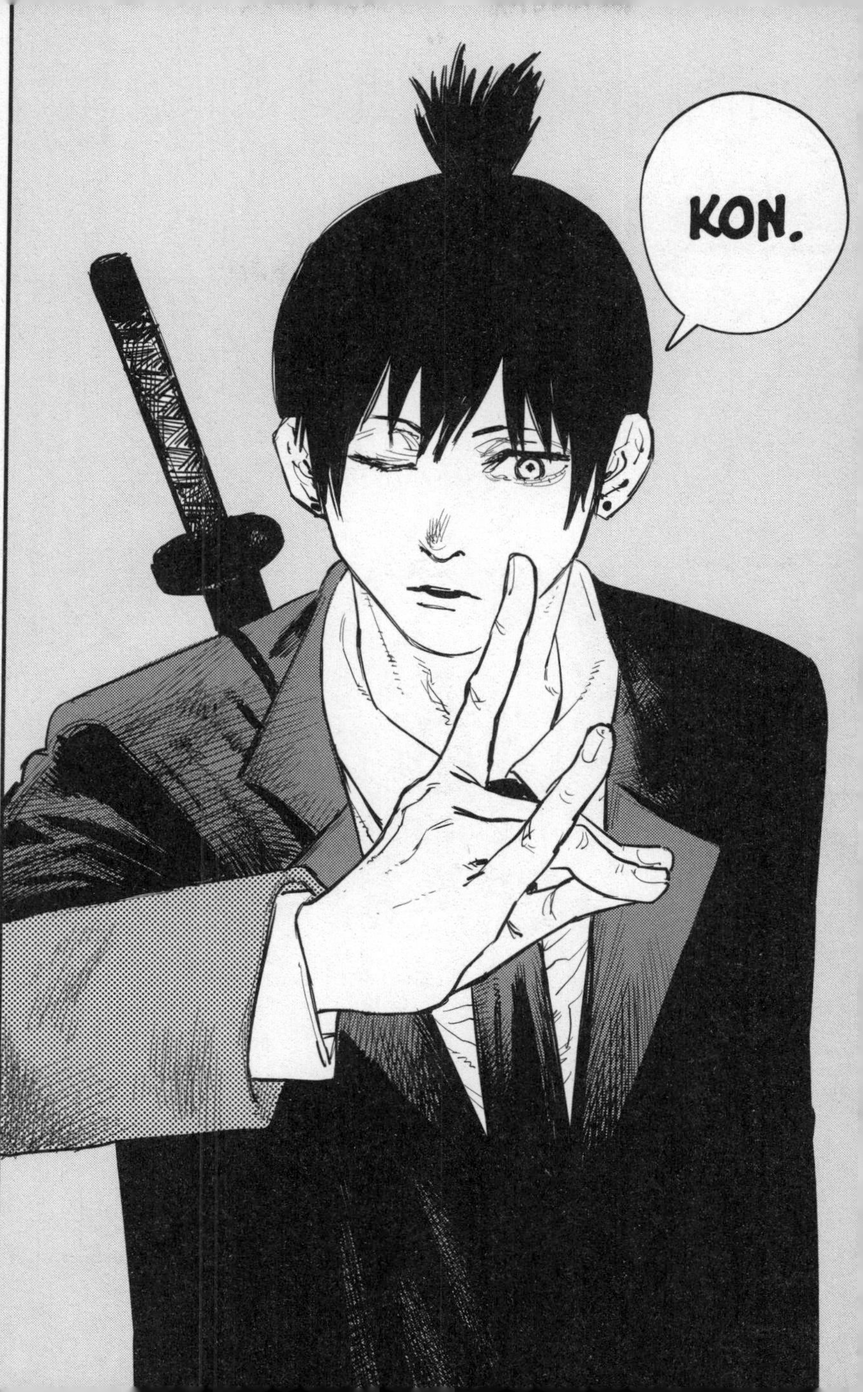
KON.

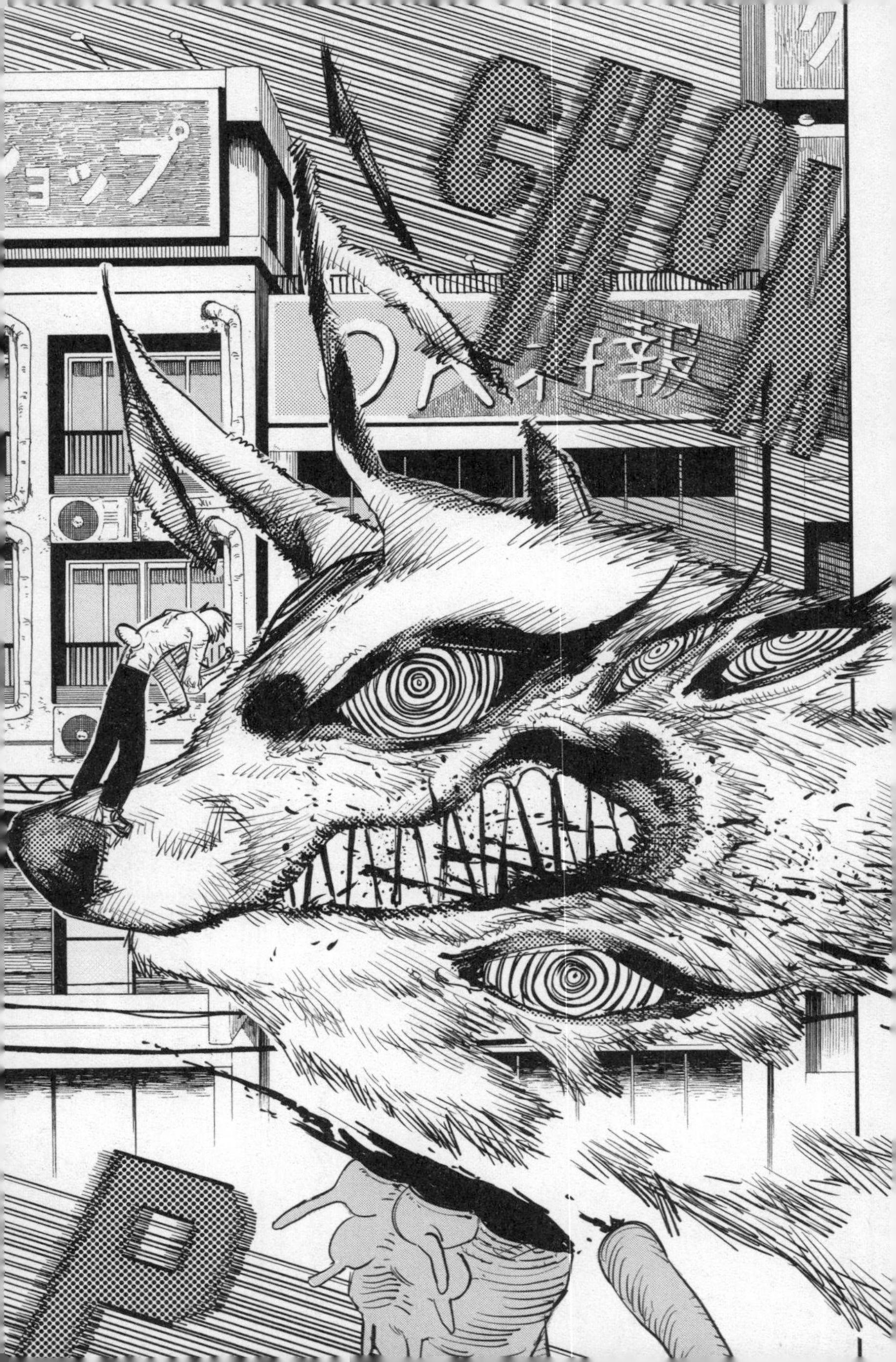
CHOMP

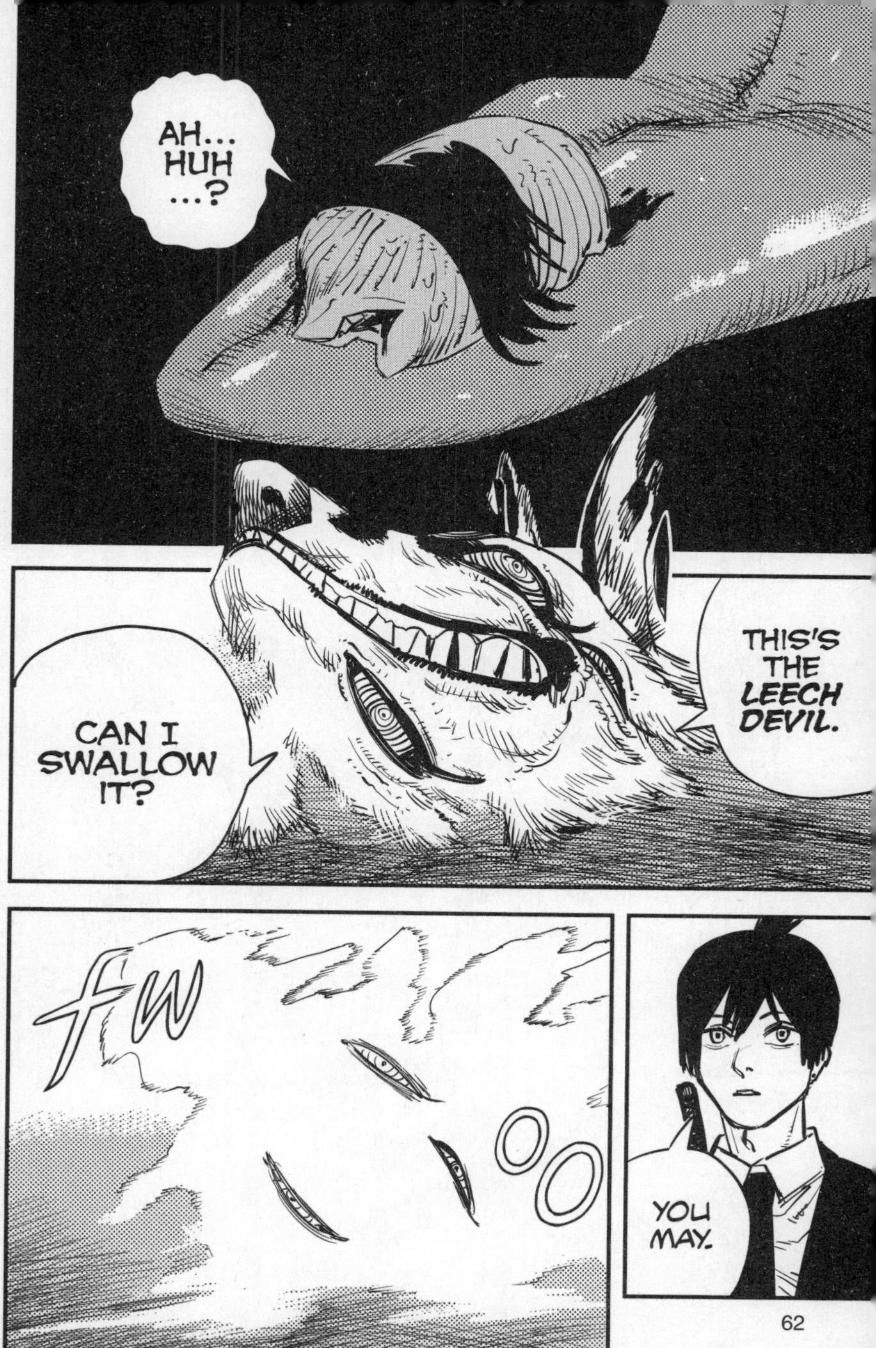
AH... HUH ...?
THIS'S THE *LEECH DEVIL.*
CAN I SWALLOW IT?
YOU MAY.
fw
oo

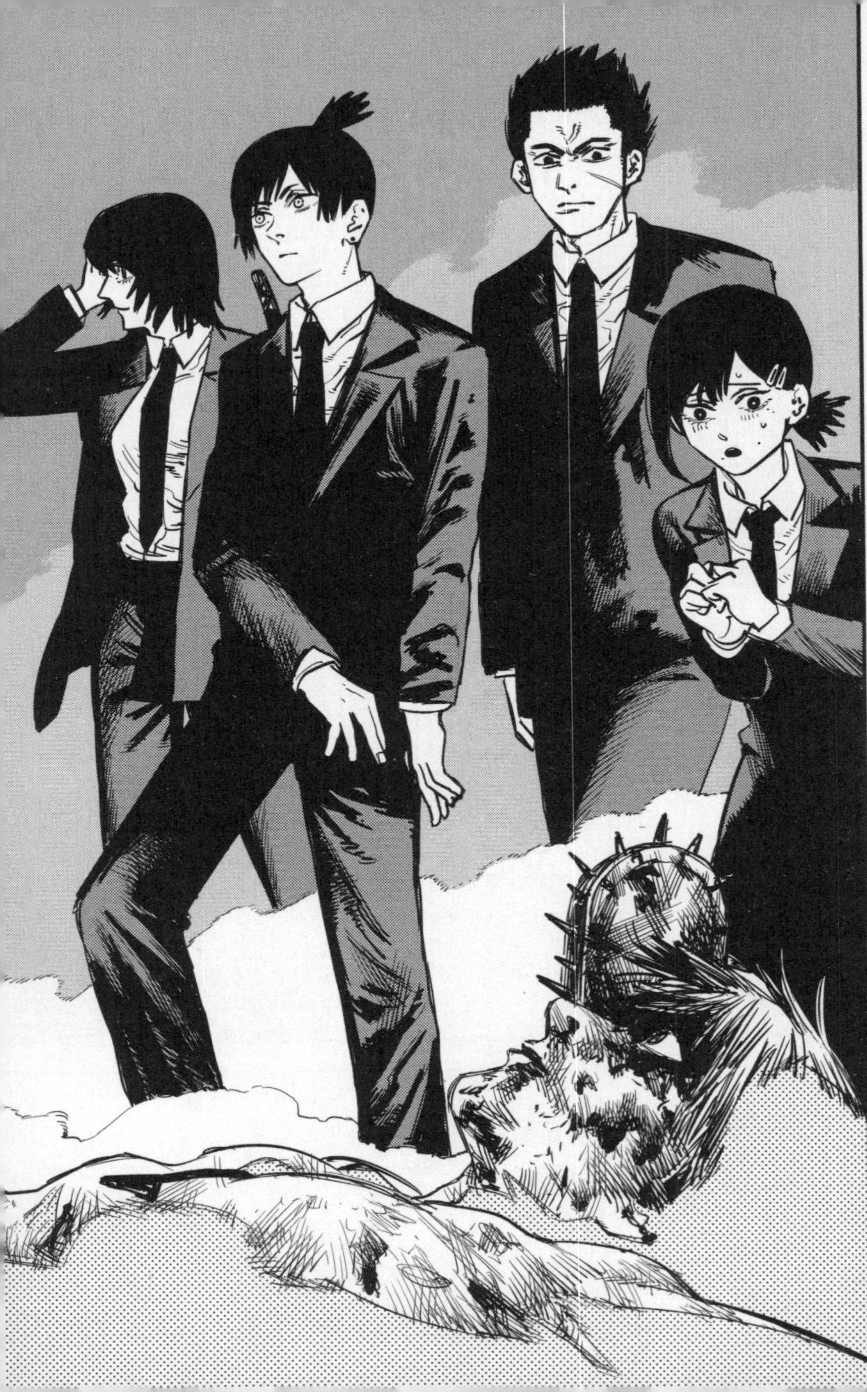

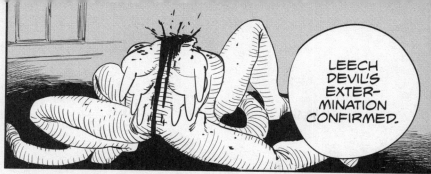

LEECH DEVIL'S EXTERMINATION CONFIRMED.

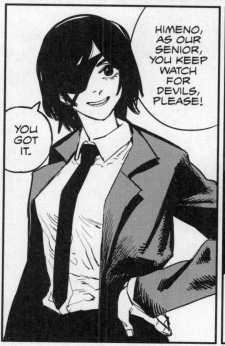

HIMENO, AS OUR SENIOR, YOU KEEP WATCH FOR DEVILS, PLEASE!

YOU GOT IT.

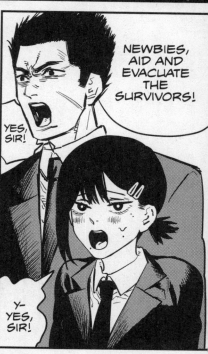

NEWBIES, AID AND EVACUATE THE SURVIVORS!

YES, SIR!

Y-YES, SIR!

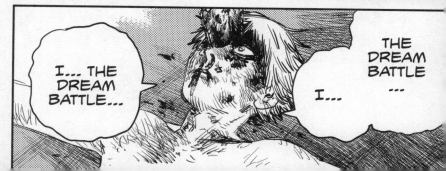

I... THE DREAM BATTLE...

THE DREAM BATTLE ...

I...

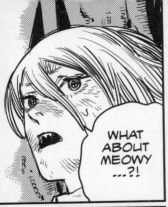

WHAT ABOUT MEOWY ...?!

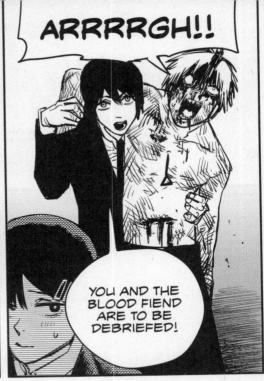

ARRRRGH!!

YOU AND THE BLOOD FIEND ARE TO BE DEBRIEFED!

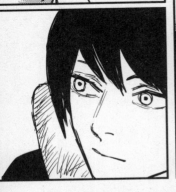

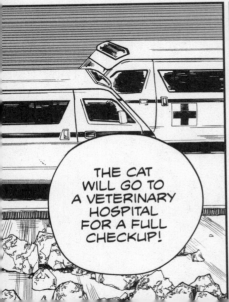

THE CAT WILL GO TO A VETERINARY HOSPITAL FOR A FULL CHECKUP!

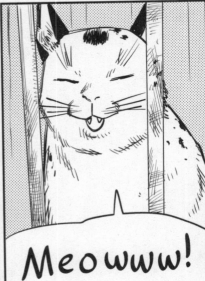

Meowww!

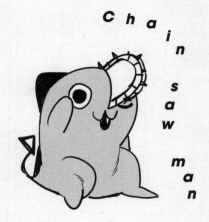

Chain saw man

# Chapter 11: Compromise

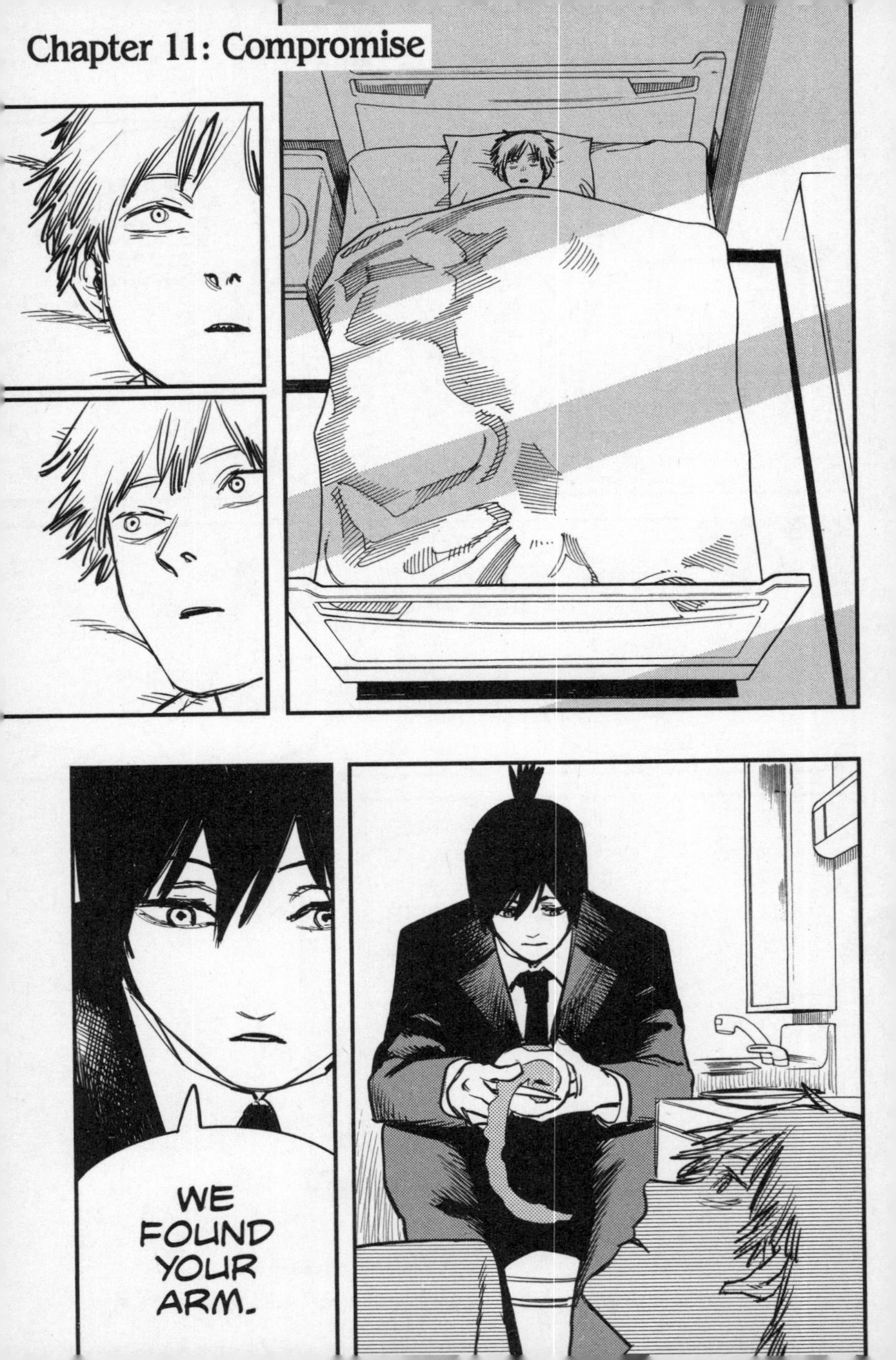
WE FOUND YOUR ARM.

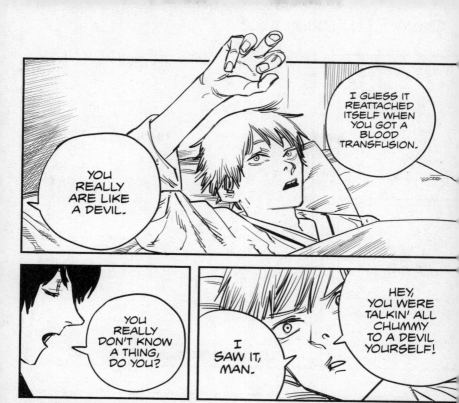

I GUESS IT REATTACHED ITSELF WHEN YOU GOT A BLOOD TRANSFUSION.

YOU REALLY ARE LIKE A DEVIL.

YOU REALLY DON'T KNOW A THING, DO YOU?

I SAW IT, MAN.

HEY, YOU WERE TALKIN' ALL CHUMMY TO A DEVIL YOURSELF!

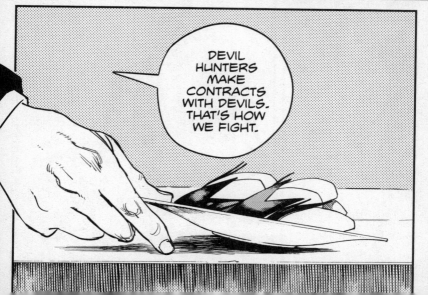

DEVIL HUNTERS MAKE CONTRACTS WITH DEVILS. THAT'S HOW WE FIGHT.

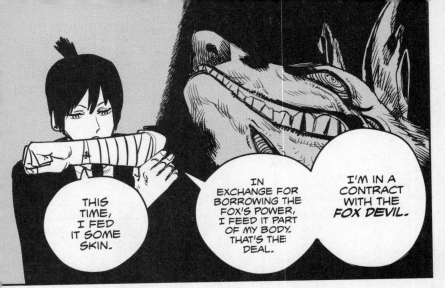

I'M IN A CONTRACT WITH THE *FOX DEVIL.*

IN EXCHANGE FOR BORROWING THE FOX'S POWER, I FEED IT PART OF MY BODY. THAT'S THE DEAL.

THIS TIME, I FED IT SOME SKIN.

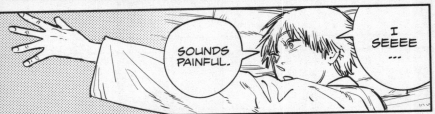

SOUNDS PAINFUL.

I SEEEE ...

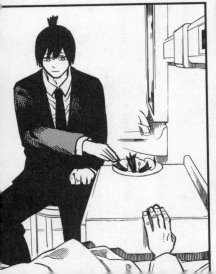

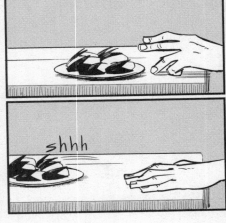

shhh

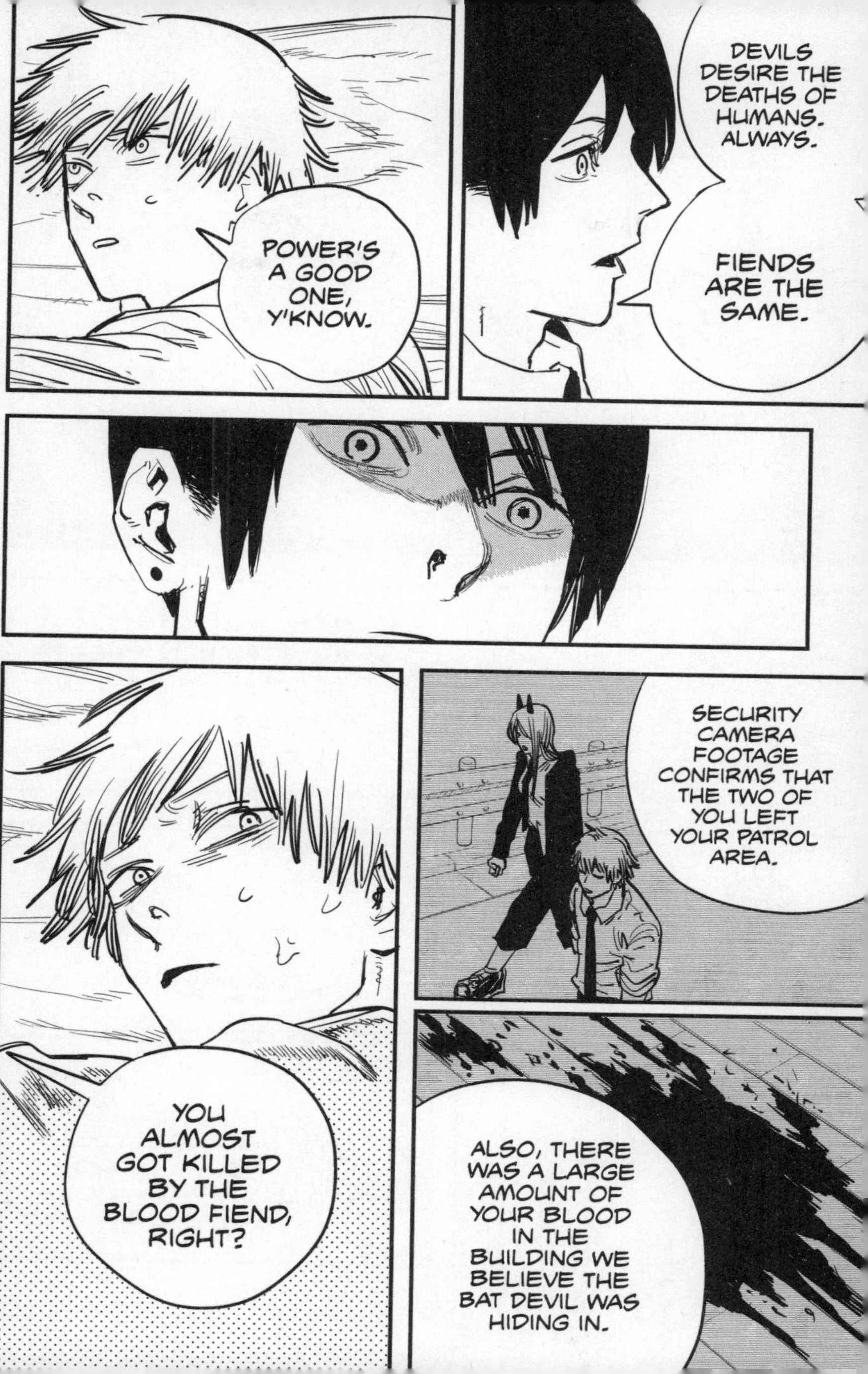
DEVILS DESIRE THE DEATHS OF HUMANS. ALWAYS.
FIENDS ARE THE SAME.
POWER'S A GOOD ONE, Y'KNOW.
SECURITY CAMERA FOOTAGE CONFIRMS THAT THE TWO OF YOU LEFT YOUR PATROL AREA.
ALSO, THERE WAS A LARGE AMOUNT OF YOUR BLOOD IN THE BUILDING WE BELIEVE THE BAT DEVIL WAS HIDING IN.
YOU ALMOST GOT KILLED BY THE BLOOD FIEND, RIGHT?

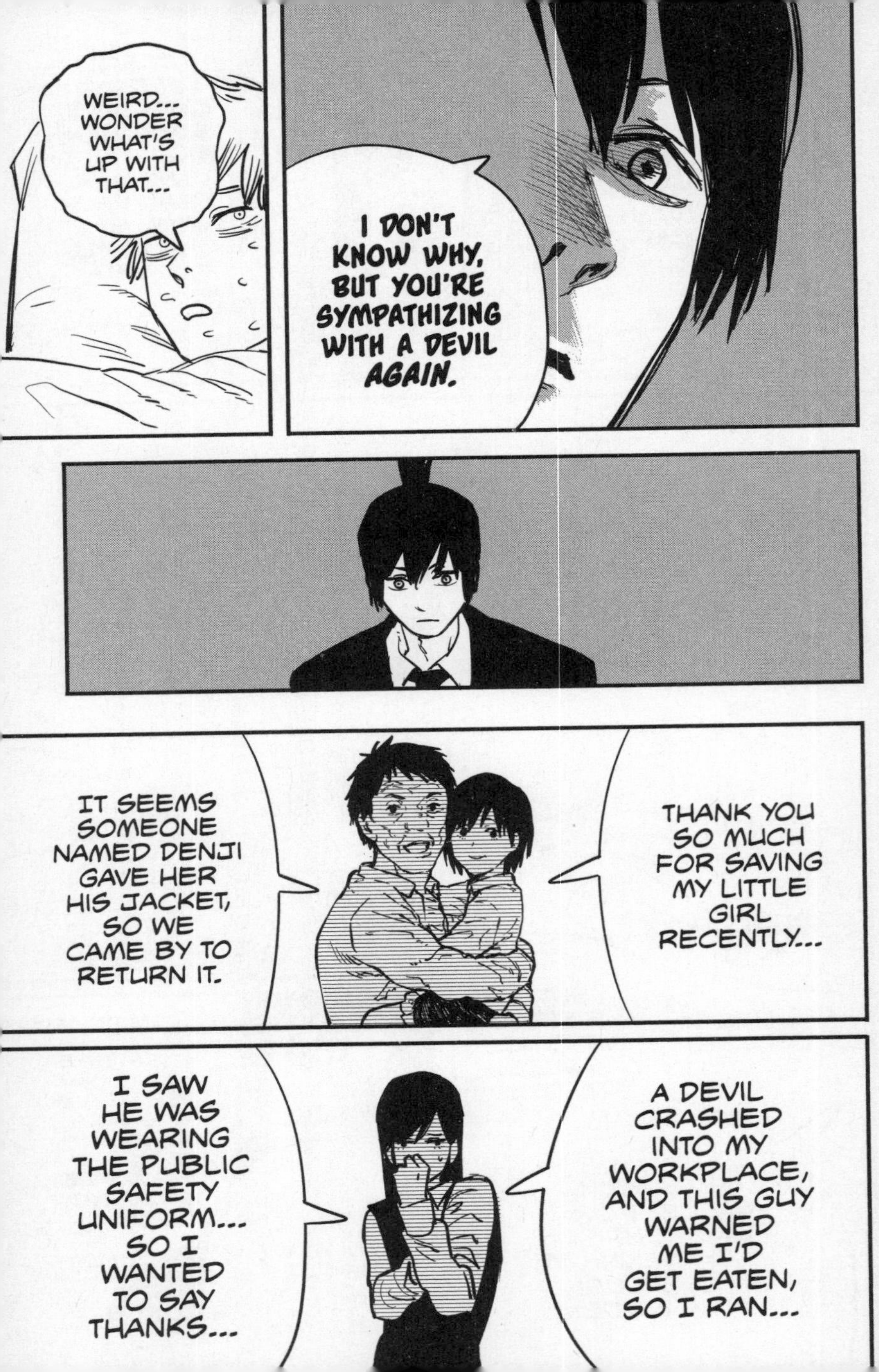
I DON'T KNOW WHY, BUT YOU'RE SYMPATHIZING WITH A DEVIL AGAIN.
WEIRD... WONDER WHAT'S UP WITH THAT...
THANK YOU SO MUCH FOR SAVING MY LITTLE GIRL RECENTLY...
IT SEEMS SOMEONE NAMED DENJI GAVE HER HIS JACKET, SO WE CAME BY TO RETURN IT.
A DEVIL CRASHED INTO MY WORKPLACE, AND THIS GUY WARNED ME I'D GET EATEN, SO I RAN...
I SAW HE WAS WEARING THE PUBLIC SAFETY UNIFORM... SO I WANTED TO SAY THANKS...

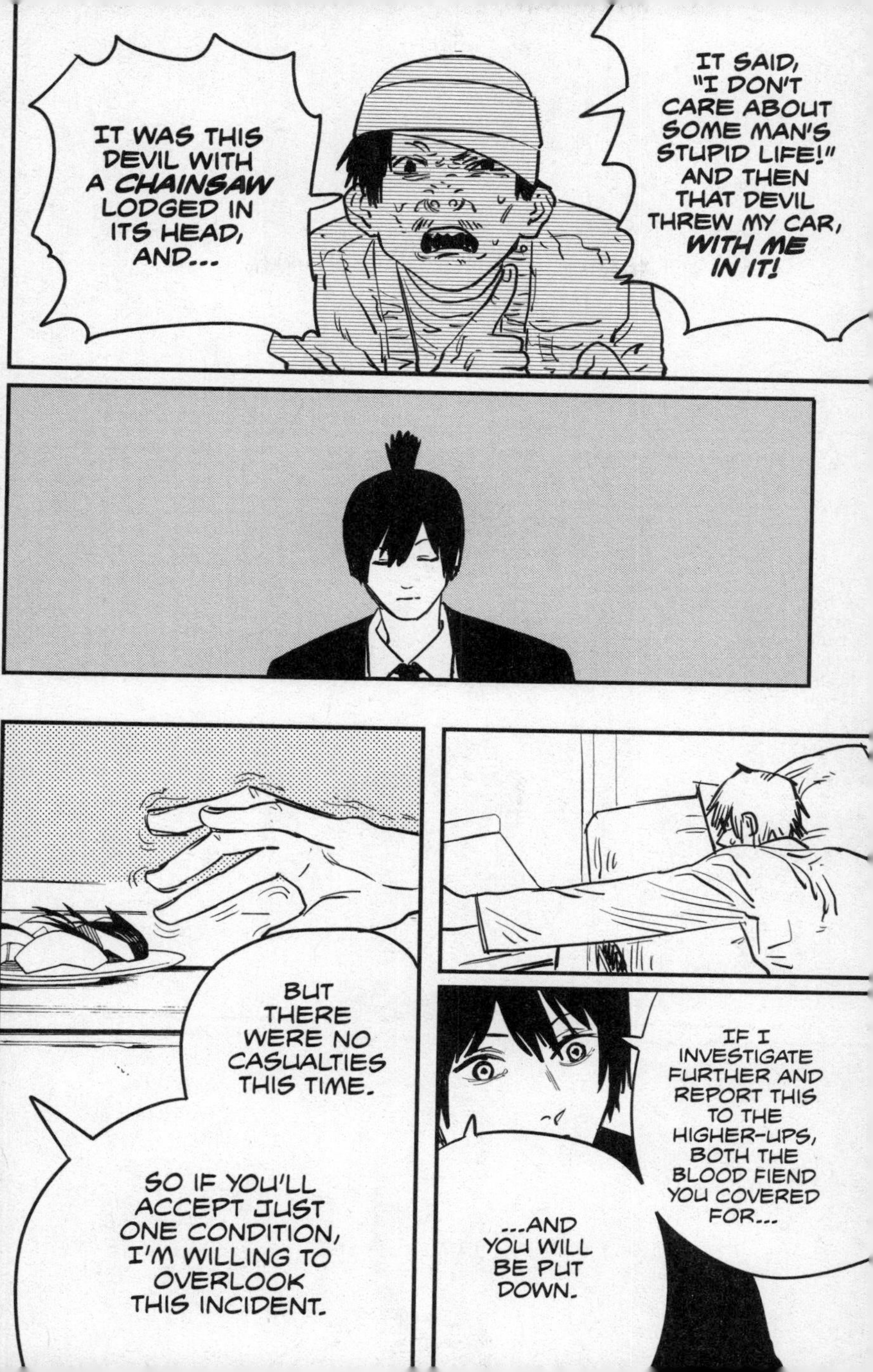
IT SAID, "I DON'T CARE ABOUT SOME MAN'S STUPID LIFE!" AND THEN THAT DEVIL THREW MY CAR, WITH ME IN IT!
IT WAS THIS DEVIL WITH A CHAINSAW LODGED IN ITS HEAD, AND...
IF I INVESTIGATE FURTHER AND REPORT THIS TO THE HIGHER-UPS, BOTH THE BLOOD FIEND YOU COVERED FOR...
...AND YOU WILL BE PUT DOWN.
BUT THERE WERE NO CASUALTIES THIS TIME.
SO IF YOU'LL ACCEPT JUST ONE CONDITION, I'M WILLING TO OVERLOOK THIS INCIDENT.

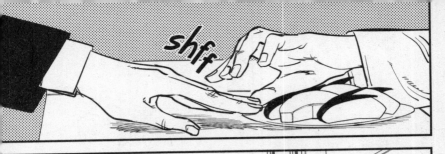

shff

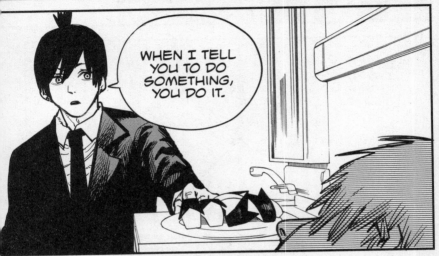

WHEN I TELL YOU TO DO SOMETHING, YOU DO IT.

ANSWER ME IF YOU UNDERSTAND.

HOW'S THAT SOUND?

YOU'RE A DUMB BRAT WITH NO MORALS.

I'VE BEEN DOING THIS FOR LONGER THAN YOU, AND I'D LIKE TO THINK I STAND FOR SOCIAL JUSTICE.

IF YOU JUST DO AS I SAY, YOU CAN PROTECT THE STANDARD OF LIVING YOU HAVE NOW.

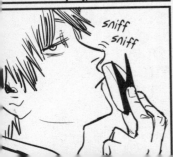

sniff sniff

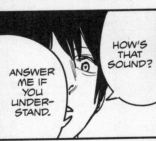

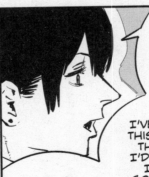

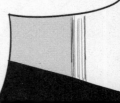

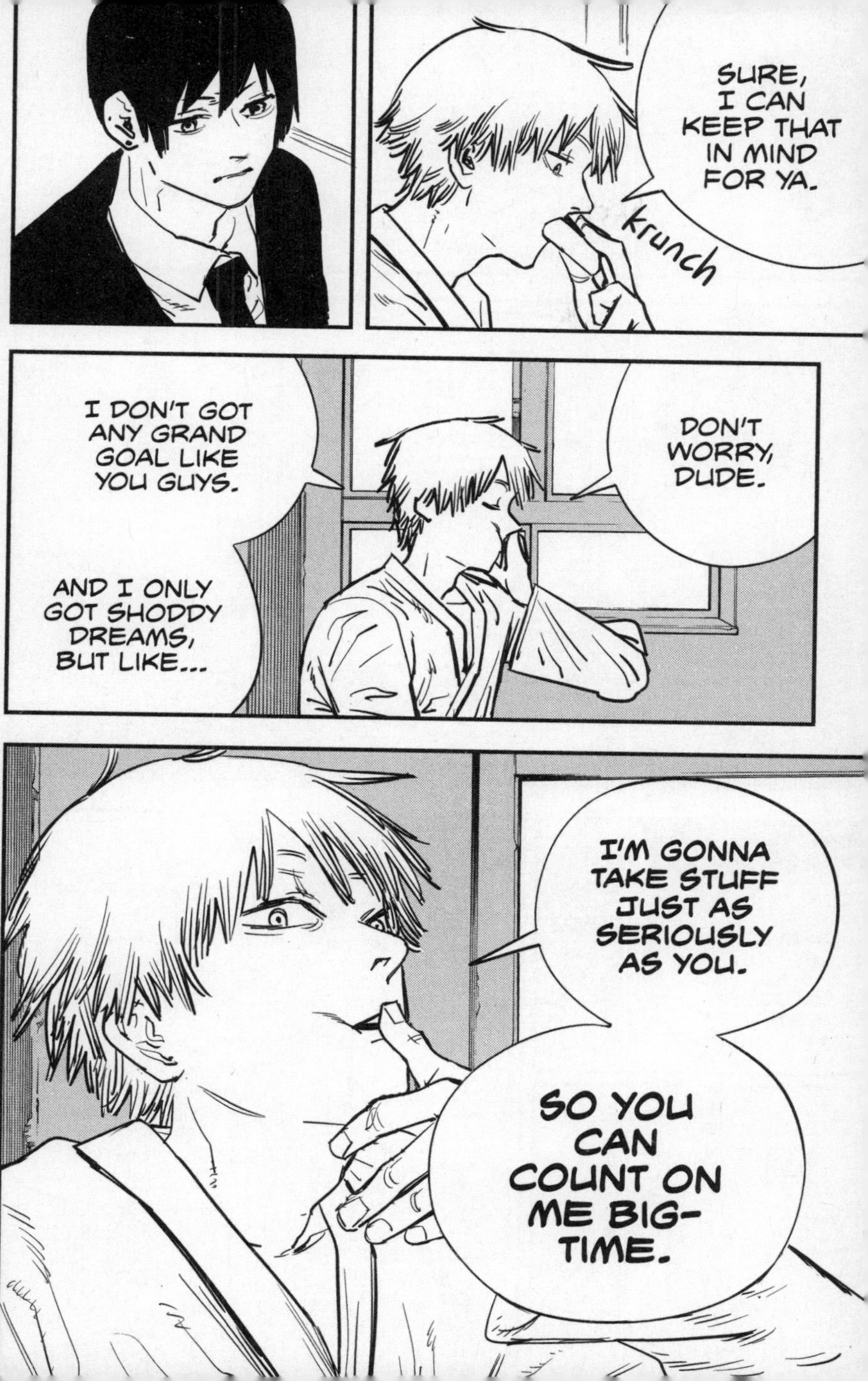
SURE, I CAN KEEP THAT IN MIND FOR YA.
krunch
DON'T WORRY, DUDE.
I DON'T GOT ANY GRAND GOAL LIKE YOU GUYS.
AND I ONLY GOT SHODDY DREAMS, BUT LIKE...
I'M GONNA TAKE STUFF JUST AS SERIOUSLY AS YOU.
SO YOU CAN COUNT ON ME BIG-TIME.

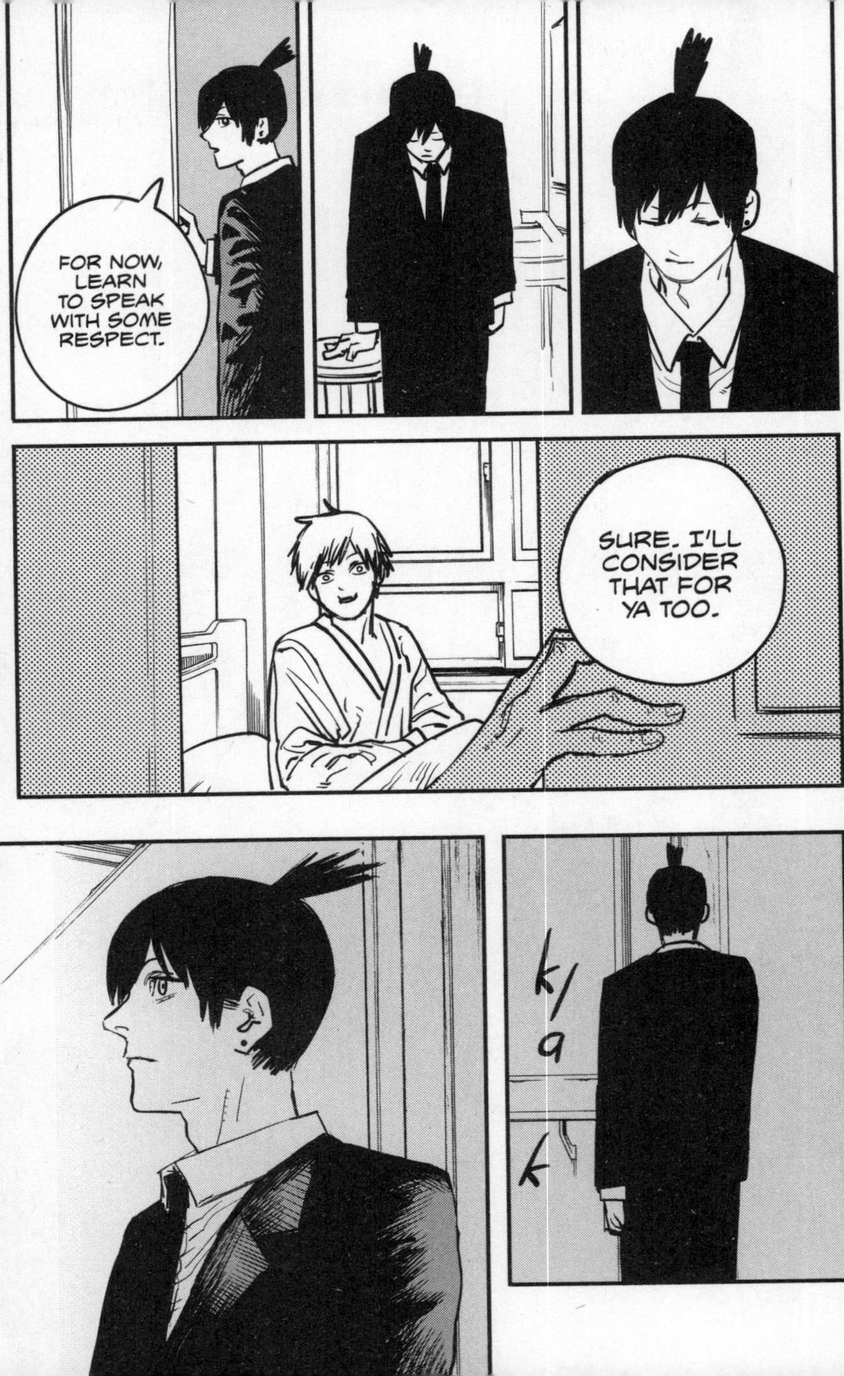
FOR NOW, LEARN TO SPEAK WITH SOME RESPECT.
SURE. I'LL CONSIDER THAT FOR YA TOO.
k/a
k

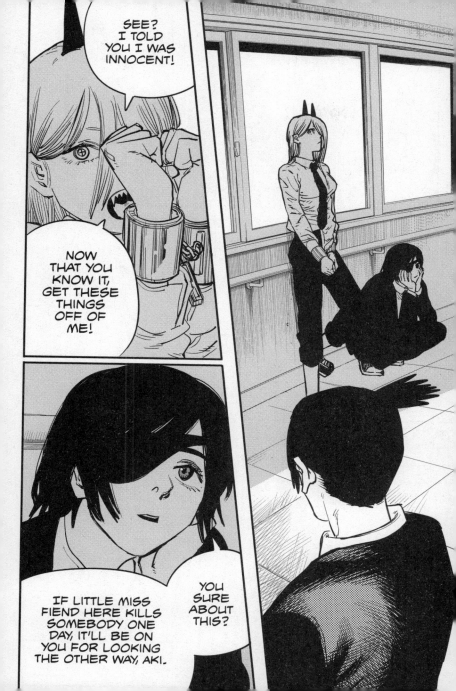

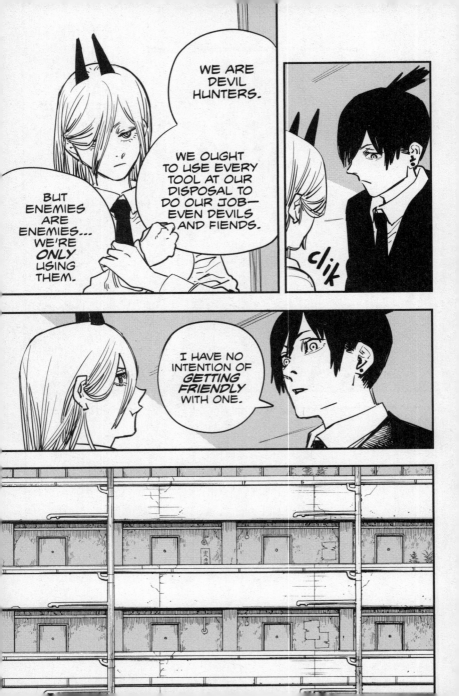

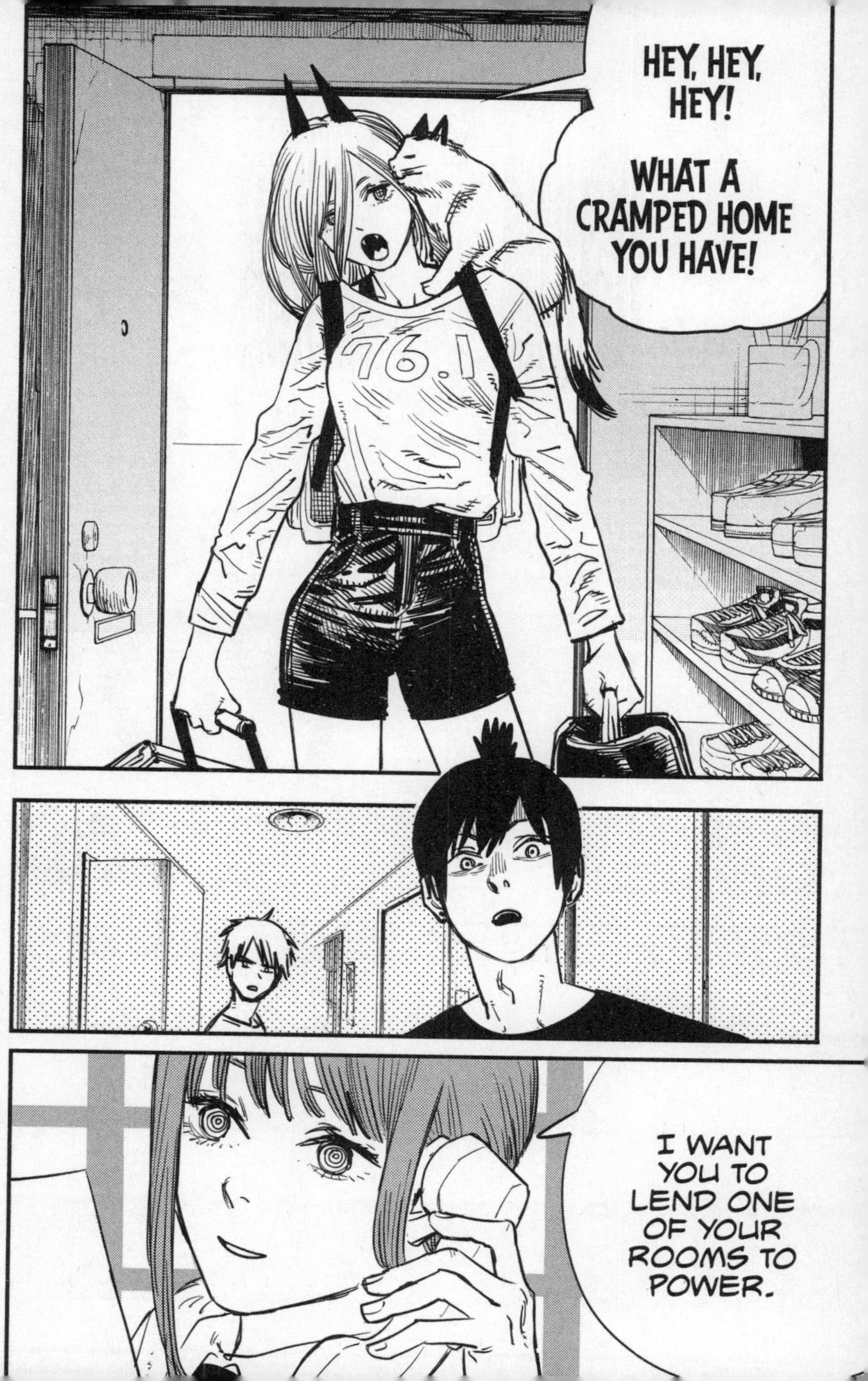
HEY, HEY, HEY! WHAT A CRAMPED HOME YOU HAVE!
I WANT YOU TO LEND ONE OF YOUR ROOMS TO POWER.

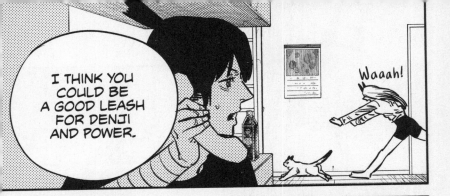

I THINK YOU COULD BE A GOOD LEASH FOR DENJI AND POWER.

Waaah!

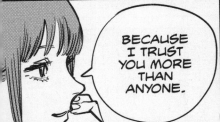

BECAUSE I TRUST YOU MORE THAN ANYONE.

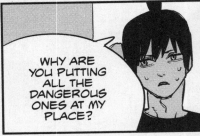

WHY ARE YOU PUTTING ALL THE DANGEROUS ONES AT MY PLACE?

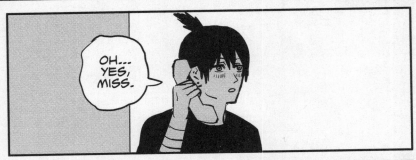

OH... YES, MISS.

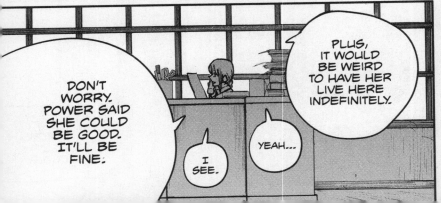

DON'T WORRY. POWER SAID SHE COULD BE GOOD. IT'LL BE FINE.

PLUS, IT WOULD BE WEIRD TO HAVE HER LIVE HERE INDEFINITELY.

I SEE.

YEAH...

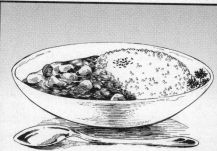

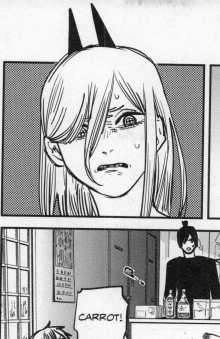

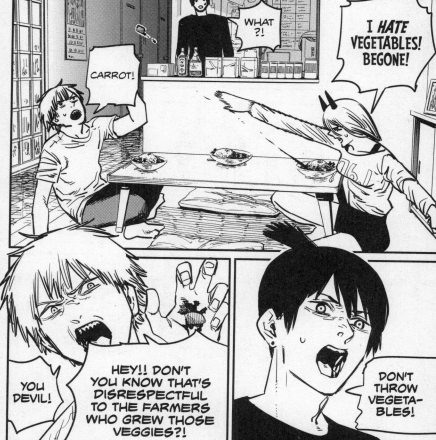

WHAT ?!

I *HATE* VEGETABLES! BEGONE!

CARROT!

HEY!! DON'T YOU KNOW THAT'S DISRESPECTFUL TO THE FARMERS WHO GREW THOSE VEGGIES?!

YOU DEVIL!

DON'T THROW VEGETABLES!

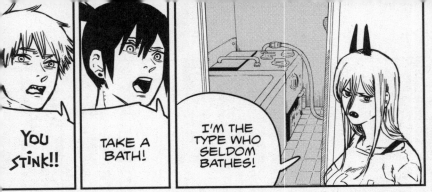

YOU
STINK!!

TAKE A
BATH!

I'M THE
TYPE WHO
SELDOM
BATHES!

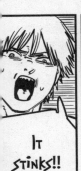

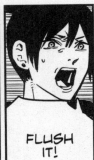

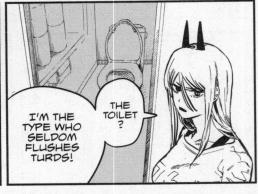

IT
STINKS!!

FLUSH
IT!

I'M THE
TYPE WHO
SELDOM
FLUSHES
TURDS!

THE
TOILET
?

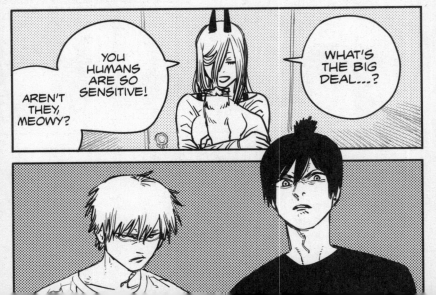

AREN'T
THEY,
MEOWY?

YOU
HUMANS
ARE SO
SENSITIVE!

WHAT'S
THE BIG
DEAL....?

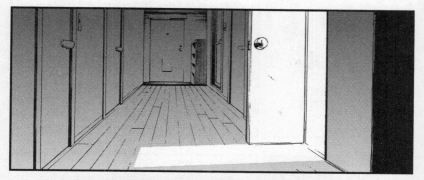

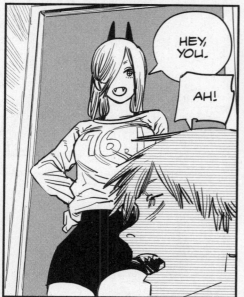

HEY, YOU.

AH!

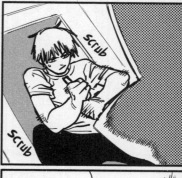

Scrub

Scrub

WHAT, DEVILS CAN'T EVEN FLUSH THEIR TURDS?!

SHE PICKS OUT HER VEGGIES TOO!

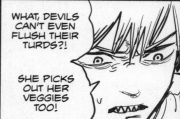

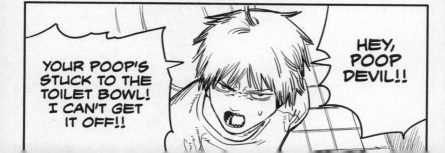

YOUR POOP'S STUCK TO THE TOILET BOWL! I CAN'T GET IT OFF!!

HEY, POOP DEVIL!!

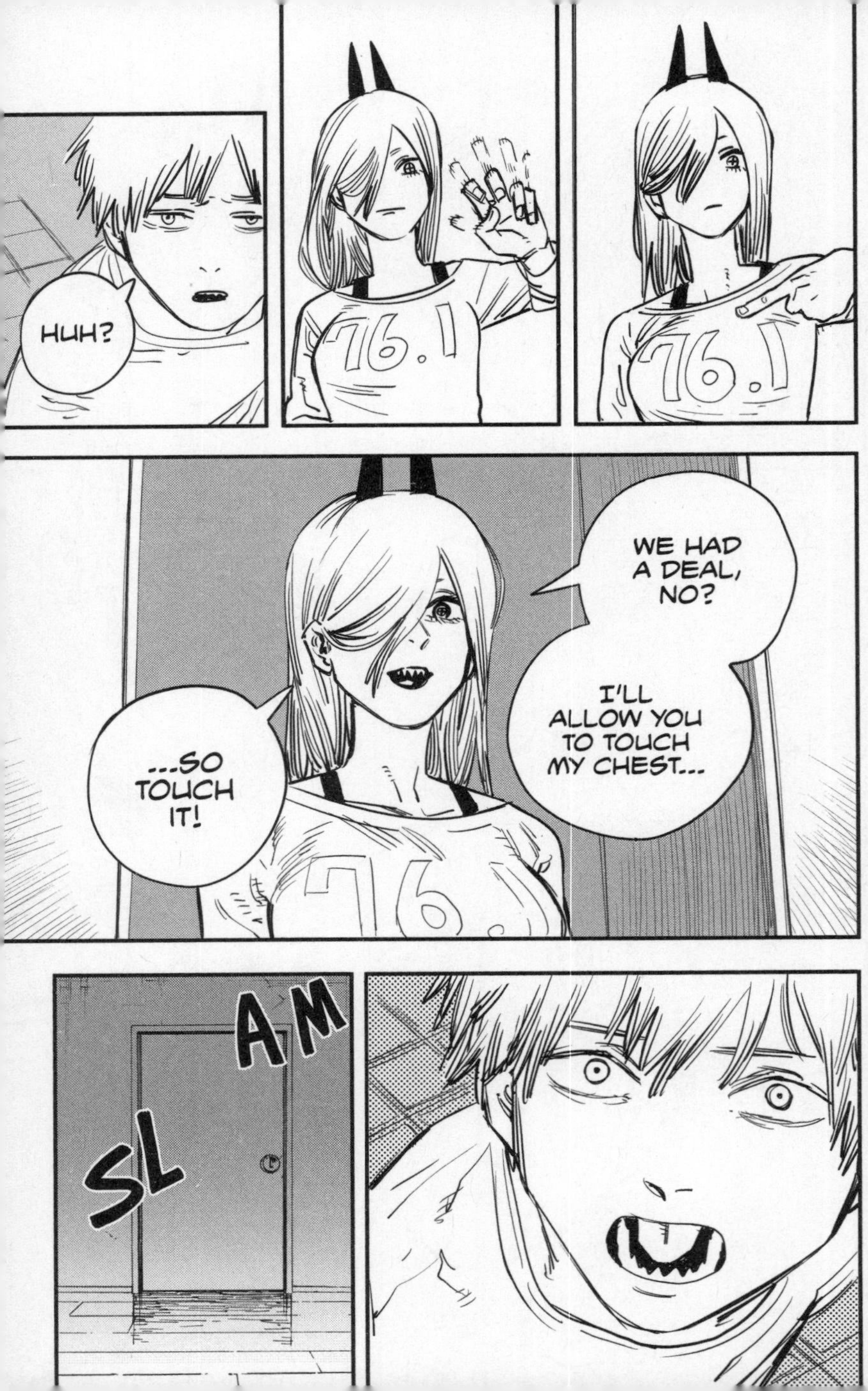
HUH?
WE HAD A DEAL, NO?
I'LL ALLOW YOU TO TOUCH MY CHEST...
...SO TOUCH IT!
SLAM

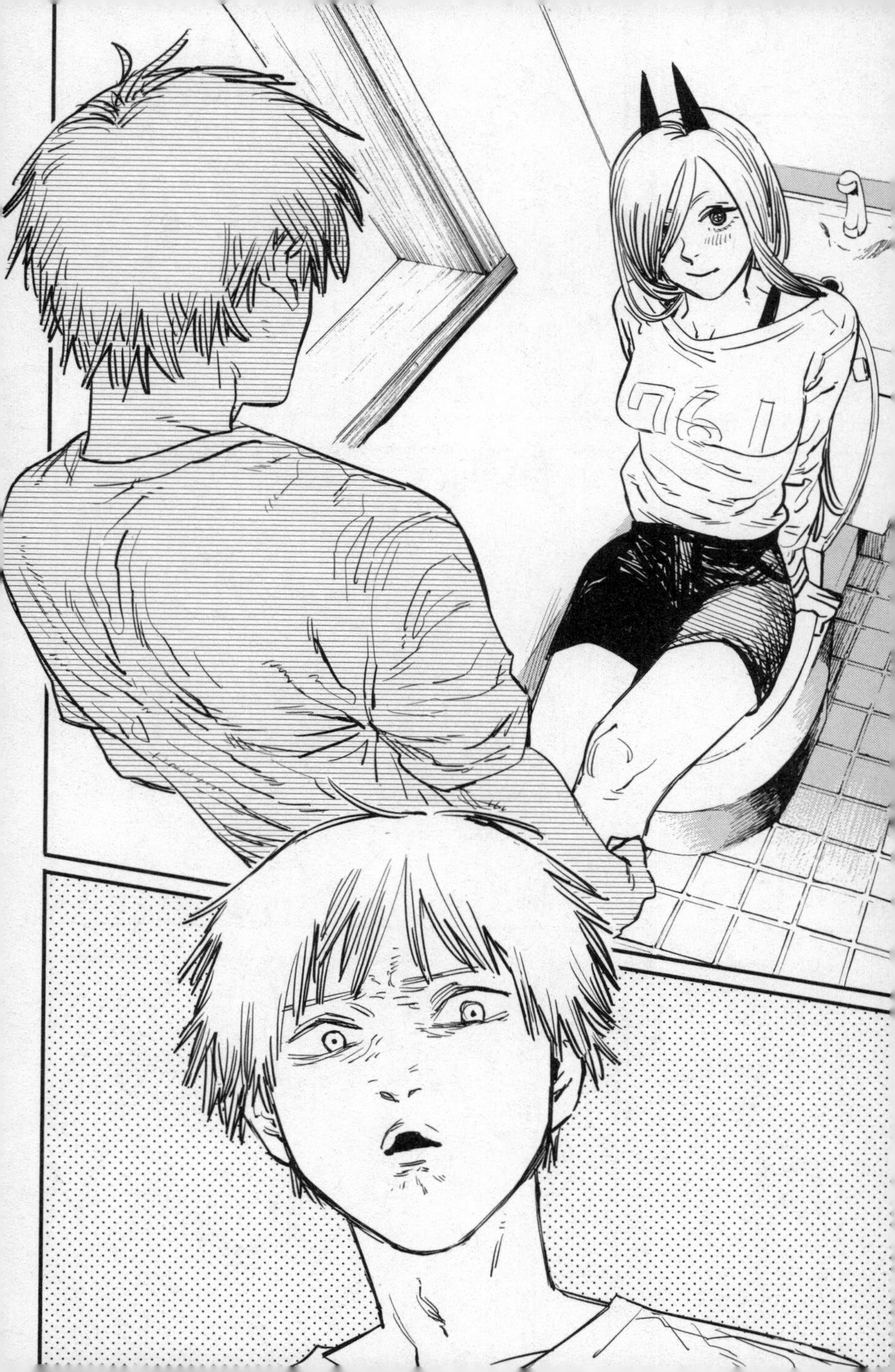

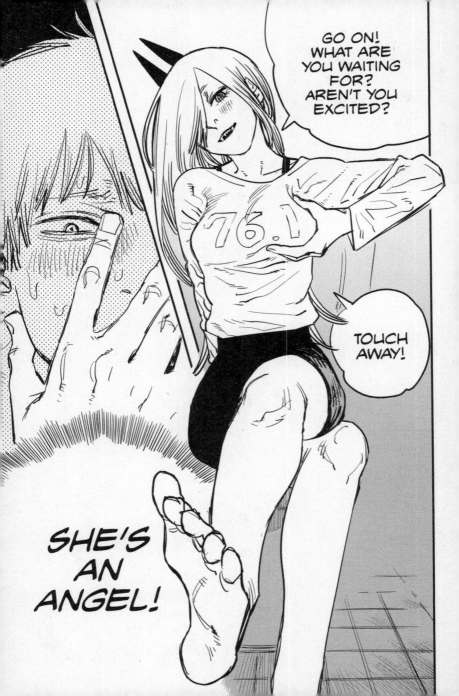

Chainsaw
man

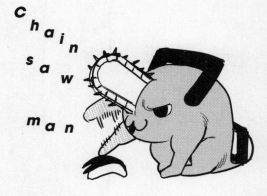

# Chapter 12: Squeeze

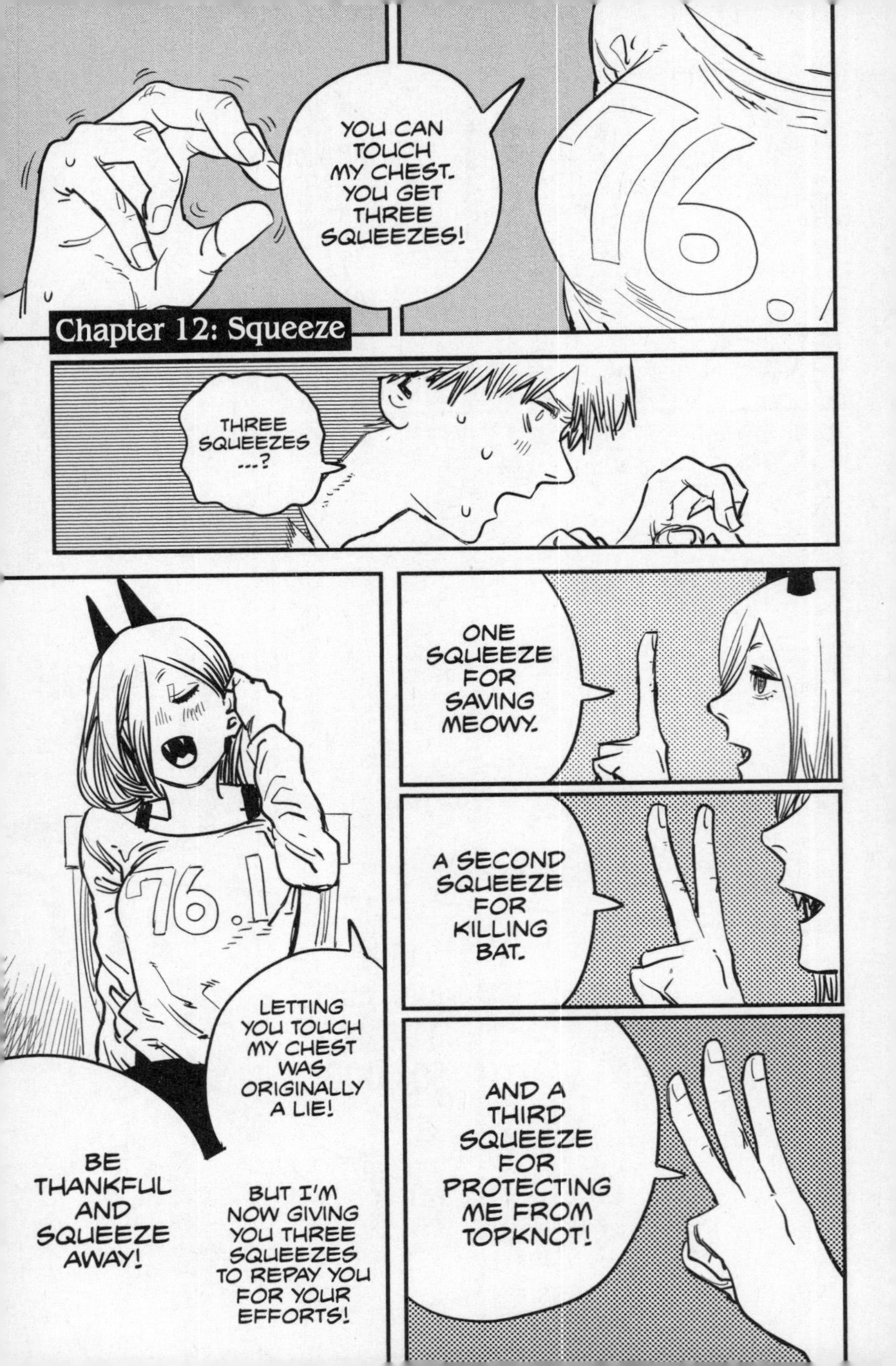
YOU CAN TOUCH MY CHEST. YOU GET THREE SQUEEZES!
THREE SQUEEZES ...?
ONE SQUEEZE FOR SAVING MEOWY.
A SECOND SQUEEZE FOR KILLING BAT.
AND A THIRD SQUEEZE FOR PROTECTING ME FROM TOPKNOT!
LETTING YOU TOUCH MY CHEST WAS ORIGINALLY A LIE!
BUT I'M NOW GIVING YOU THREE SQUEEZES TO REPAY YOU FOR YOUR EFFORTS!
BE THANKFUL AND SQUEEZE AWAY!

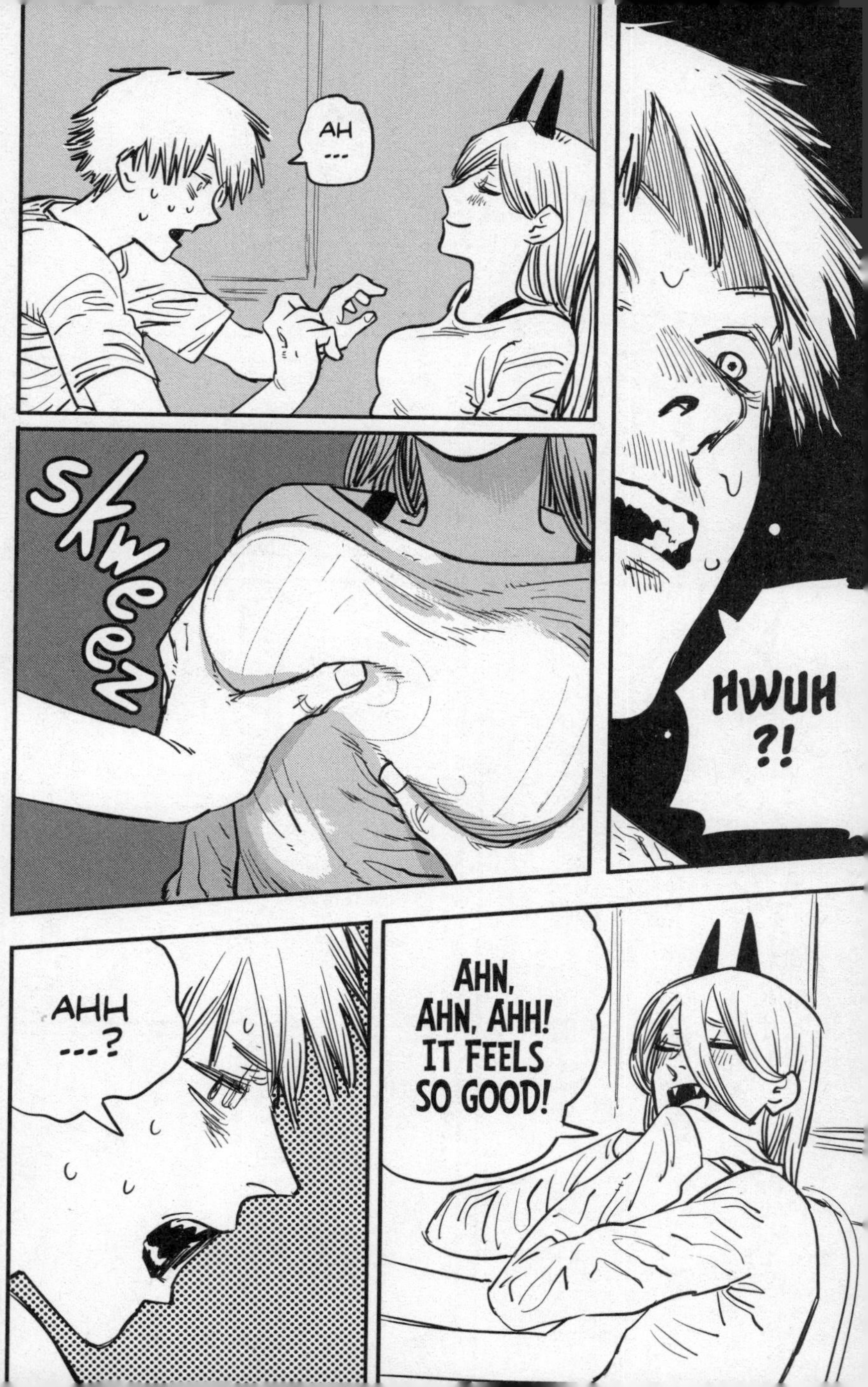
HWUH ?!
AH ---
SKWEEZ
AHN, AHN, AHH! IT FEELS SO GOOD!
AHH ---?

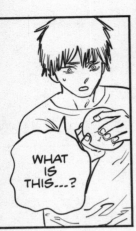

WHAT IS THIS....?

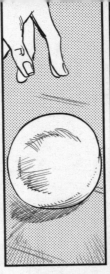

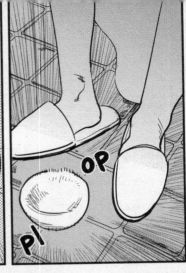

OP

PI

A WONDROUS ITEM THAT MAKES CHESTS BIGGER.

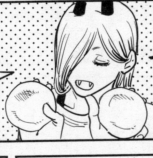

'TIS A BREAST PAD.

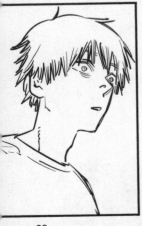

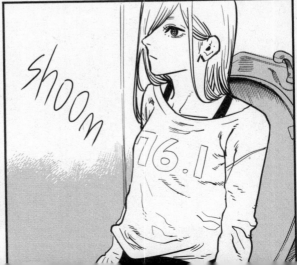

SHOOM

76.1

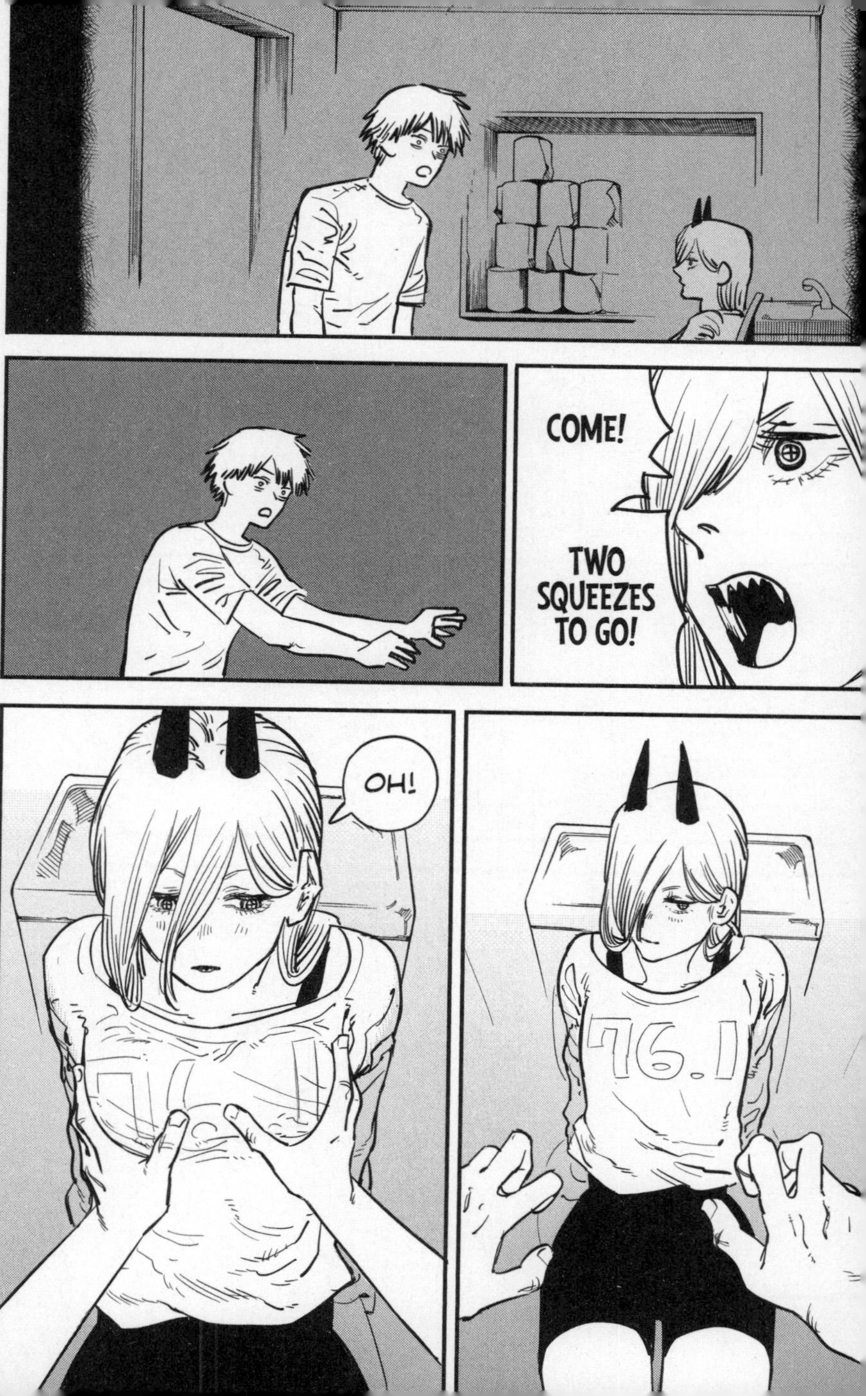
COME!
TWO SQUEEZES TO GO!
OH!
76.1

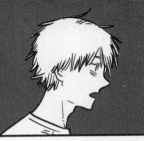

OKAY! ONE SQUEEZE LEFT!

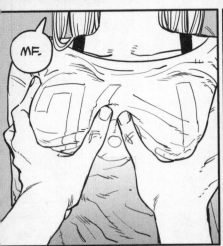
MF.

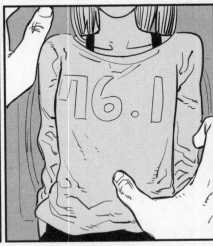
76.1

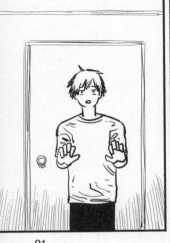

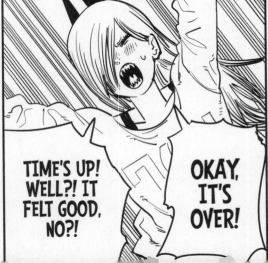
TIME'S UP! WELL?! IT FELT GOOD, NO?!

OKAY, IT'S OVER!

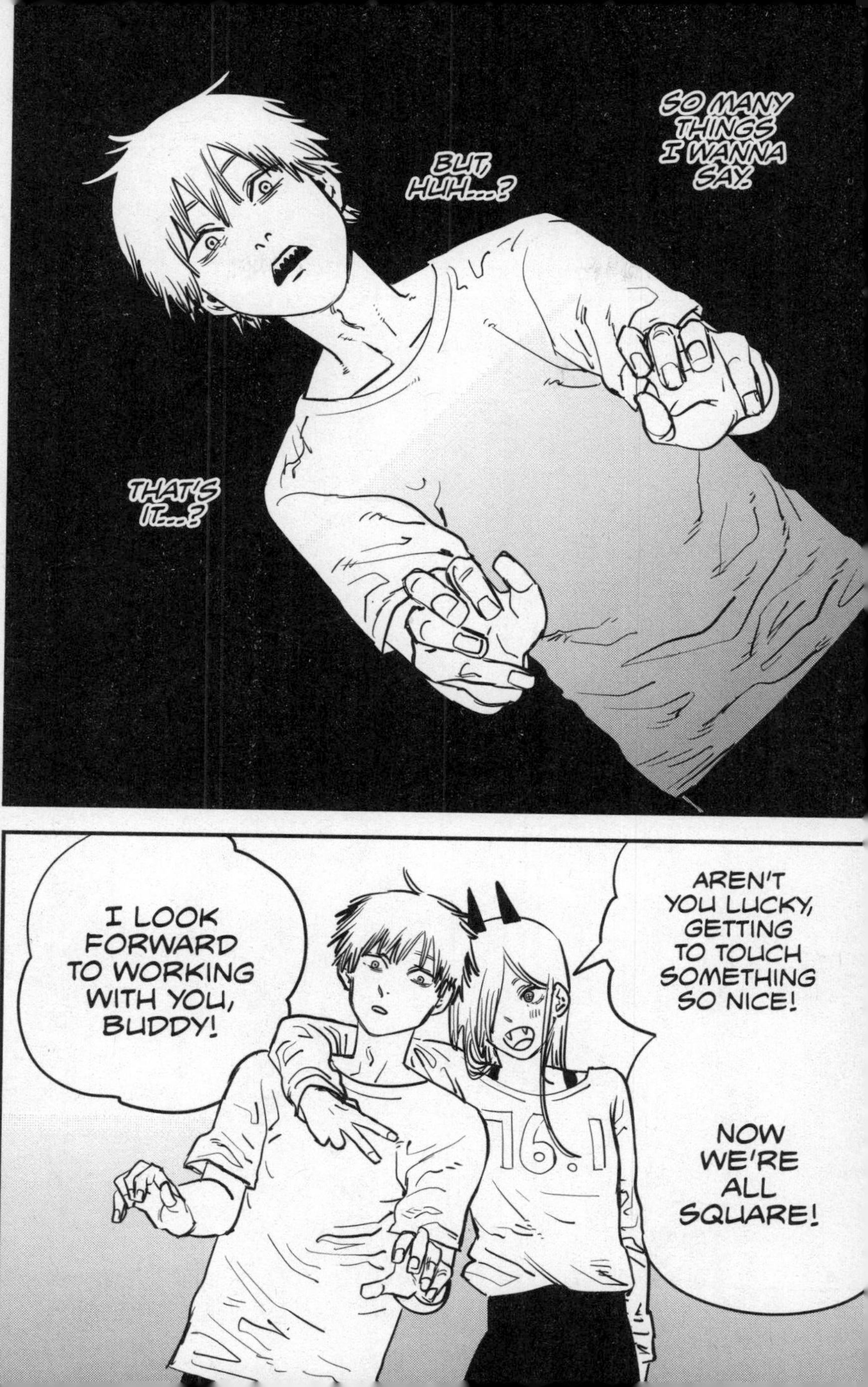
SO MANY THINGS I WANNA SAY.
BUT, HUH...?
THAT'S IT...?
AREN'T YOU LUCKY, GETTING TO TOUCH SOMETHING SO NICE!
NOW WE'RE ALL SQUARE!
I LOOK FORWARD TO WORKING WITH YOU, BUDDY!

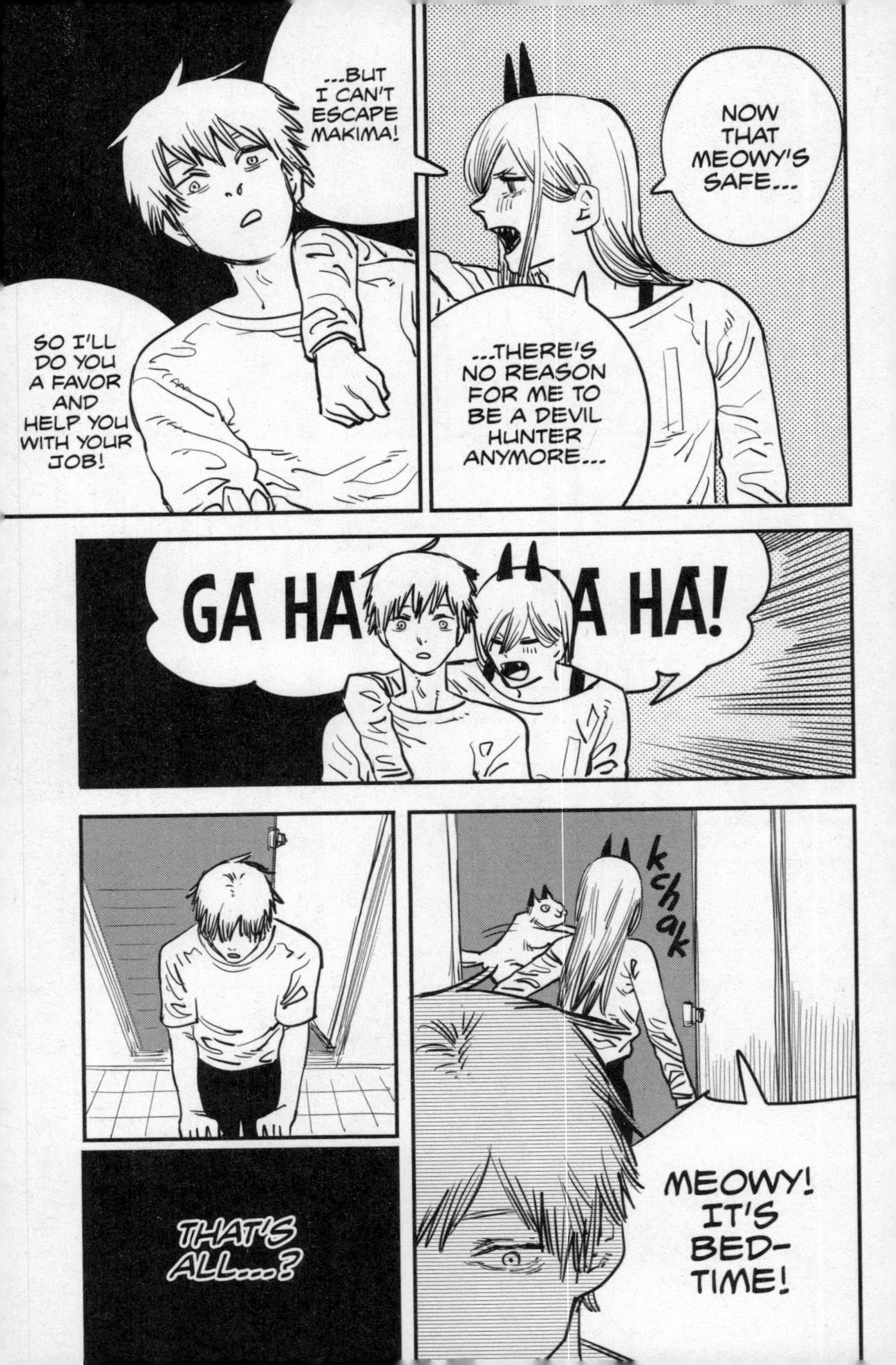
NOW THAT MEOWY'S SAFE...
...THERE'S NO REASON FOR ME TO BE A DEVIL HUNTER ANYMORE...
...BUT I CAN'T ESCAPE MAKIMA!
SO I'LL DO YOU A FAVOR AND HELP YOU WITH YOUR JOB!
GA HA A HA!
kchak
MEOWY! IT'S BED-TIME!
THAT'S ALL...?

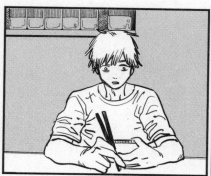
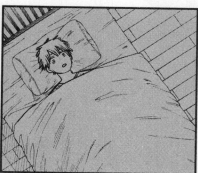

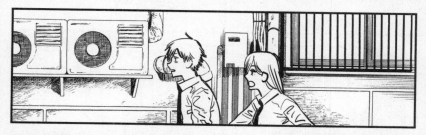

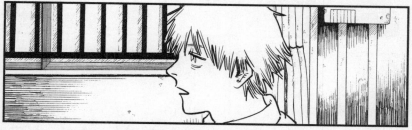

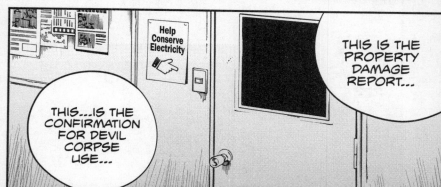

THIS IS THE PROPERTY DAMAGE REPORT...

THIS...IS THE CONFIRMATION FOR DEVIL CORPSE USE...

Help Conserve Electricity

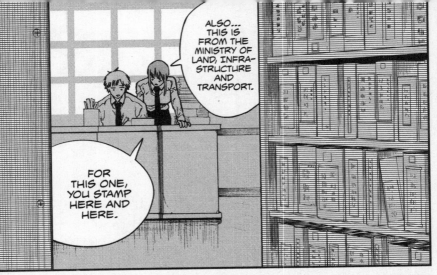

ALSO...
THIS IS
FROM THE
MINISTRY OF
LAND, INFRA-
STRUCTURE
AND
TRANSPORT.

FOR
THIS ONE,
YOU STAMP
HERE AND
HERE.

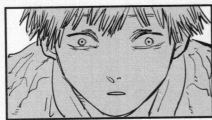

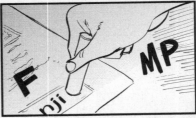

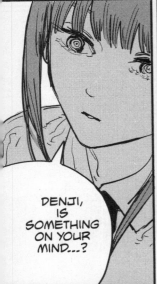

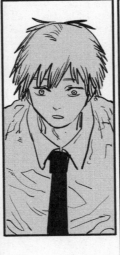

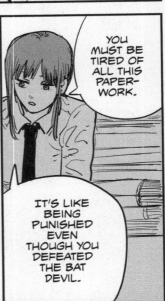

YOU
MUST BE
TIRED OF
ALL THIS
PAPER-
WORK.

IT'S LIKE
BEING
PUNISHED
EVEN
THOUGH YOU
DEFEATED
THE BAT
DEVIL.

DENJI,
IS
SOMETHING
ON YOUR
MIND...?

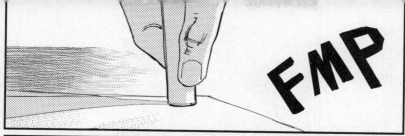
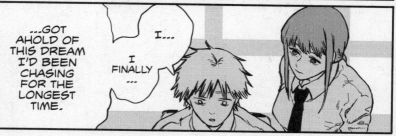
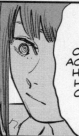
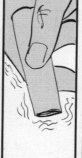
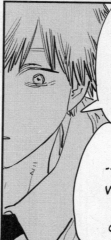
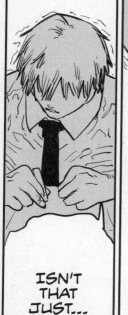

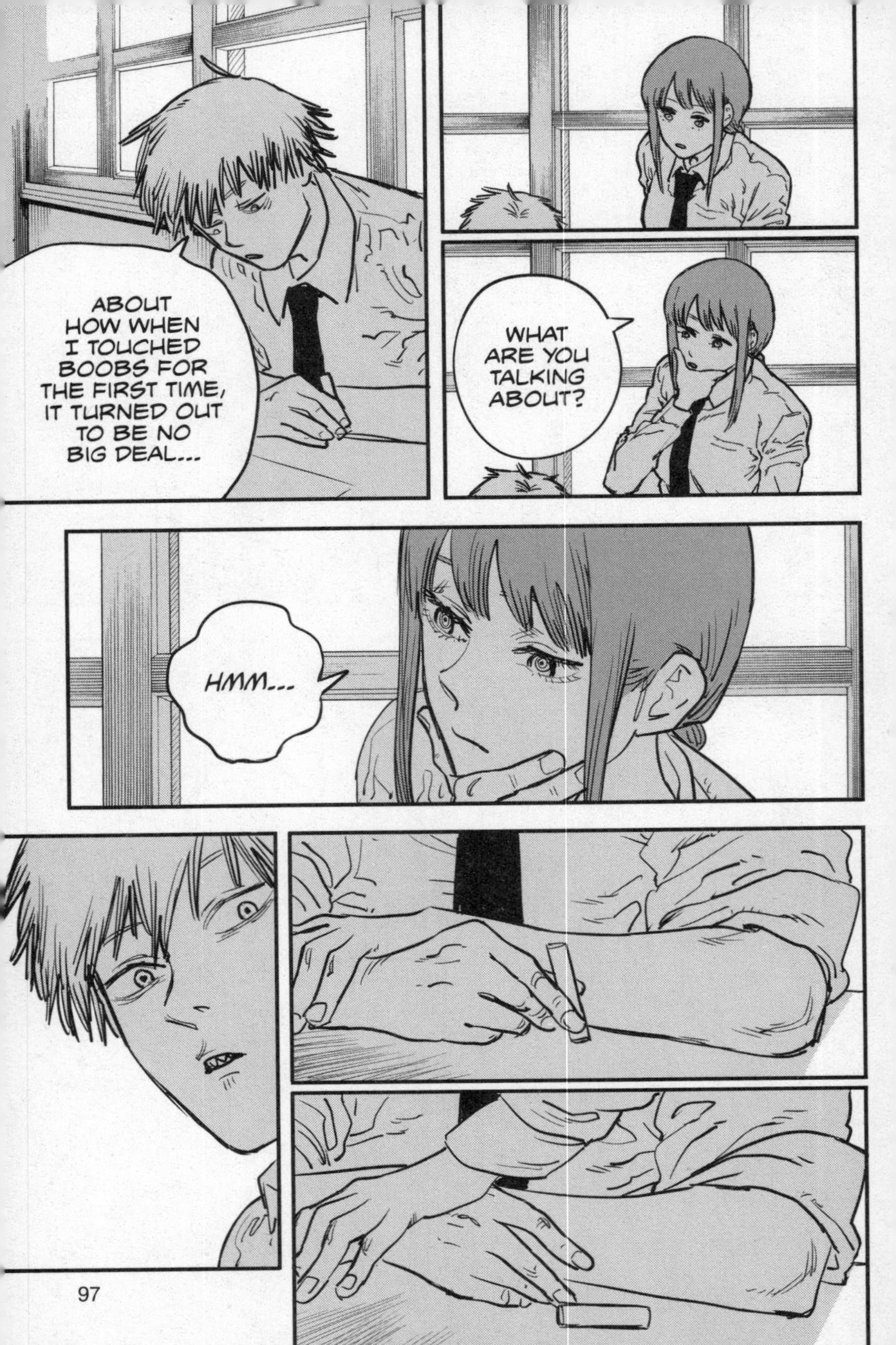
WHAT ARE YOU TALKING ABOUT?
ABOUT HOW WHEN I TOUCHED BOOBS FOR THE FIRST TIME, IT TURNED OUT TO BE NO BIG DEAL...
HMM...

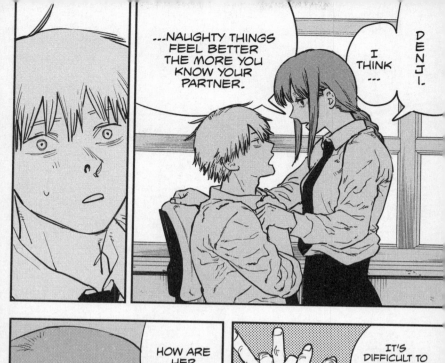

...NAUGHTY THINGS FEEL BETTER THE MORE YOU KNOW YOUR PARTNER.

I THINK...

DENJI.

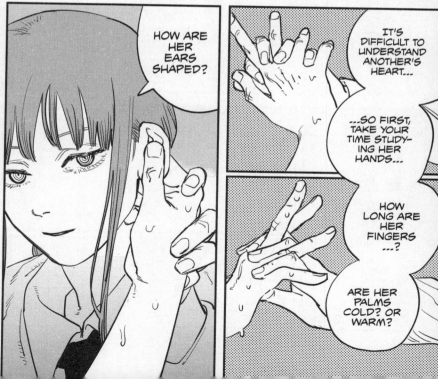

HOW ARE HER EARS SHAPED?

IT'S DIFFICULT TO UNDERSTAND ANOTHER'S HEART...

...SO FIRST, TAKE YOUR TIME STUDYING HER HANDS...

HOW LONG ARE HER FINGERS...?

ARE HER PALMS COLD? OR WARM?

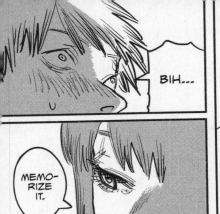

BIH...

MEMORIZE IT.

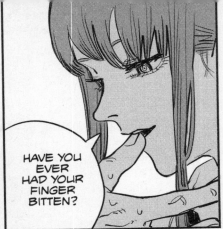

HAVE YOU EVER HAD YOUR FINGER BITTEN?

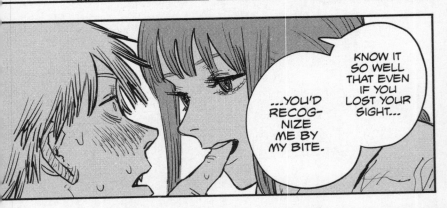

...YOU'D RECOGNIZE ME BY MY BITE.

KNOW IT SO WELL THAT EVEN IF YOU LOST YOUR SIGHT...

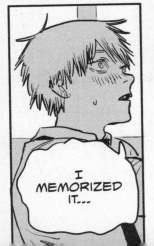

I MEMORIZED IT...

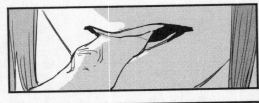

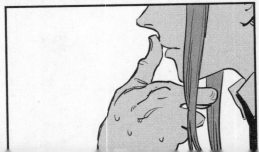

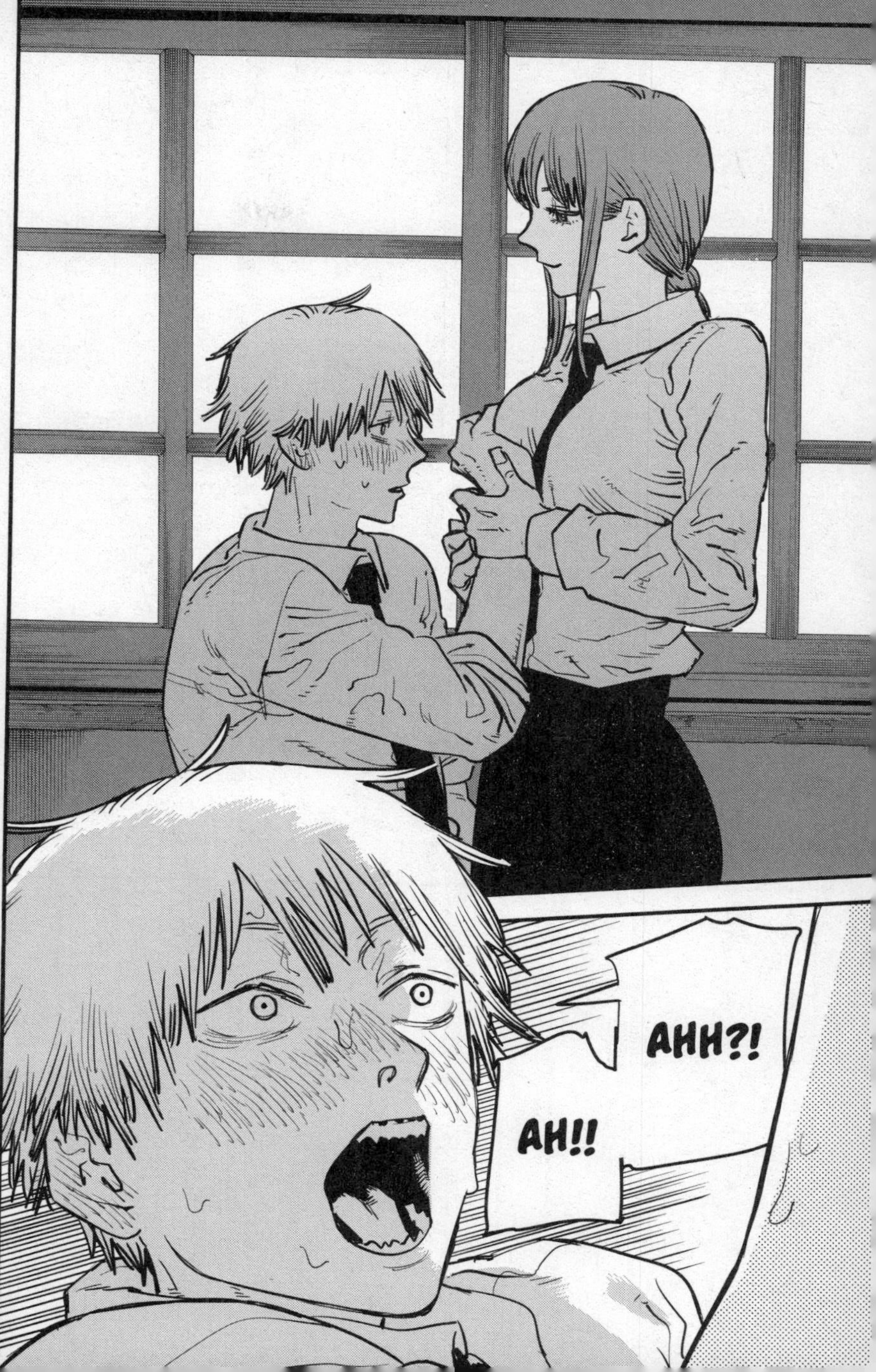
AHH?!
AH!!

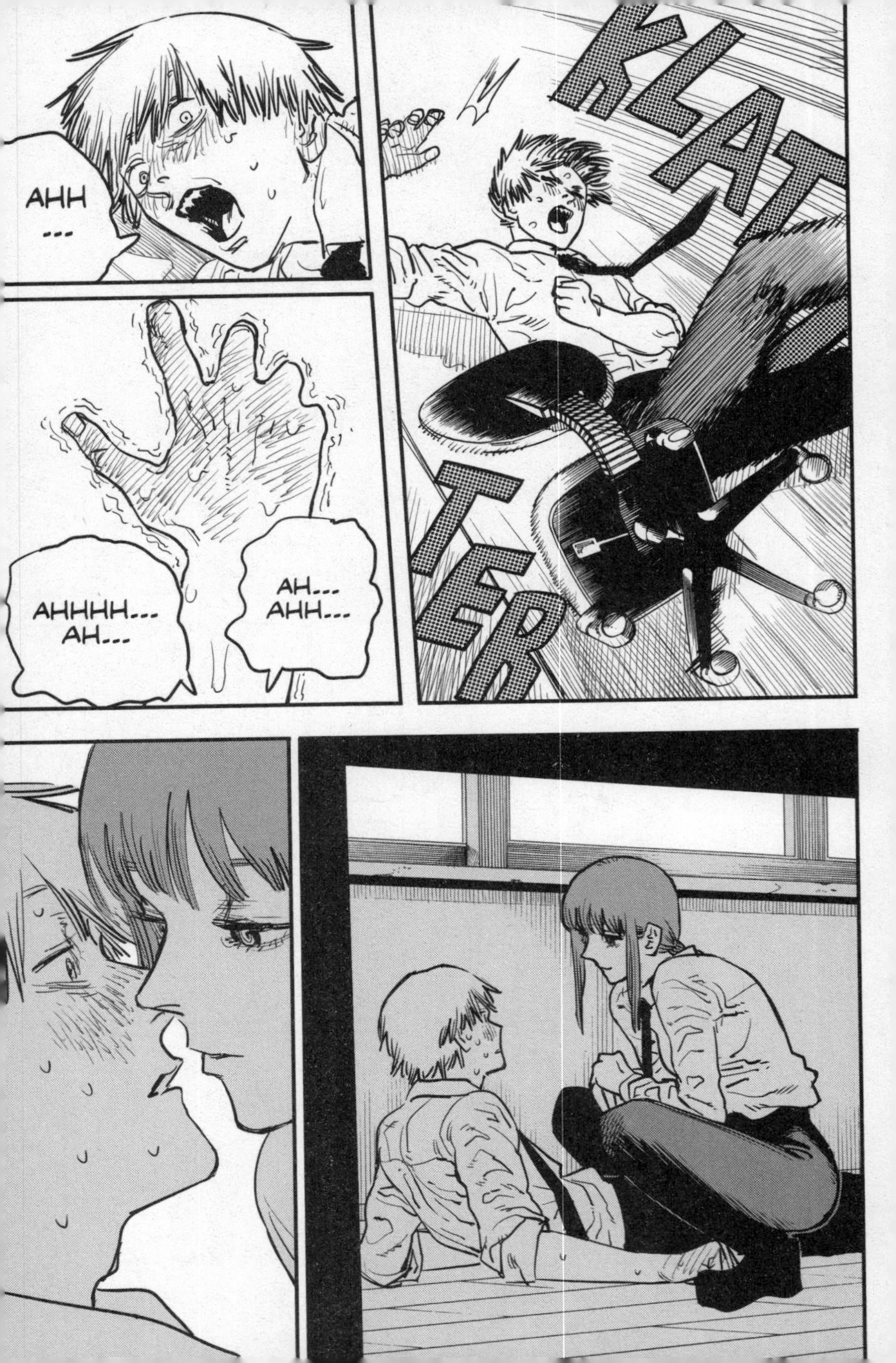

KLATTER
AHH ...
AH... AHH...
AHHHH... AH...

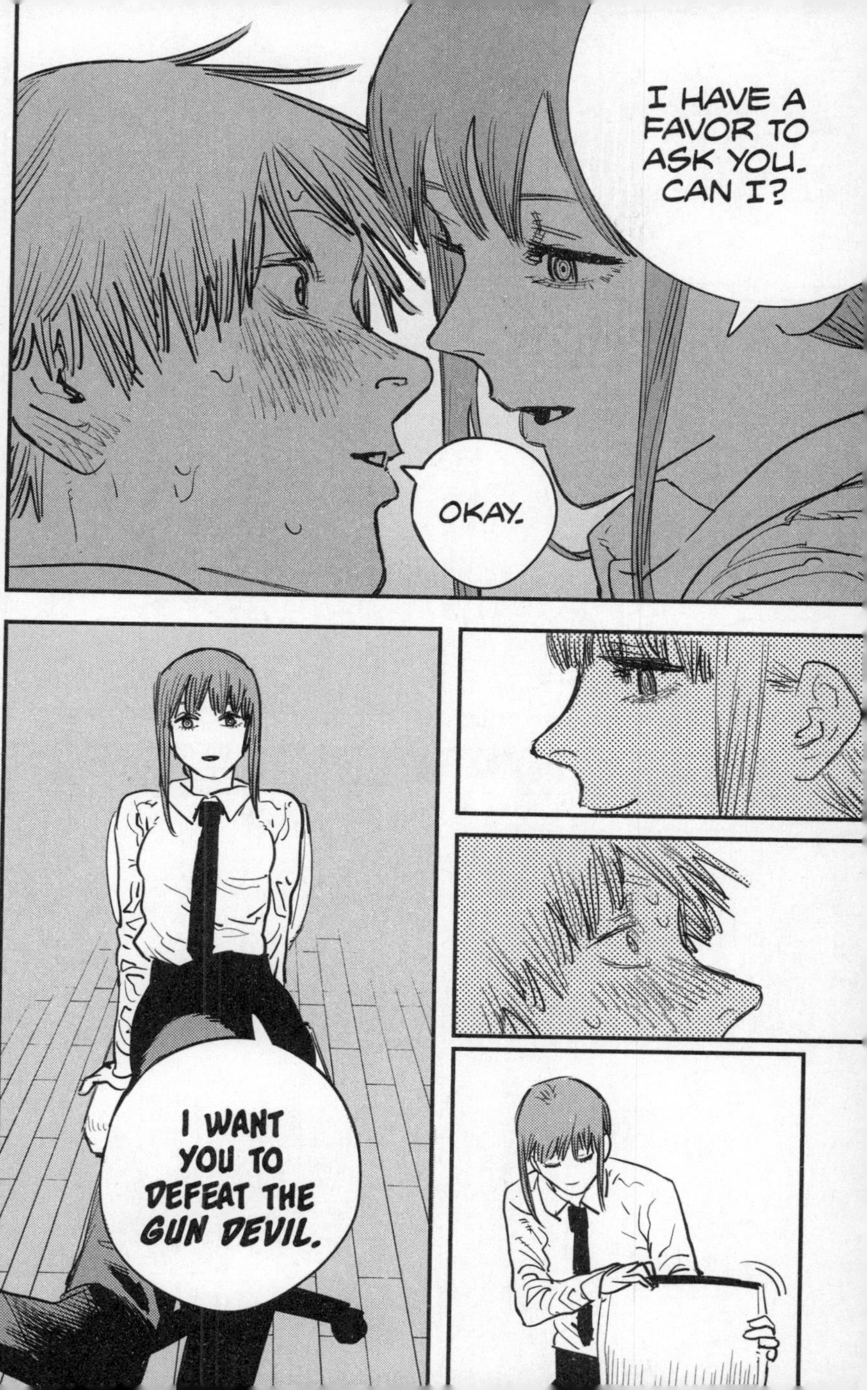
I HAVE A FAVOR TO ASK YOU. CAN I?
OKAY.
I WANT YOU TO DEFEAT THE GUN DEVIL.

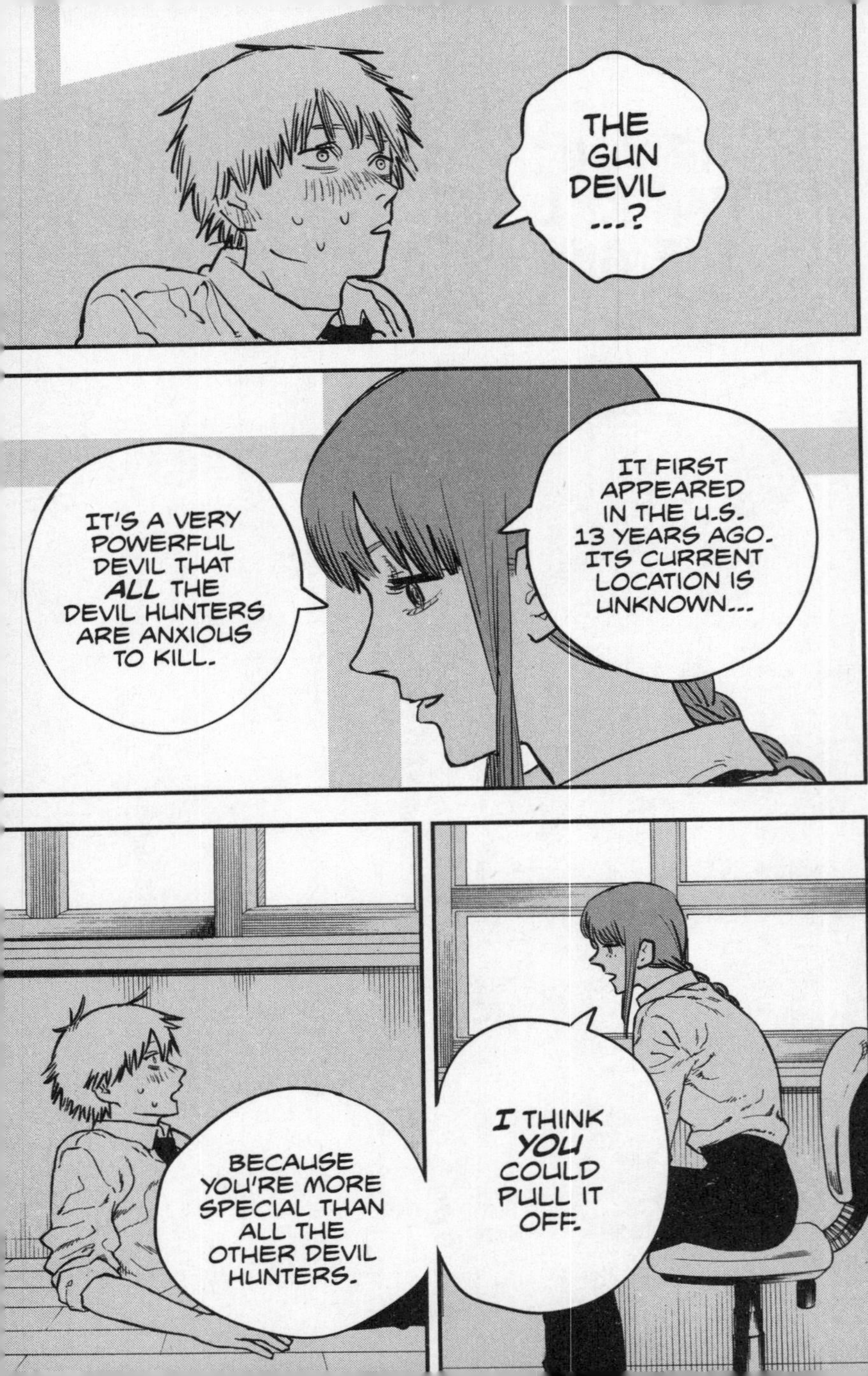
THE GUN DEVIL ...?
IT FIRST APPEARED IN THE U.S. 13 YEARS AGO. ITS CURRENT LOCATION IS UNKNOWN...
IT'S A VERY POWERFUL DEVIL THAT ALL THE DEVIL HUNTERS ARE ANXIOUS TO KILL.
I THINK YOU COULD PULL IT OFF.
BECAUSE YOU'RE MORE SPECIAL THAN ALL THE OTHER DEVIL HUNTERS.

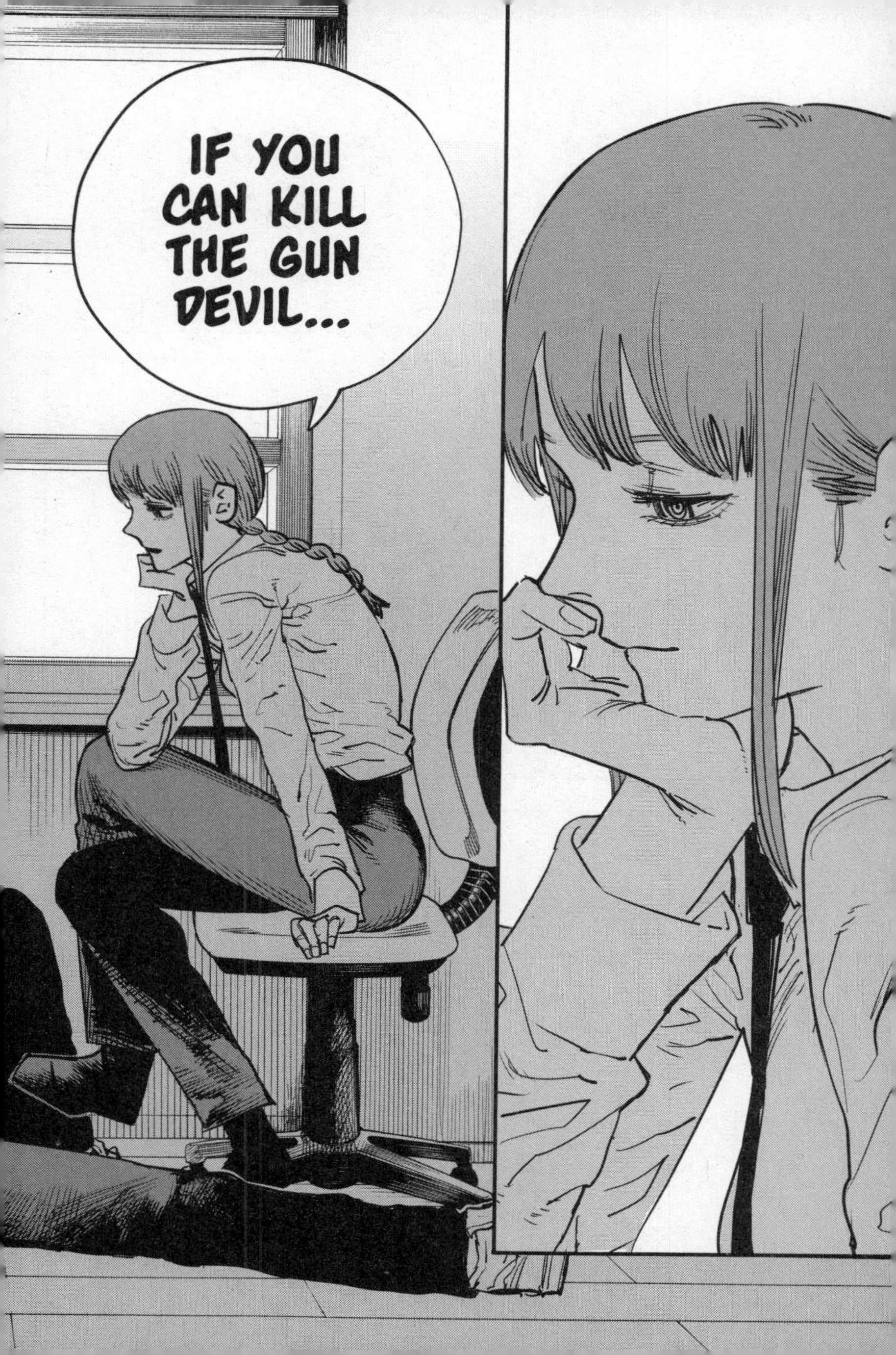
IF YOU CAN KILL THE GUN DEVIL...

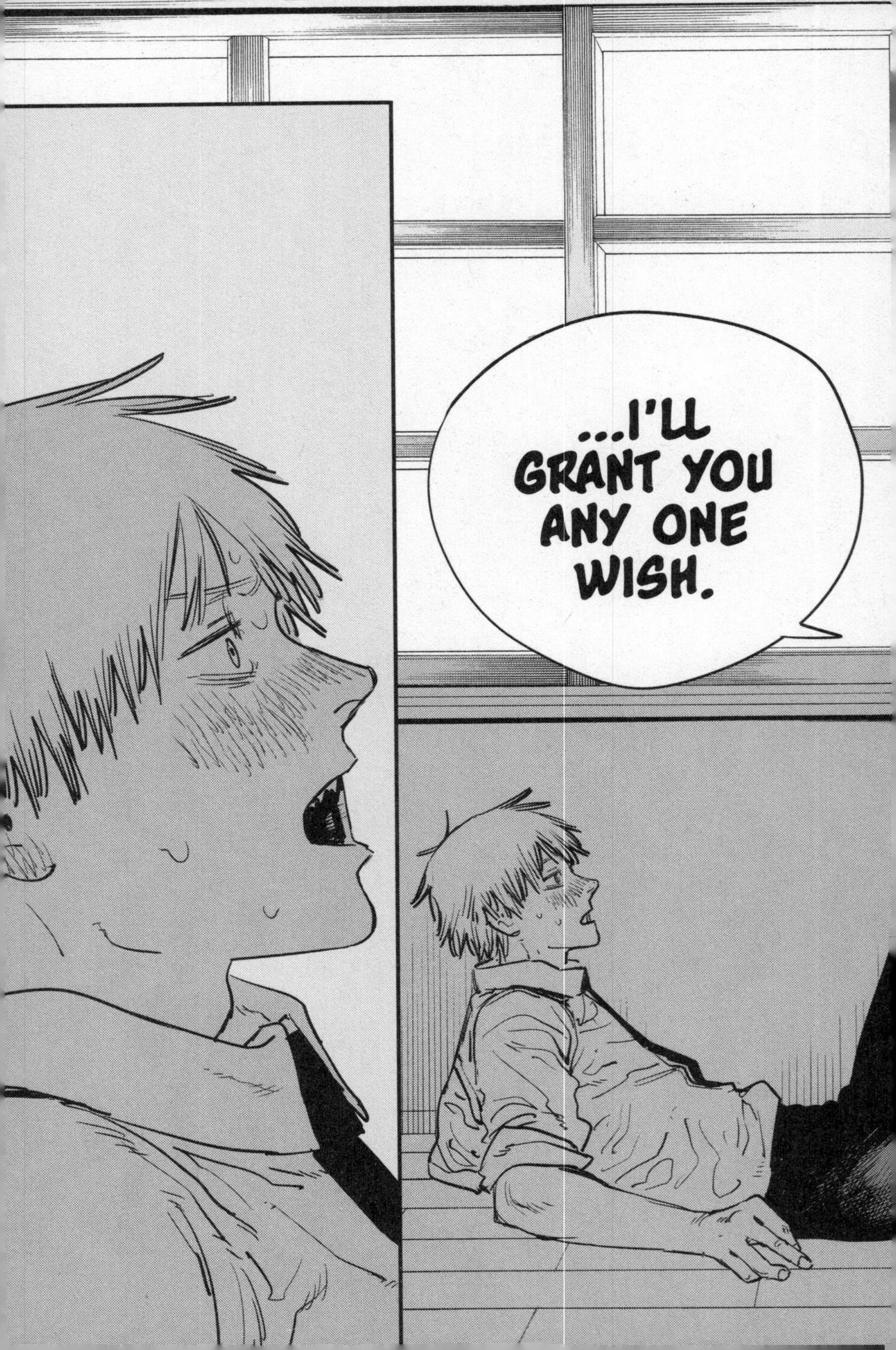
...I'LL GRANT YOU ANY ONE WISH.

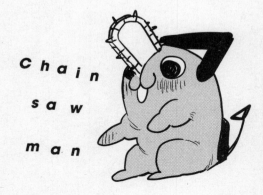

Chain

saw

man

# Chapter 13: Gun Devil

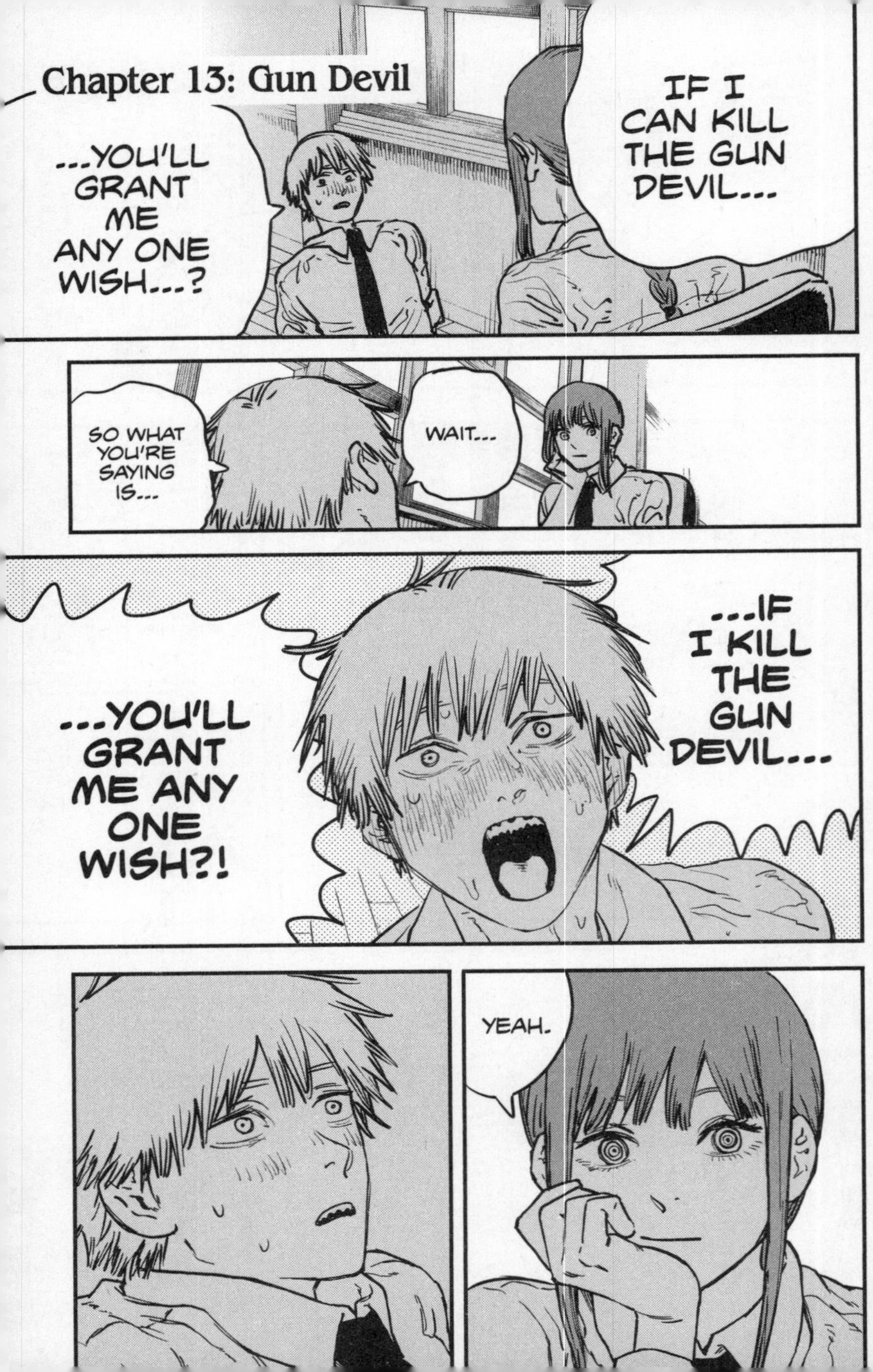
IF I CAN KILL THE GUN DEVIL...
...YOU'LL GRANT ME ANY ONE WISH...?
WAIT...
SO WHAT YOU'RE SAYING IS...
...IF I KILL THE GUN DEVIL...
...YOU'LL GRANT ME ANY ONE WISH?!
YEAH.

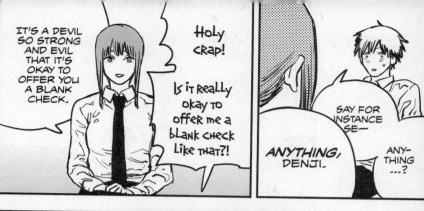

IT'S A DEVIL SO STRONG AND EVIL THAT IT'S OKAY TO OFFER YOU A BLANK CHECK.

Holy crap!

Is it really okay to offer me a blank check like that?!

SAY FOR INSTANCE SE—

ANYTHING, DENJI.

ANYTHING...?

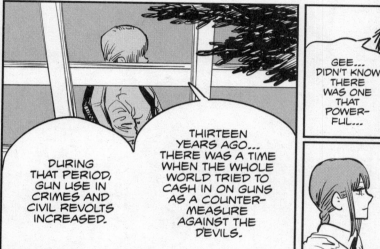

GEE... DIDN'T KNOW THERE WAS ONE THAT POWERFUL...

THIRTEEN YEARS AGO... THERE WAS A TIME WHEN THE WHOLE WORLD TRIED TO CASH IN ON GUNS AS A COUNTERMEASURE AGAINST THE DEVILS.

DURING THAT PERIOD, GUN USE IN CRIMES AND CIVIL REVOLTS INCREASED.

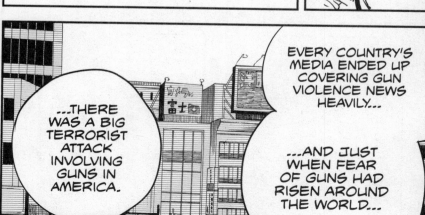

EVERY COUNTRY'S MEDIA ENDED UP COVERING GUN VIOLENCE NEWS HEAVILY...

...THERE WAS A BIG TERRORIST ATTACK INVOLVING GUNS IN AMERICA.

...AND JUST WHEN FEAR OF GUNS HAD RISEN AROUND THE WORLD...

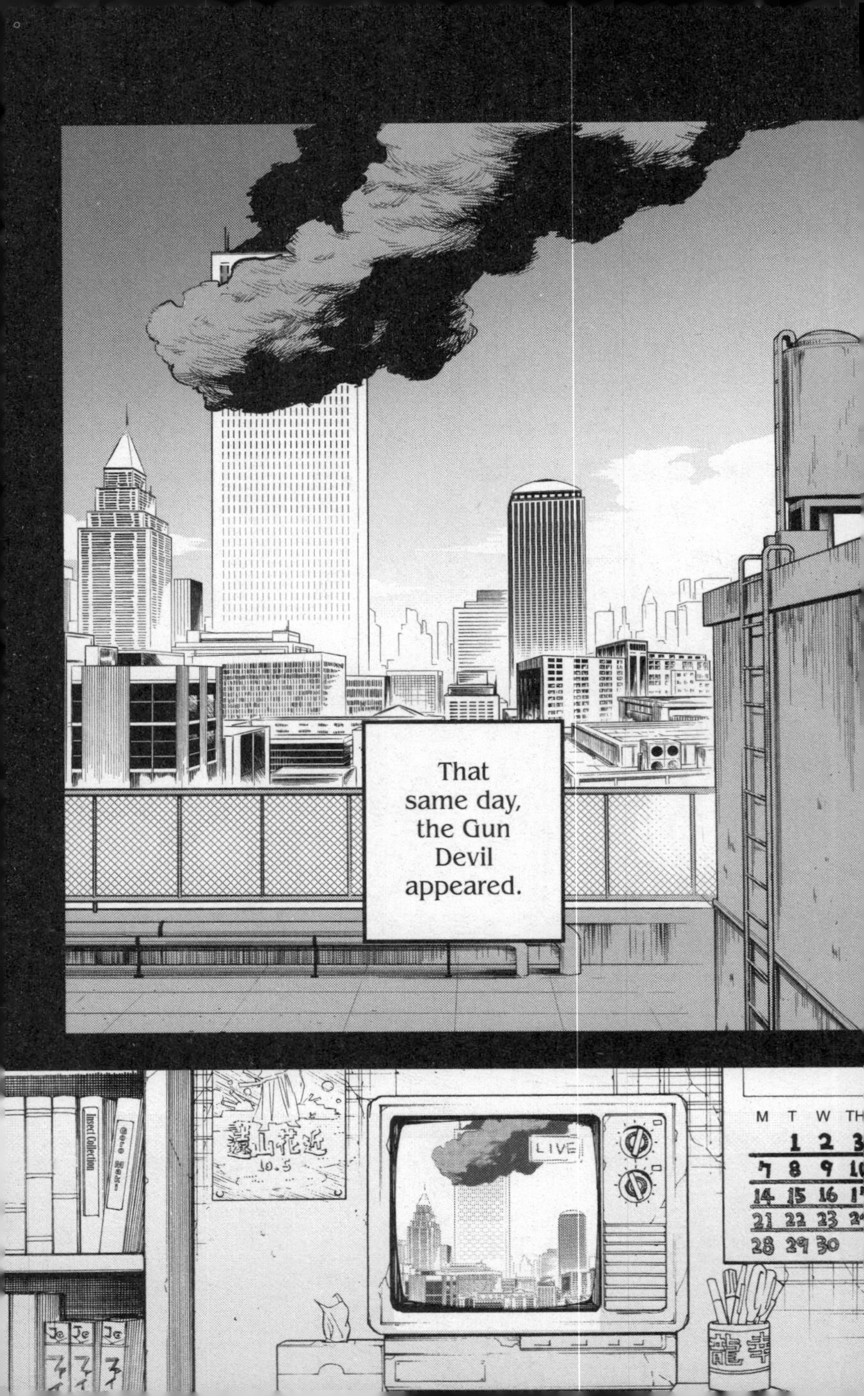
That same day, the Gun Devil appeared.
Insect Collection
LIVE
M T W TH

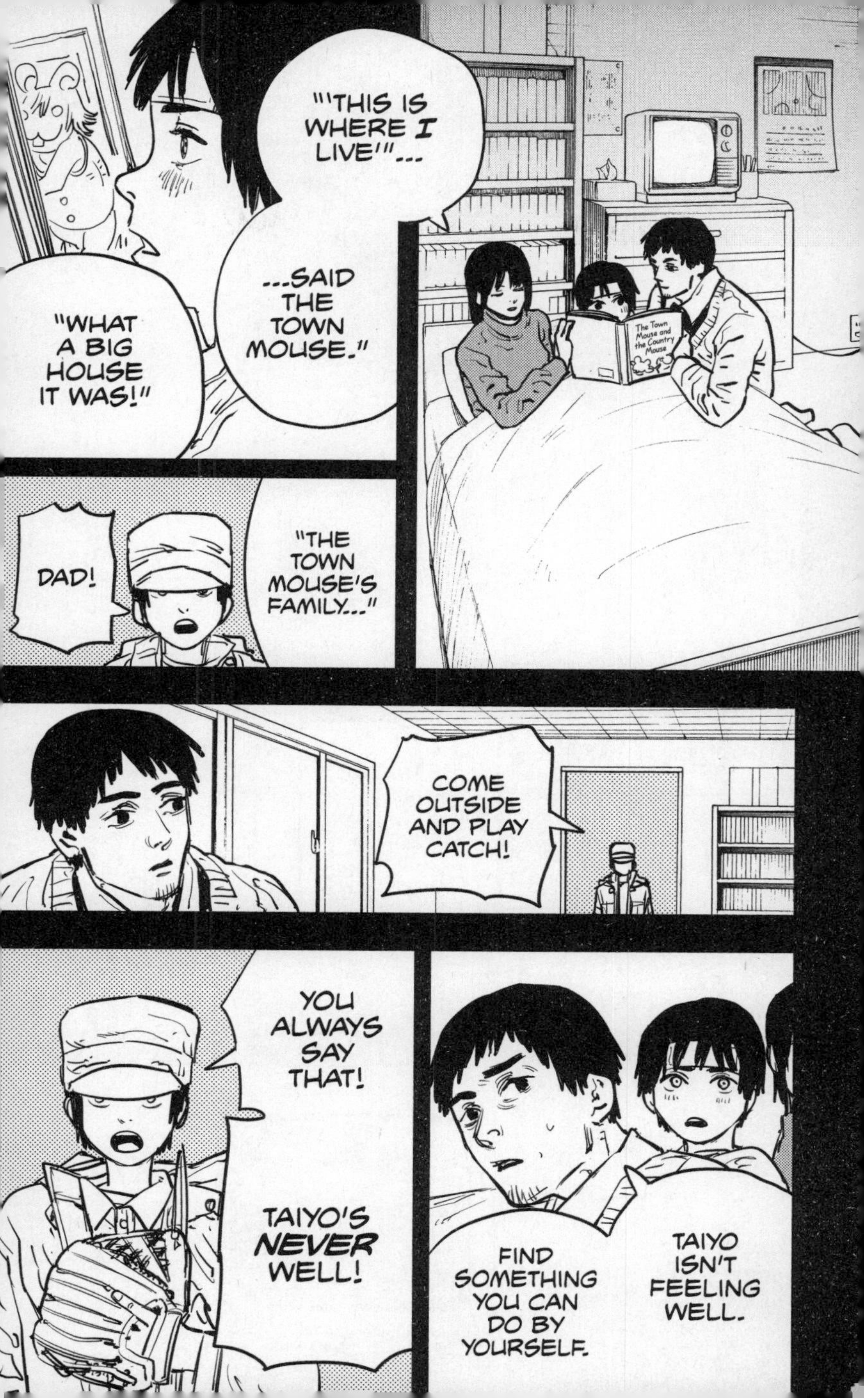
The Town Mouse and the Country Mouse
"'THIS IS WHERE *I* LIVE'"...
...SAID THE TOWN MOUSE."
"WHAT A BIG HOUSE IT WAS!"
"THE TOWN MOUSE'S FAMILY..."
DAD!
COME OUTSIDE AND PLAY CATCH!
TAIYO ISN'T FEELING WELL.
FIND SOMETHING YOU CAN DO BY YOURSELF.
YOU ALWAYS SAY THAT!
TAIYO'S ***NEVER*** WELL!

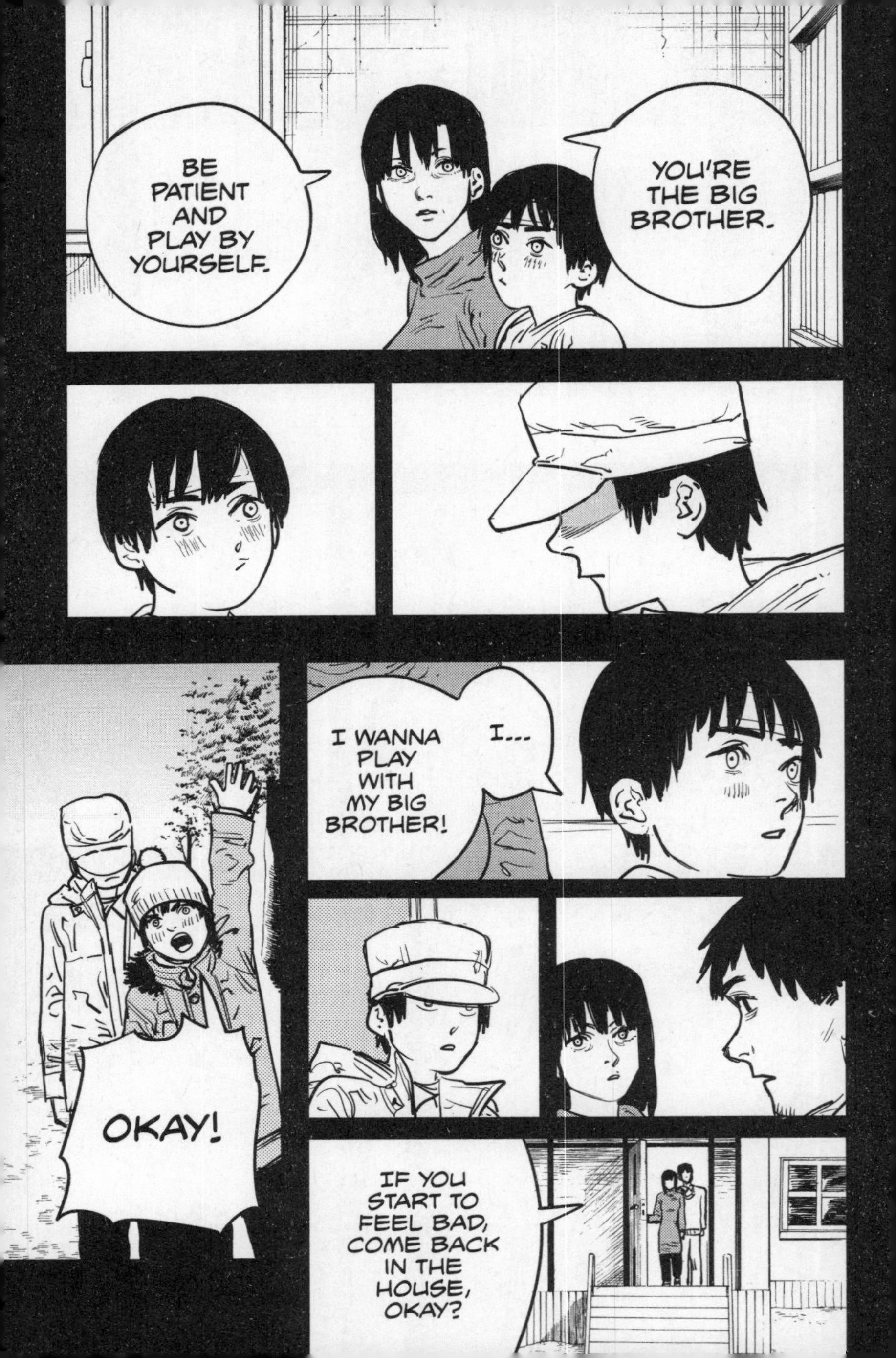
YOU'RE THE BIG BROTHER.
BE PATIENT AND PLAY BY YOURSELF.
I...
I WANNA PLAY WITH MY BIG BROTHER!
IF YOU START TO FEEL BAD, COME BACK IN THE HOUSE, OKAY?
OKAY!

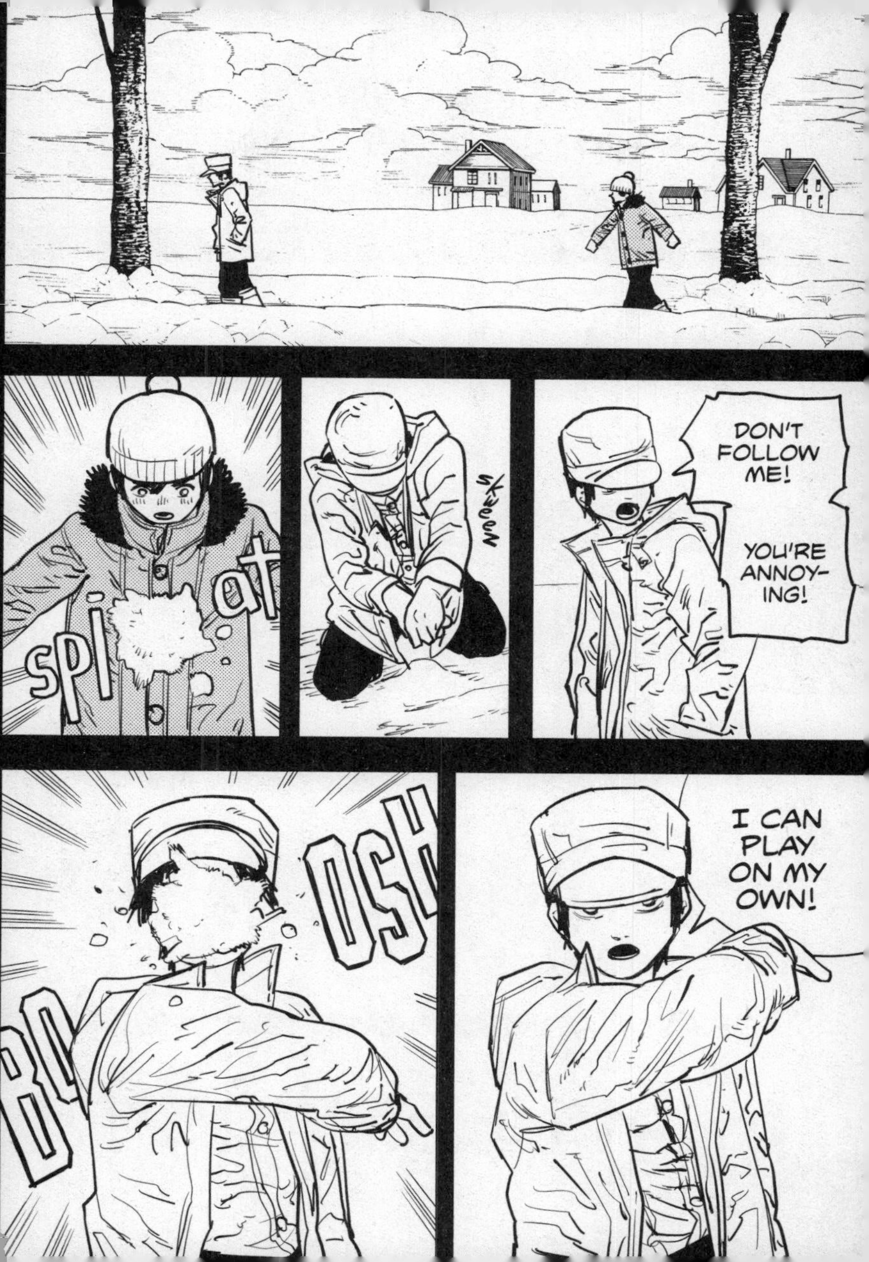
DON'T FOLLOW ME!
YOU'RE ANNOYING!
skween
splat
I CAN PLAY ON MY OWN!
BO OSH

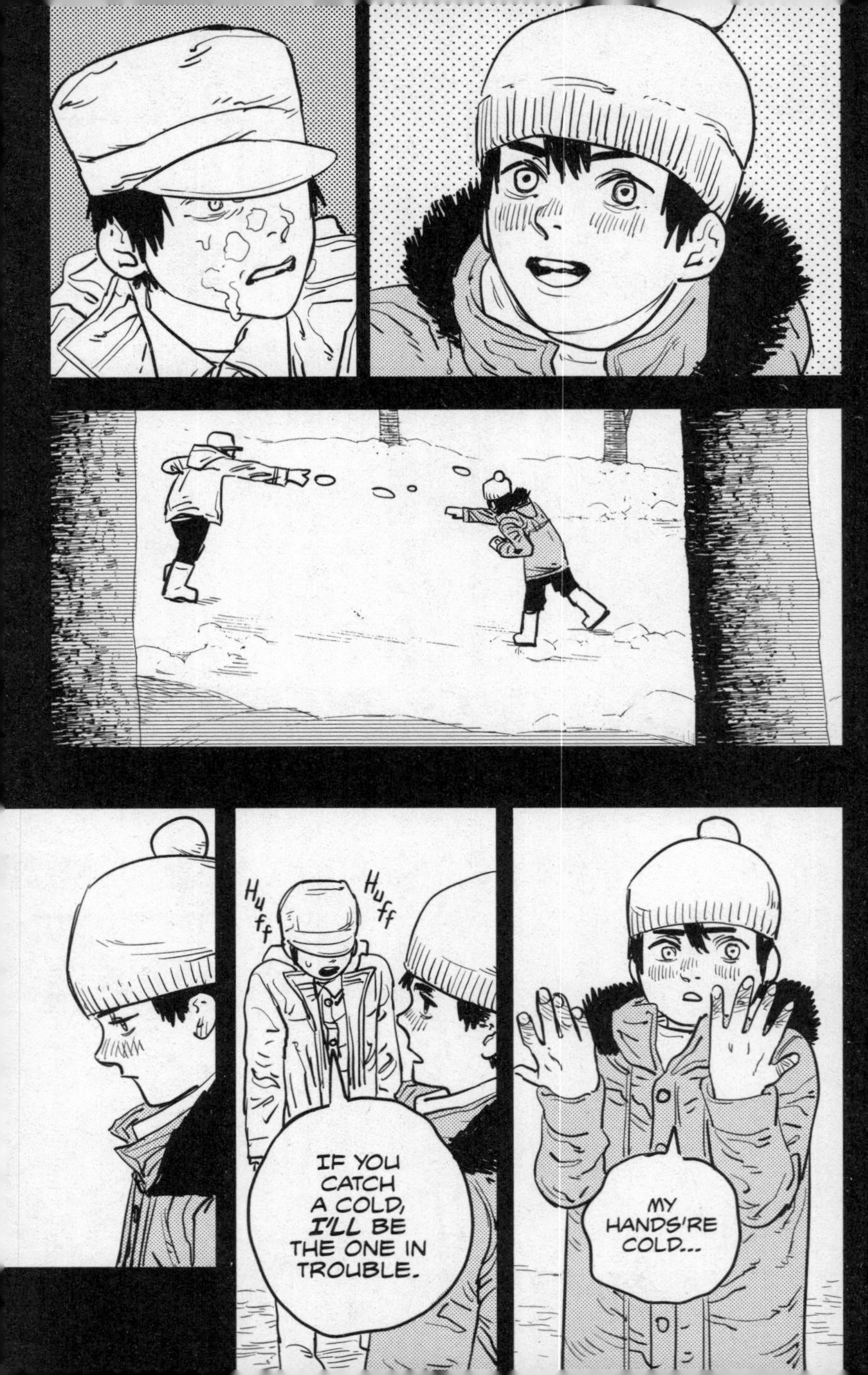
MY HANDS'RE COLD...
Huff
Huff
IF YOU CATCH A COLD, *I'LL* BE THE ONE IN TROUBLE.

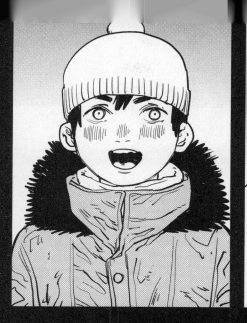

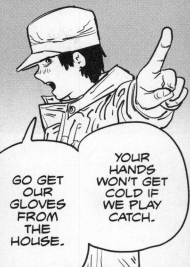

YOUR HANDS WON'T GET COLD IF WE PLAY CATCH.

GO GET OUR GLOVES FROM THE HOUSE.

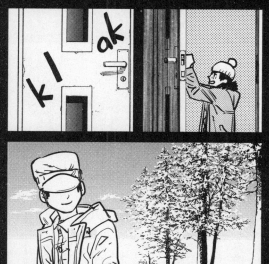

Kl ak

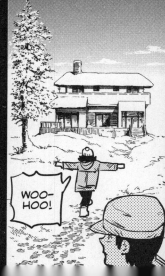

WOO-HOO!

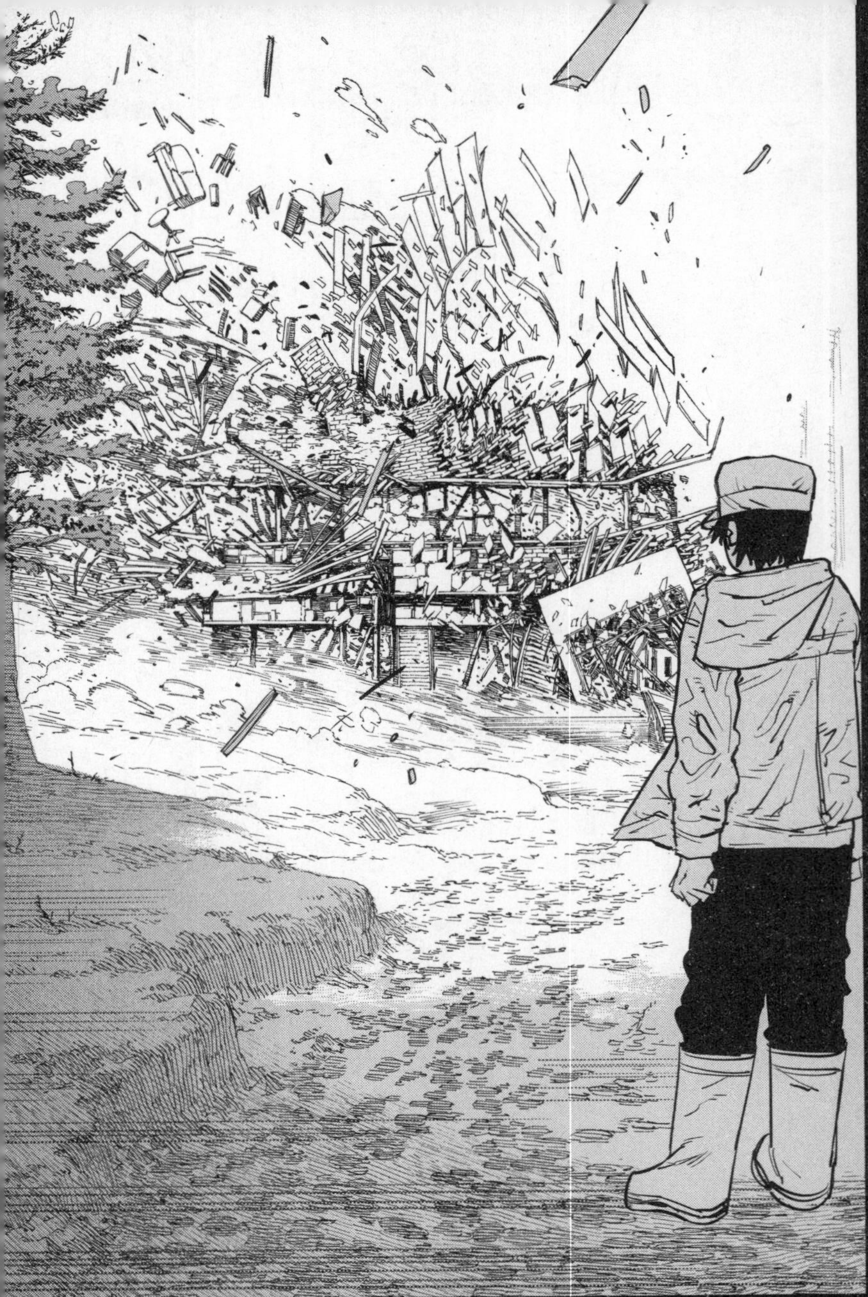

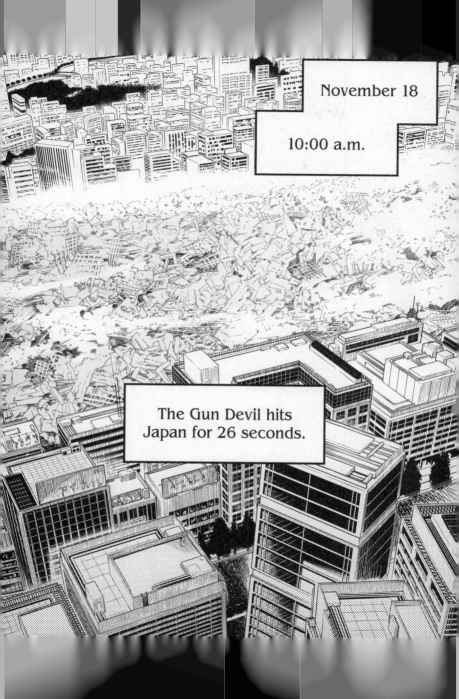

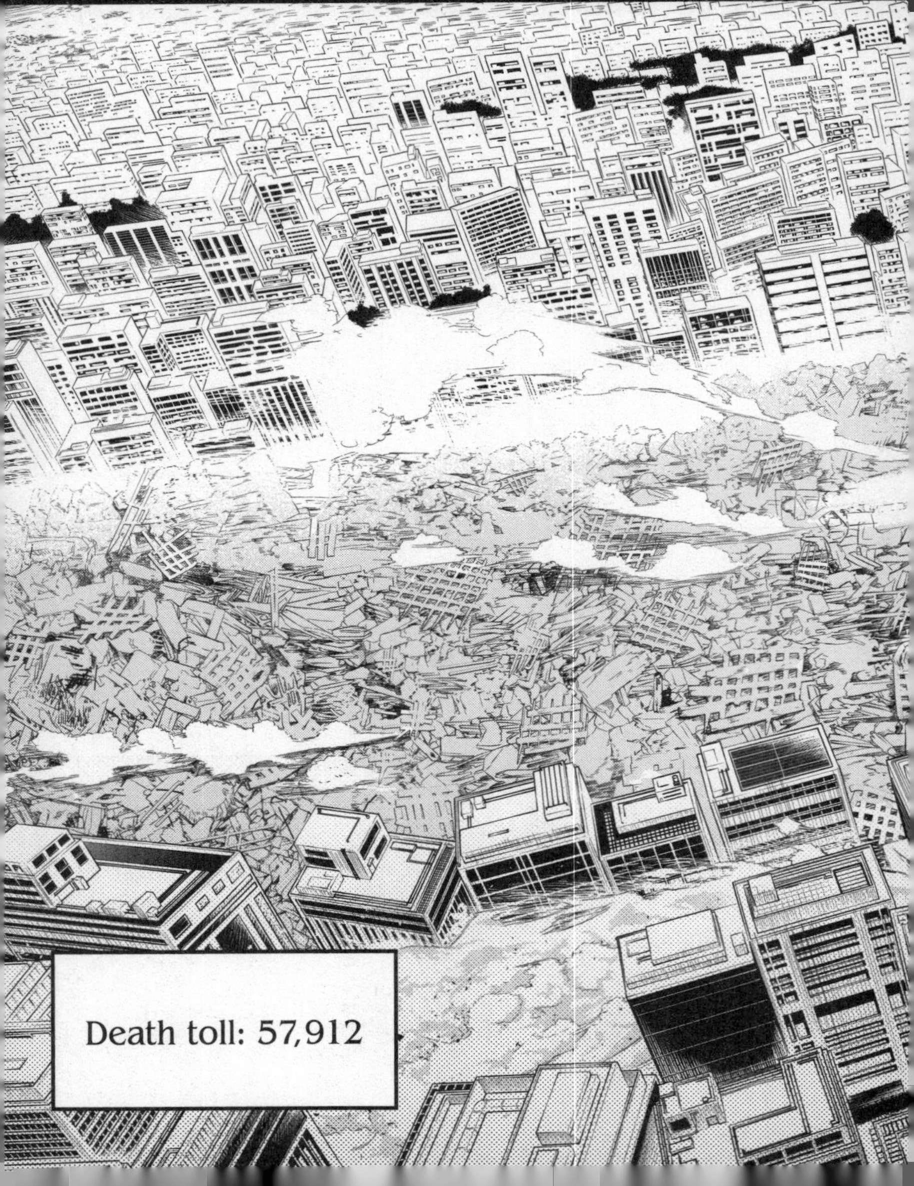
Death toll: 57,912

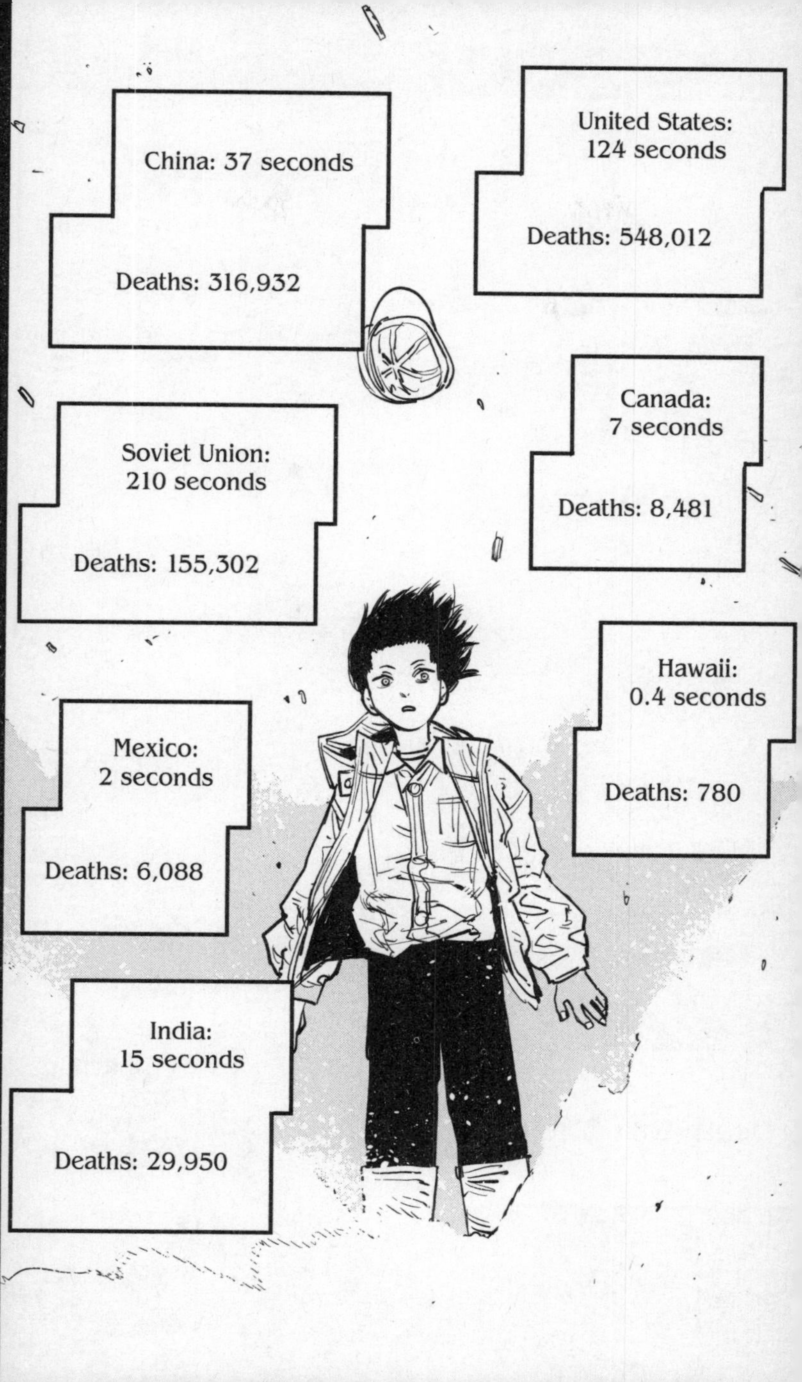
United States:
124 seconds
Deaths: 548,012
China: 37 seconds
Deaths: 316,932
Canada:
7 seconds
Deaths: 8,481
Soviet Union:
210 seconds
Deaths: 155,302
Hawaii:
0.4 seconds
Deaths: 780
Mexico:
2 seconds
Deaths: 6,088
India:
15 seconds
Deaths: 29,950

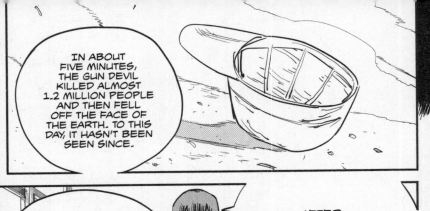

IN ABOUT FIVE MINUTES, THE GUN DEVIL KILLED ALMOST 1.2 MILLION PEOPLE AND THEN FELL OFF THE FACE OF THE EARTH. TO THIS DAY, IT HASN'T BEEN SEEN SINCE.

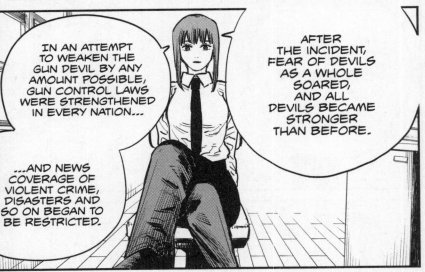

IN AN ATTEMPT TO WEAKEN THE GUN DEVIL BY ANY AMOUNT POSSIBLE, GUN CONTROL LAWS WERE STRENGTHENED IN EVERY NATION...

AFTER THE INCIDENT, FEAR OF DEVILS AS A WHOLE SOARED, AND ALL DEVILS BECAME STRONGER THAN BEFORE.

...AND NEWS COVERAGE OF VIOLENT CRIME, DISASTERS AND SO ON BEGAN TO BE RESTRICTED.

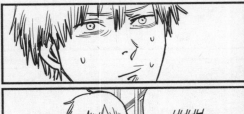

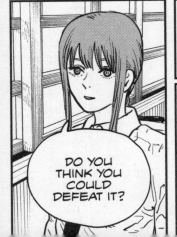

DO YOU THINK YOU COULD DEFEAT IT?

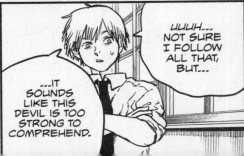

UUUH... NOT SURE I FOLLOW ALL THAT, BUT...

...IT SOUNDS LIKE THIS DEVIL IS TOO STRONG TO COMPREHEND.

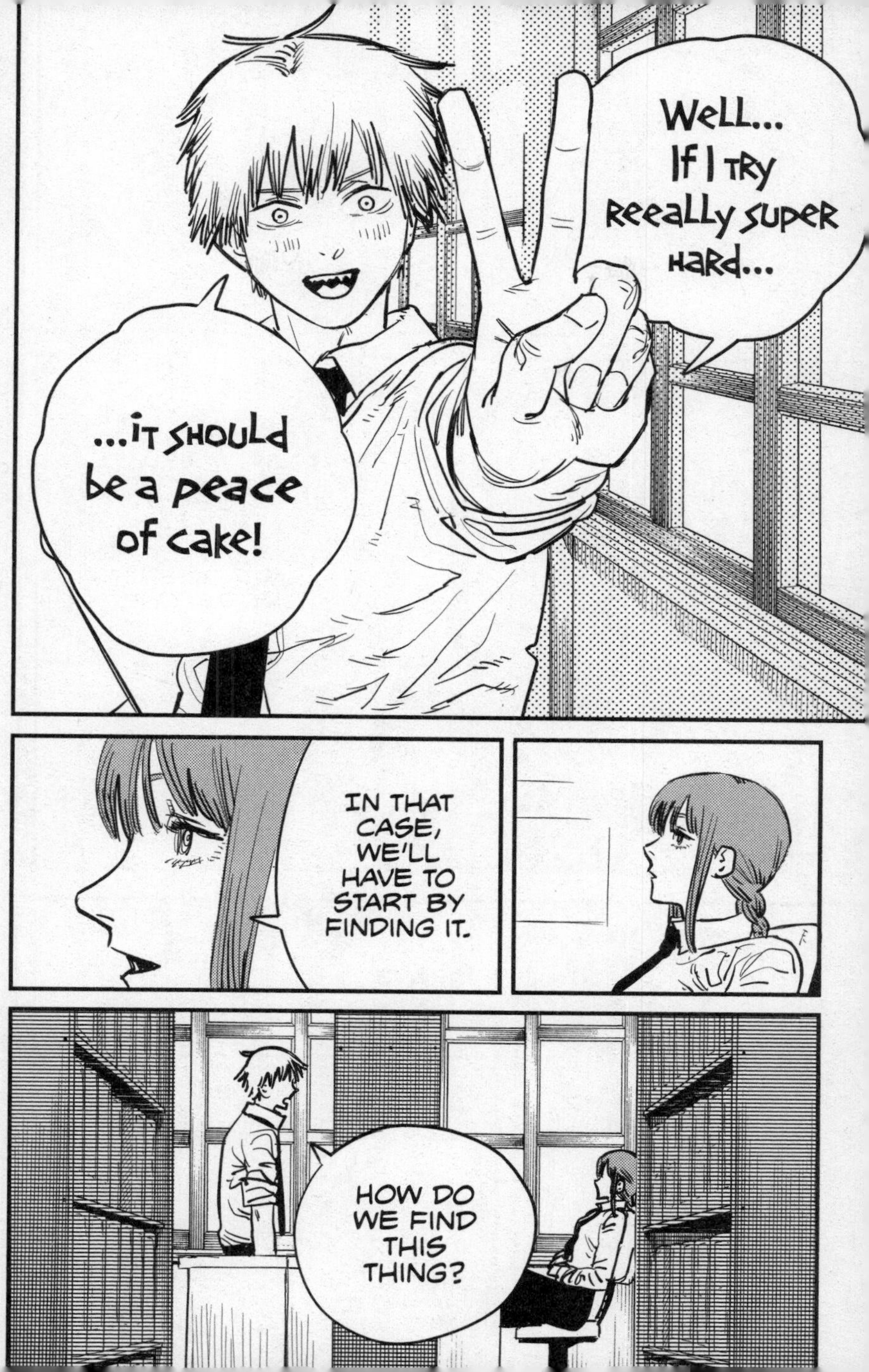
Well... If I try reeally super hard...
...it should be a peace of cake!
IN THAT CASE, WE'LL HAVE TO START BY FINDING IT.
HOW DO WE FIND THIS THING?

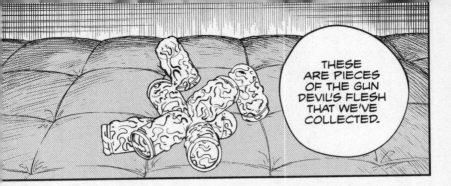

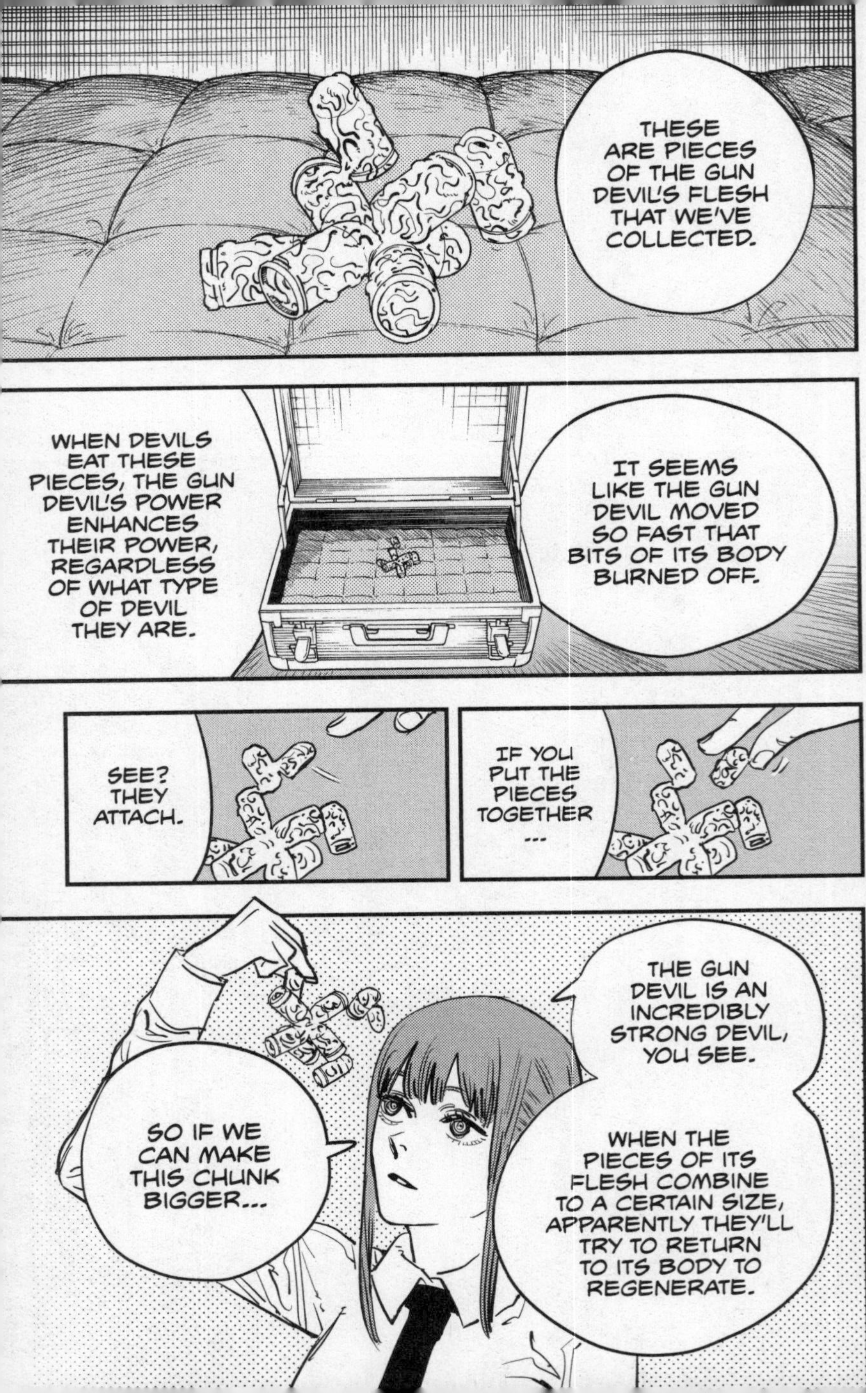

THESE ARE PIECES OF THE GUN DEVIL'S FLESH THAT WE'VE COLLECTED.

WHEN DEVILS EAT THESE PIECES, THE GUN DEVIL'S POWER ENHANCES THEIR POWER, REGARDLESS OF WHAT TYPE OF DEVIL THEY ARE.

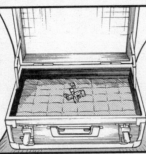

IT SEEMS LIKE THE GUN DEVIL MOVED SO FAST THAT BITS OF ITS BODY BURNED OFF.

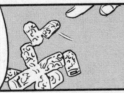

SEE? THEY ATTACH.

IF YOU PUT THE PIECES TOGETHER ...

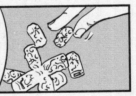

THE GUN DEVIL IS AN INCREDIBLY STRONG DEVIL, YOU SEE.

SO IF WE CAN MAKE THIS CHUNK BIGGER...

WHEN THE PIECES OF ITS FLESH COMBINE TO A CERTAIN SIZE, APPARENTLY THEY'LL TRY TO RETURN TO ITS BODY TO REGENERATE.

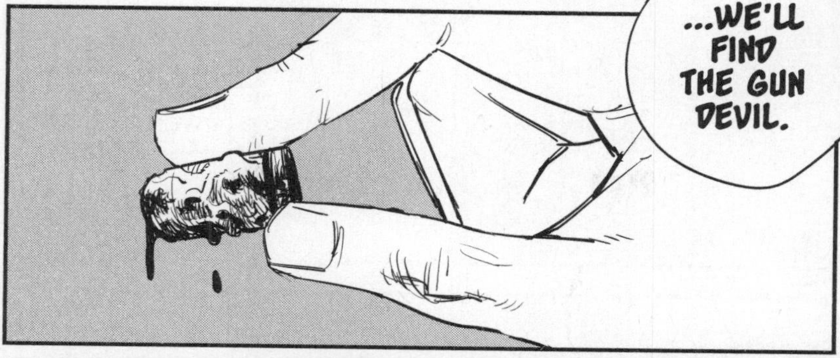
...WE'LL FIND THE GUN DEVIL.
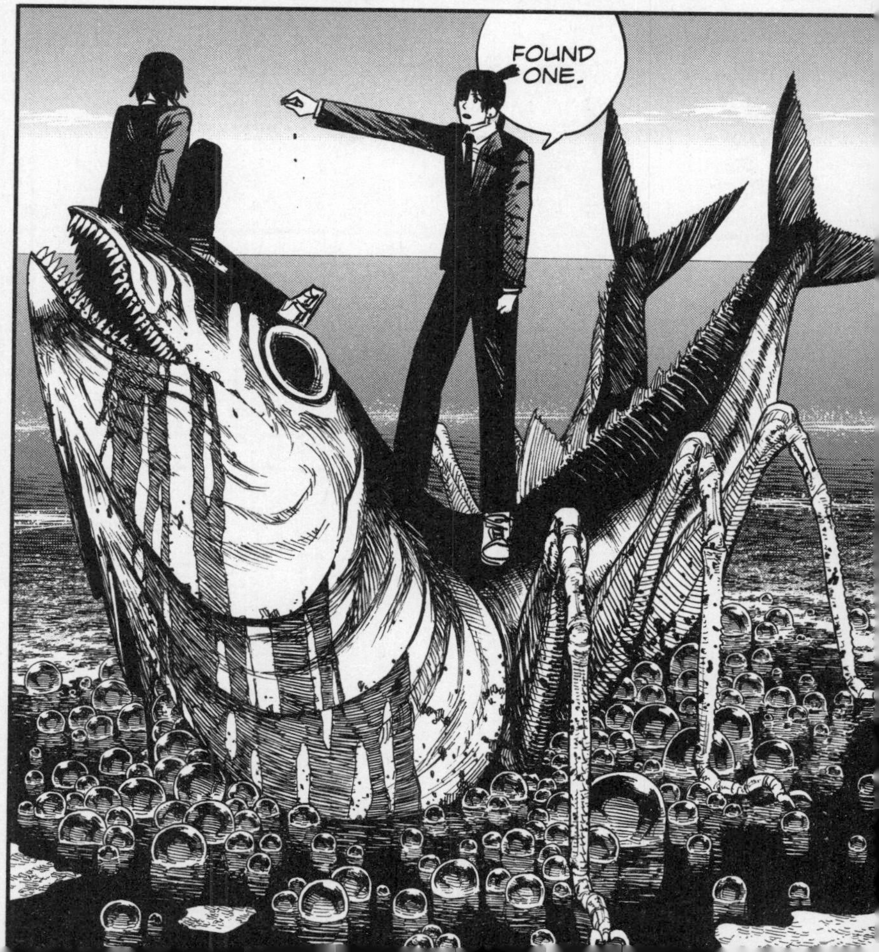
FOUND ONE.

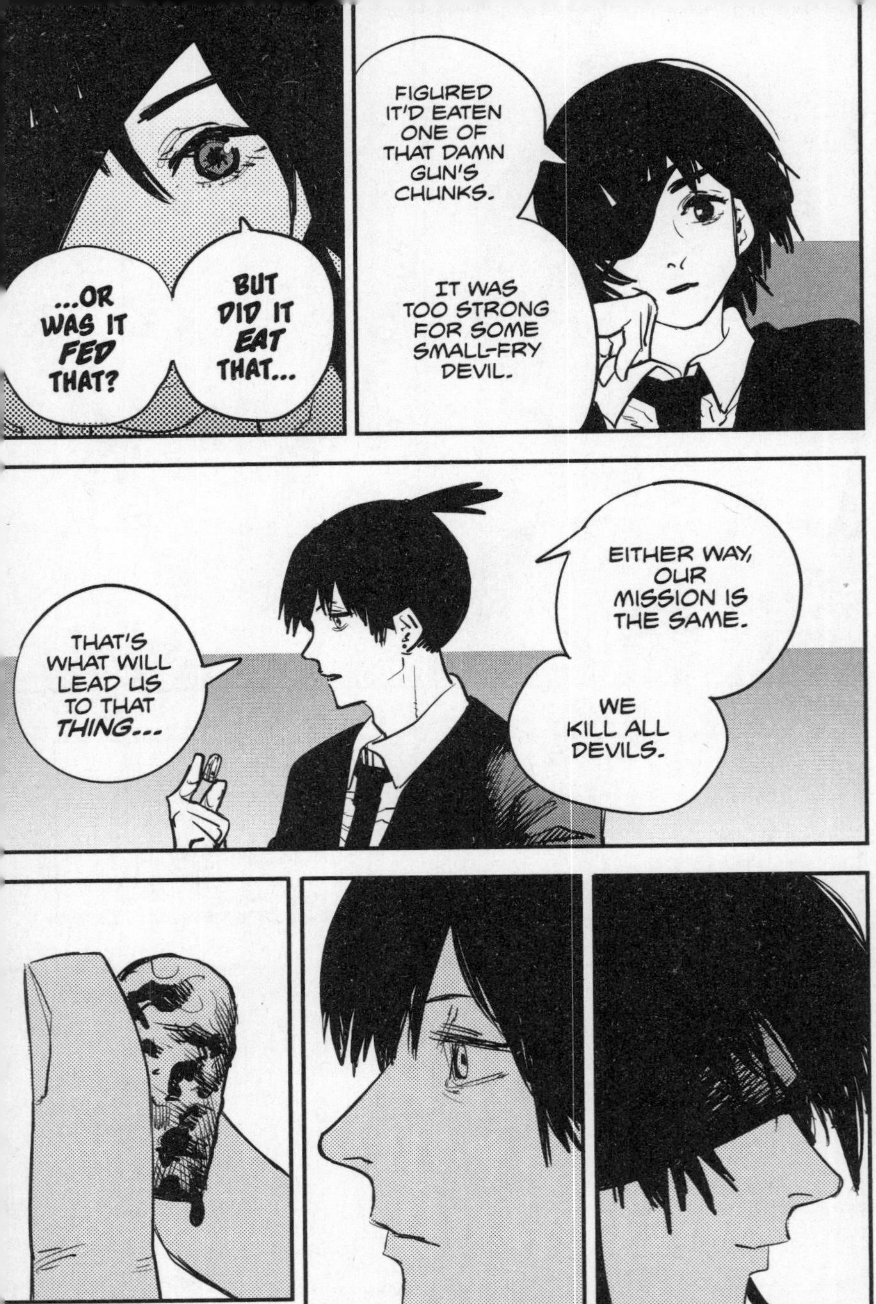
FIGURED IT'D EATEN ONE OF THAT DAMN GUN'S CHUNKS.
IT WAS TOO STRONG FOR SOME SMALL-FRY DEVIL.
BUT DID IT *EAT* THAT...
...OR WAS IT *FED* THAT?
EITHER WAY, OUR MISSION IS THE SAME.
WE KILL ALL DEVILS.
THAT'S WHAT WILL LEAD US TO THAT *THING*...

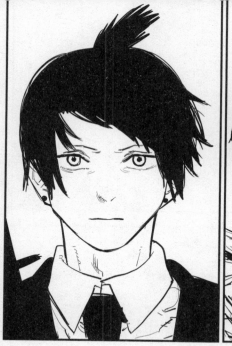
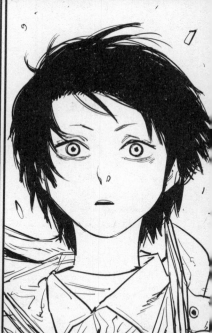

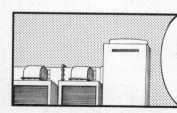

DEVIL EXTERMINATION REQUEST FOR PUBLIC SAFETY.

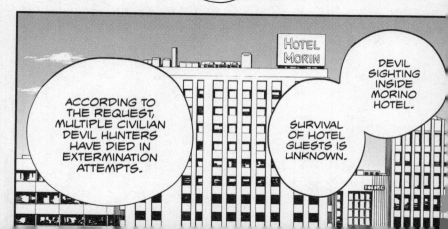

ACCORDING TO THE REQUEST, MULTIPLE CIVILIAN DEVIL HUNTERS HAVE DIED IN EXTERMINATION ATTEMPTS.

SURVIVAL OF HOTEL GUESTS IS UNKNOWN.

DEVIL SIGHTING INSIDE MORINO HOTEL.

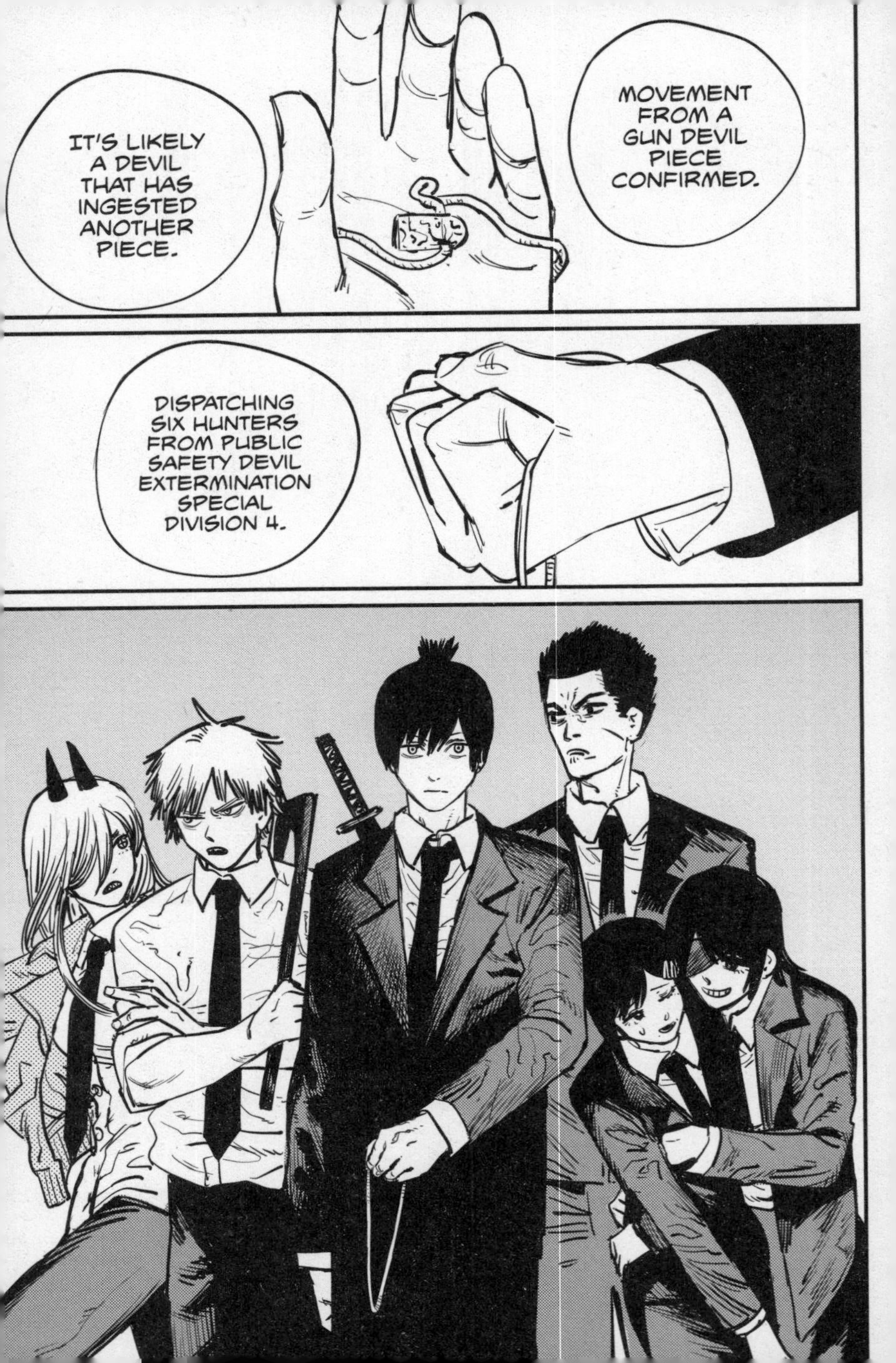
MOVEMENT FROM A GUN DEVIL PIECE CONFIRMED.
IT'S LIKELY A DEVIL THAT HAS INGESTED ANOTHER PIECE.
DISPATCHING SIX HUNTERS FROM PUBLIC SAFETY DEVIL EXTERMINATION SPECIAL DIVISION 4.

Chain

saw

man

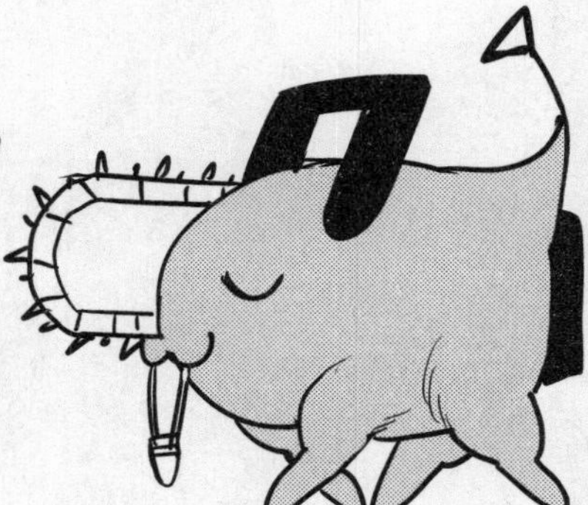

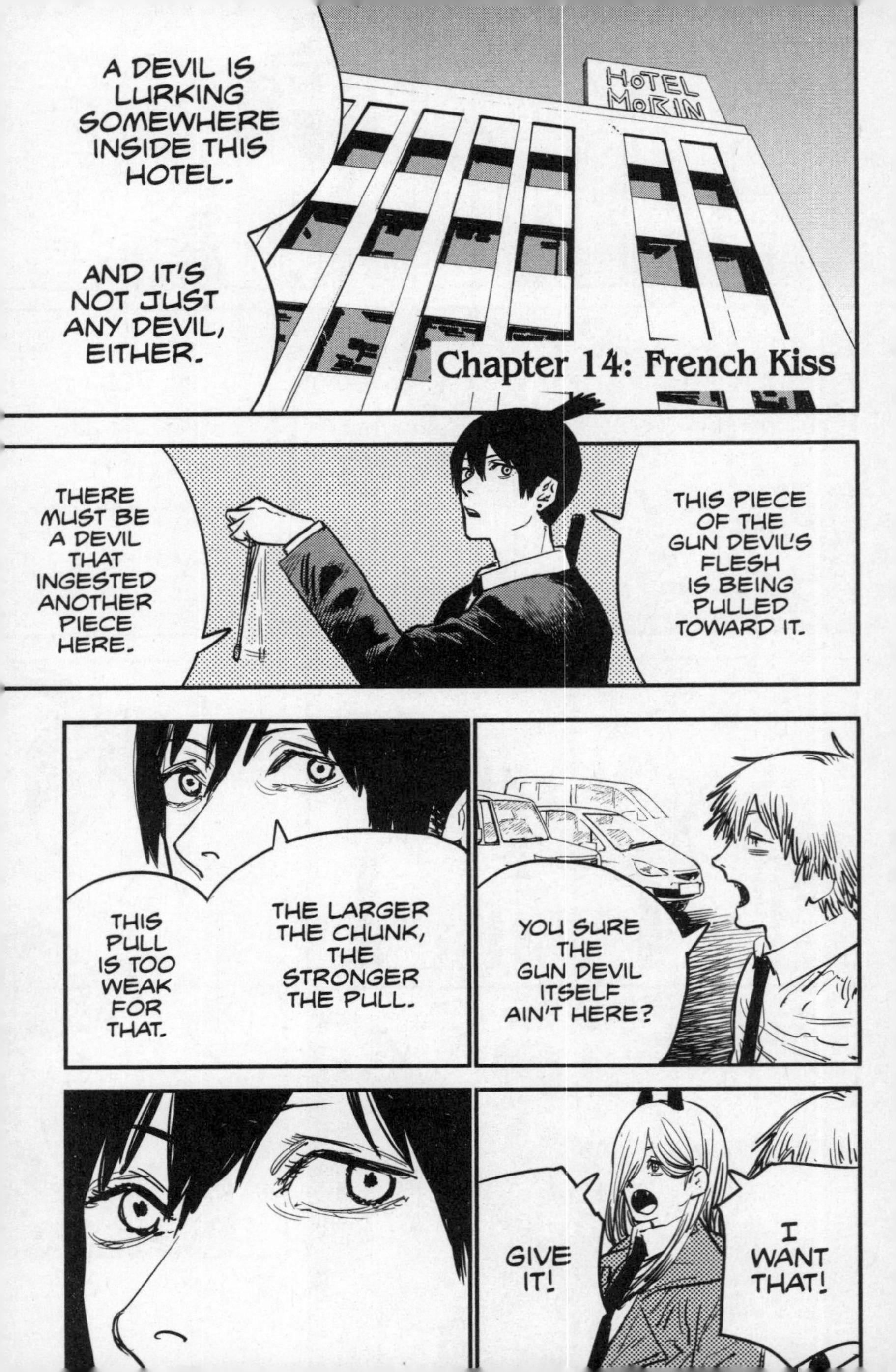
A DEVIL IS LURKING SOMEWHERE INSIDE THIS HOTEL.
AND IT'S NOT JUST ANY DEVIL, EITHER.
HOTEL MoRIN
Chapter 14: French Kiss
THIS PIECE OF THE GUN DEVIL'S FLESH IS BEING PULLED TOWARD IT.
THERE MUST BE A DEVIL THAT INGESTED ANOTHER PIECE HERE.
YOU SURE THE GUN DEVIL ITSELF AIN'T HERE?
THE LARGER THE CHUNK, THE STRONGER THE PULL.
THIS PULL IS TOO WEAK FOR THAT.
I WANT THAT!
GIVE IT!

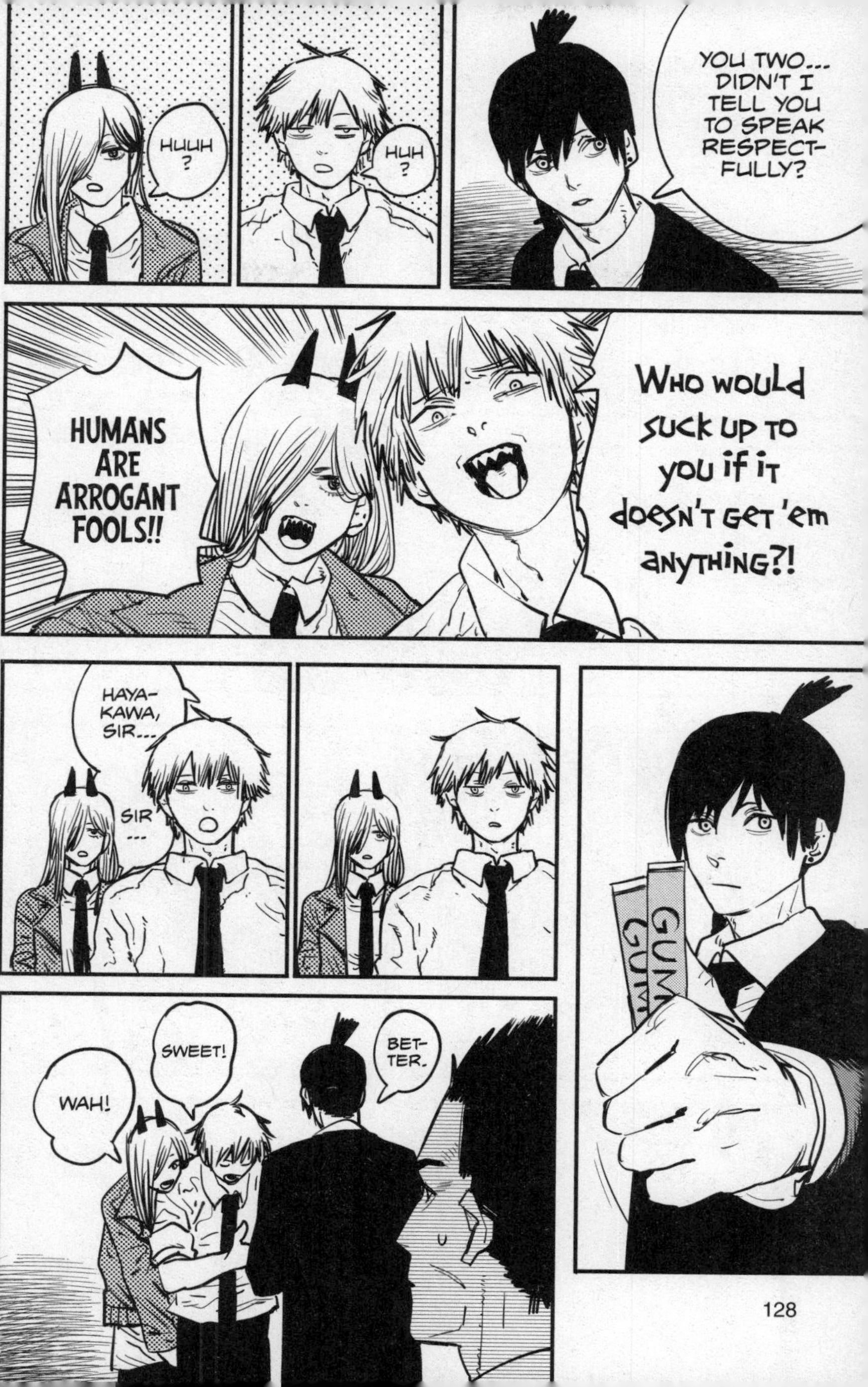
YOU TWO... DIDN'T I TELL YOU TO SPEAK RESPECT-FULLY?
HUH ?
HUUH ?
WHO WOULD SUCK UP TO YOU IF IT DOESN'T GET 'EM ANYTHING?!
HUMANS ARE ARROGANT FOOLS!!
GUM
GUM
HAYA-KAWA, SIR...
SIR ...
BET-TER.
SWEET!
WAH!

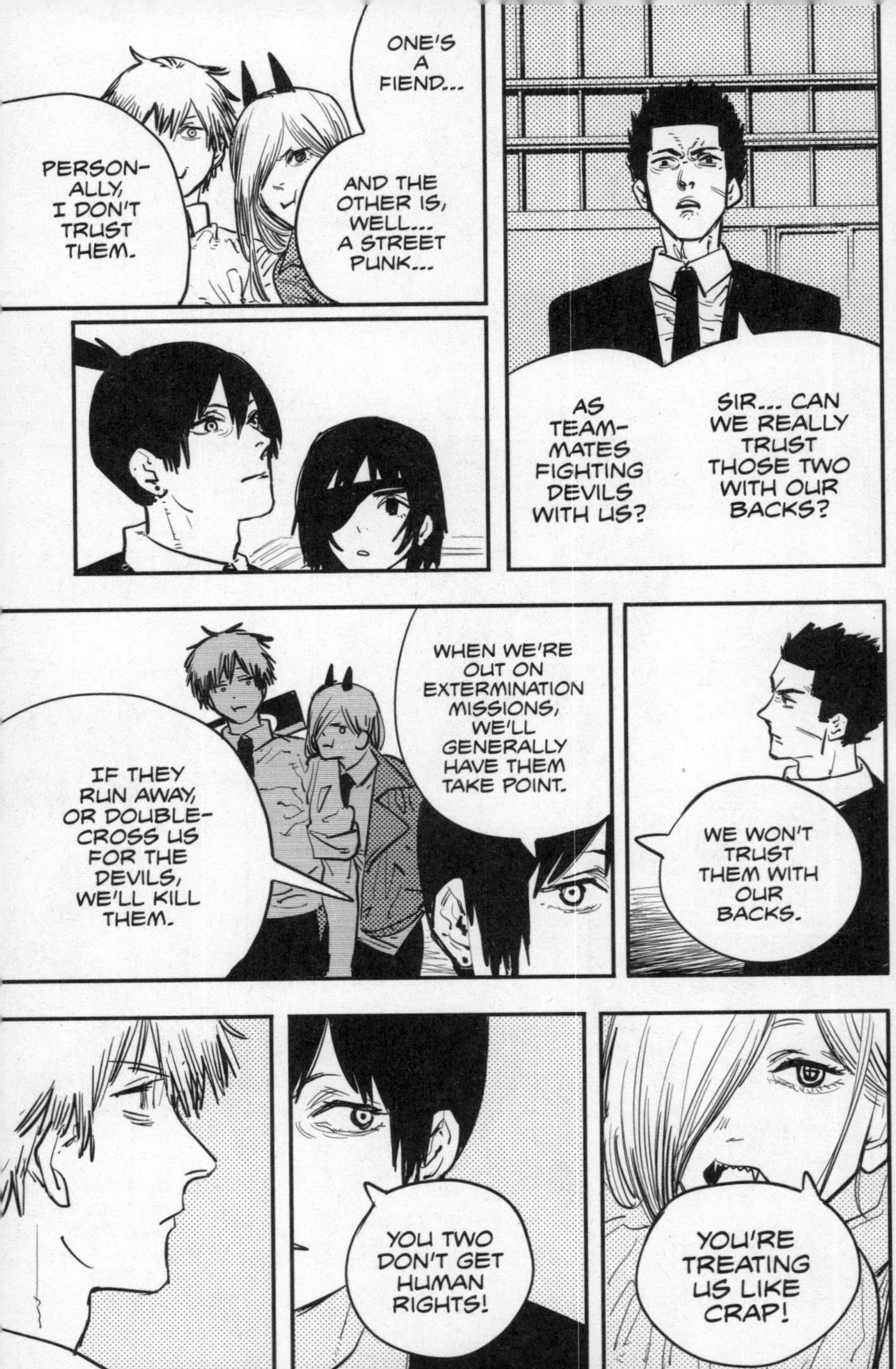
SIR... CAN WE REALLY TRUST THOSE TWO WITH OUR BACKS?
AS TEAMMATES FIGHTING DEVILS WITH US?
ONE'S A FIEND...
AND THE OTHER IS, WELL... A STREET PUNK...
PERSONALLY, I DON'T TRUST THEM.
WE WON'T TRUST THEM WITH OUR BACKS.
WHEN WE'RE OUT ON EXTERMINATION MISSIONS, WE'LL GENERALLY HAVE THEM TAKE POINT.
IF THEY RUN AWAY, OR DOUBLE-CROSS US FOR THE DEVILS, WE'LL KILL THEM.
YOU'RE TREATING US LIKE CRAP!
YOU TWO DON'T GET HUMAN RIGHTS!

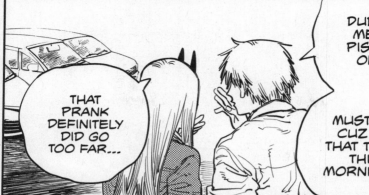

DUDE'S MEGA PISSED OFF!

MUST BE CUZ OF THAT THING THIS MORNING...

THAT PRANK DEFINITELY DID GO TOO FAR...

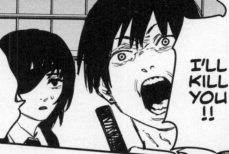

THAT! WAS WAY BEYOND A PRANK!!

I'LL KILL YOU !!

SCARY... WHAT THE HECK HAPPENED ---?

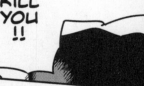

OHO!

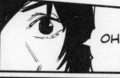

ALL RIGHT! I'LL THROW YOU A BONE!

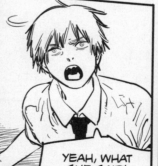

GIMME A REWARD!

YEAH, WHAT SHE SAID! THAT BAT ALMOST KILLED ME, AND NOW IT'S STRAIGHT BACK TO WORK!

C'MON, AKI, YOU CAN'T BE STRICT WITH THEM ALL THE TIME.

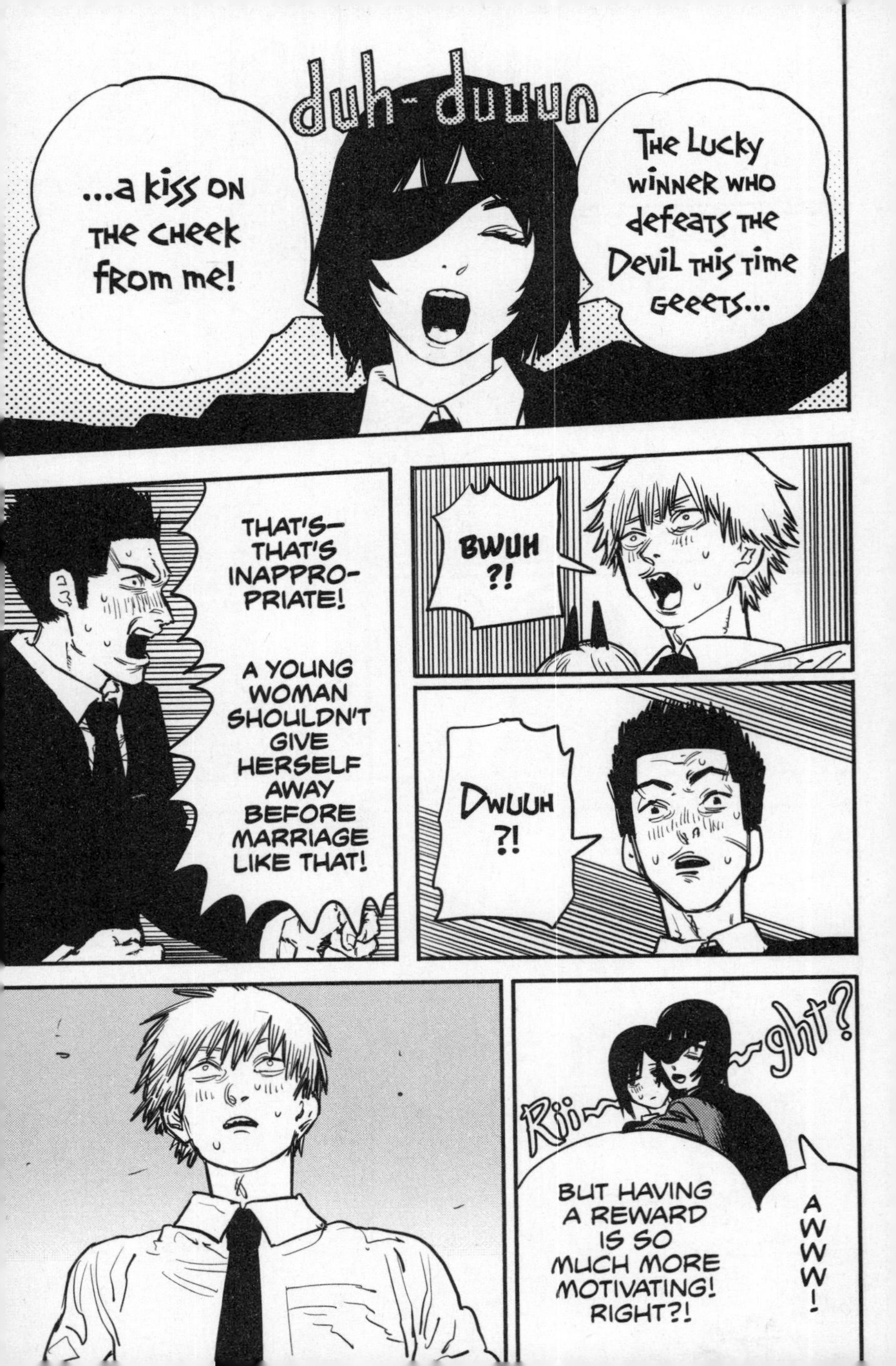
The Lucky winner who defeats the Devil this time geeets...
duh-duuun
...a kiss on the cheek from me!
BWUH ?!
DWUUH ?!
THAT'S— THAT'S INAPPROPRIATE!
A YOUNG WOMAN SHOULDN'T GIVE HERSELF AWAY BEFORE MARRIAGE LIKE THAT!
Rii~~ght?
AWWW!
BUT HAVING A REWARD IS SO MUCH MORE MOTIVATING! RIGHT?!

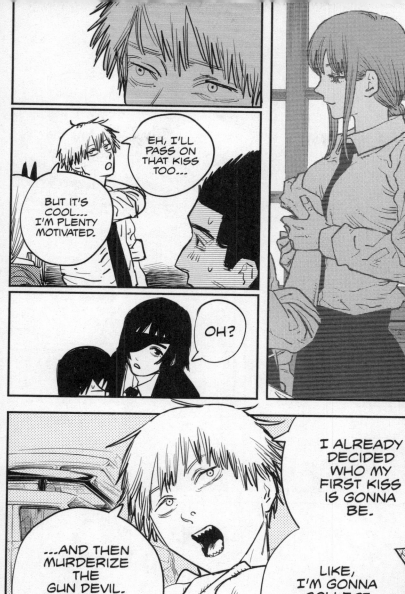

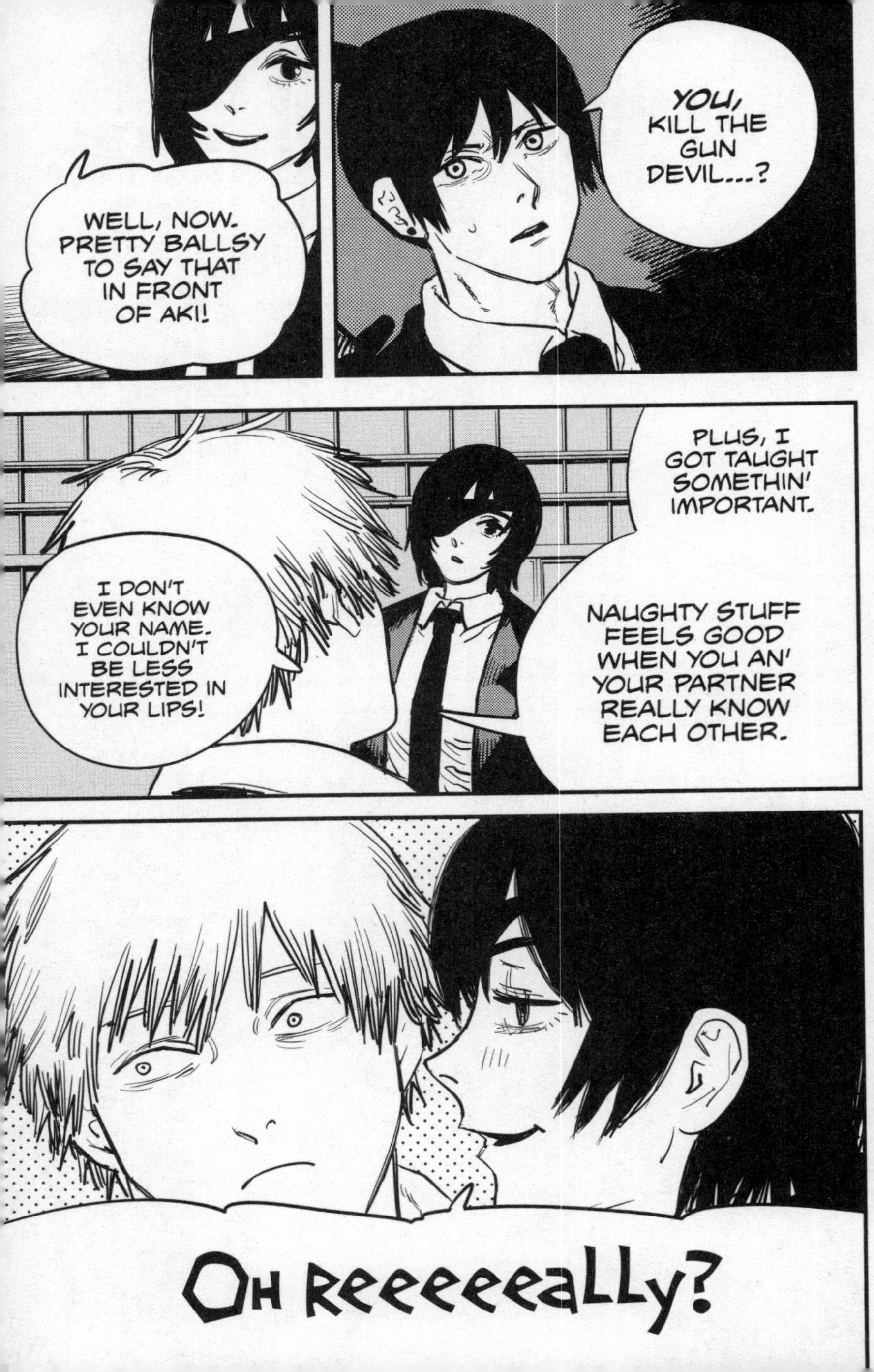
YOU, KILL THE GUN DEVIL...?
WELL, NOW. PRETTY BALLSY TO SAY THAT IN FRONT OF AKI!
PLUS, I GOT TAUGHT SOMETHIN' IMPORTANT.
NAUGHTY STUFF FEELS GOOD WHEN YOU AN' YOUR PARTNER REALLY KNOW EACH OTHER.
I DON'T EVEN KNOW YOUR NAME. I COULDN'T BE LESS INTERESTED IN YOUR LIPS!
OH REEEEEALLY?

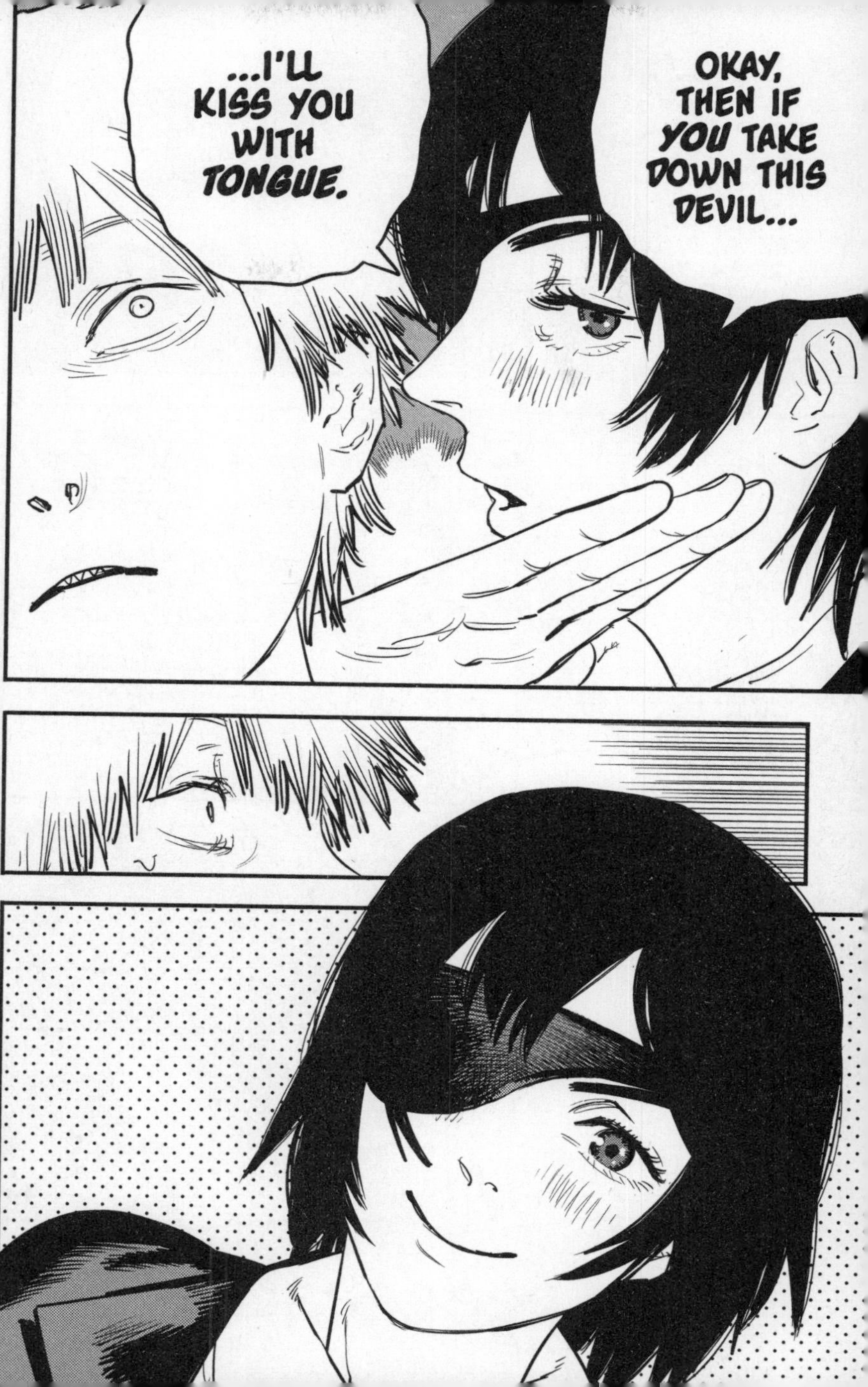
OKAY, THEN IF YOU TAKE DOWN THIS DEVIL...
...I'LL KISS YOU WITH TONGUE.

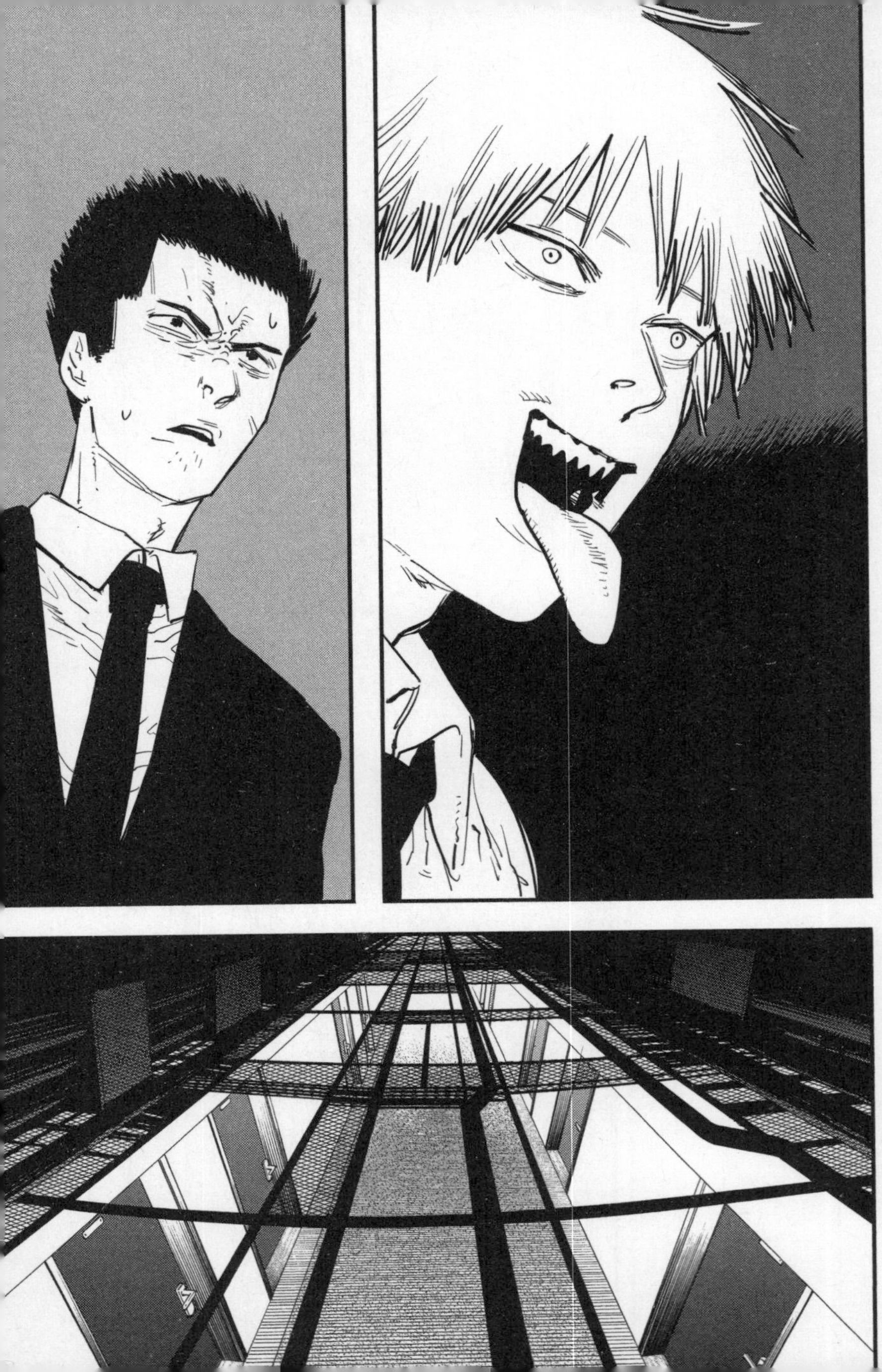

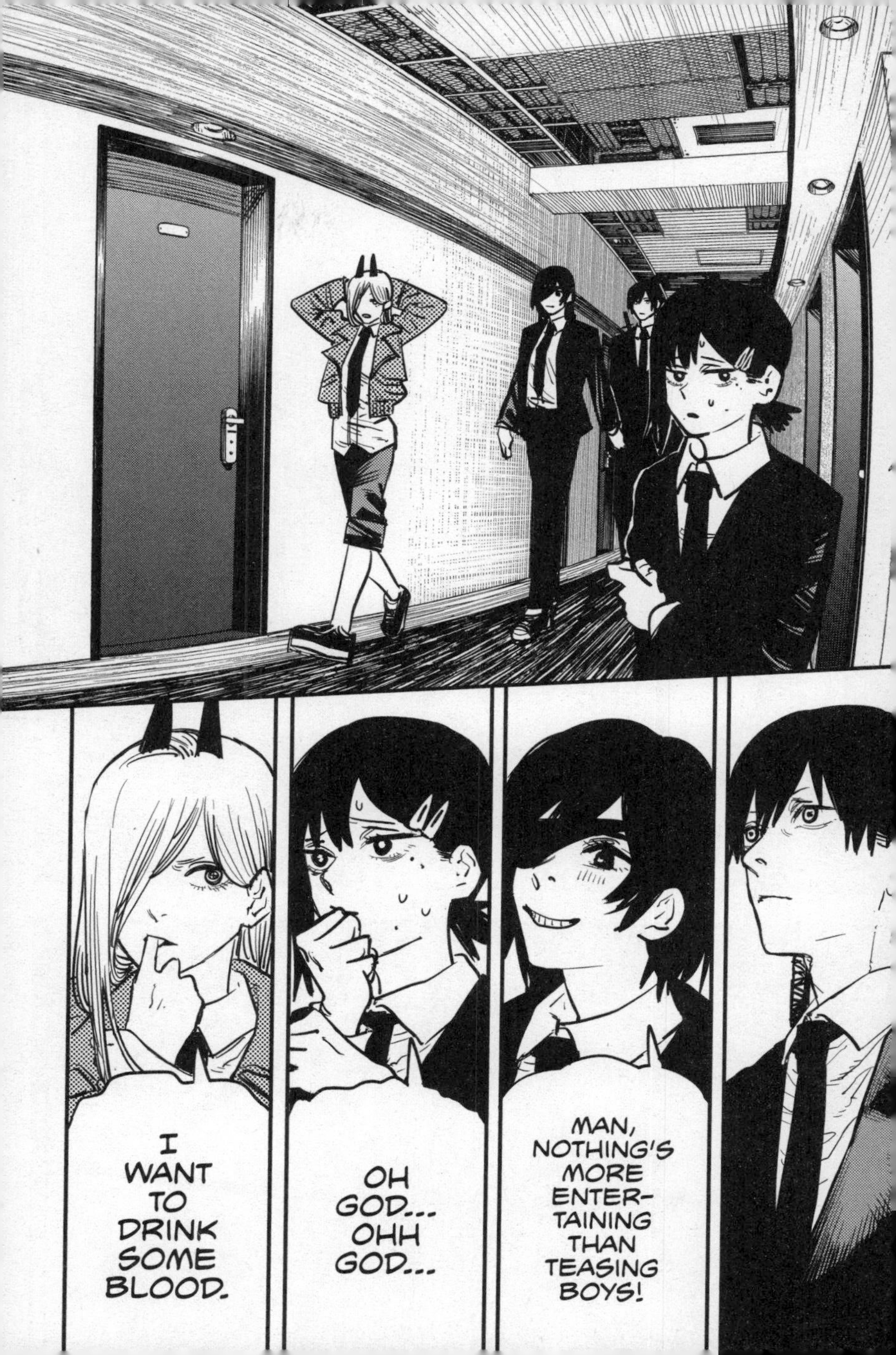
MAN, NOTHING'S MORE ENTER-TAINING THAN TEASING BOYS!
OH GOD... OHH GOD...
I WANT TO DRINK SOME BLOOD.

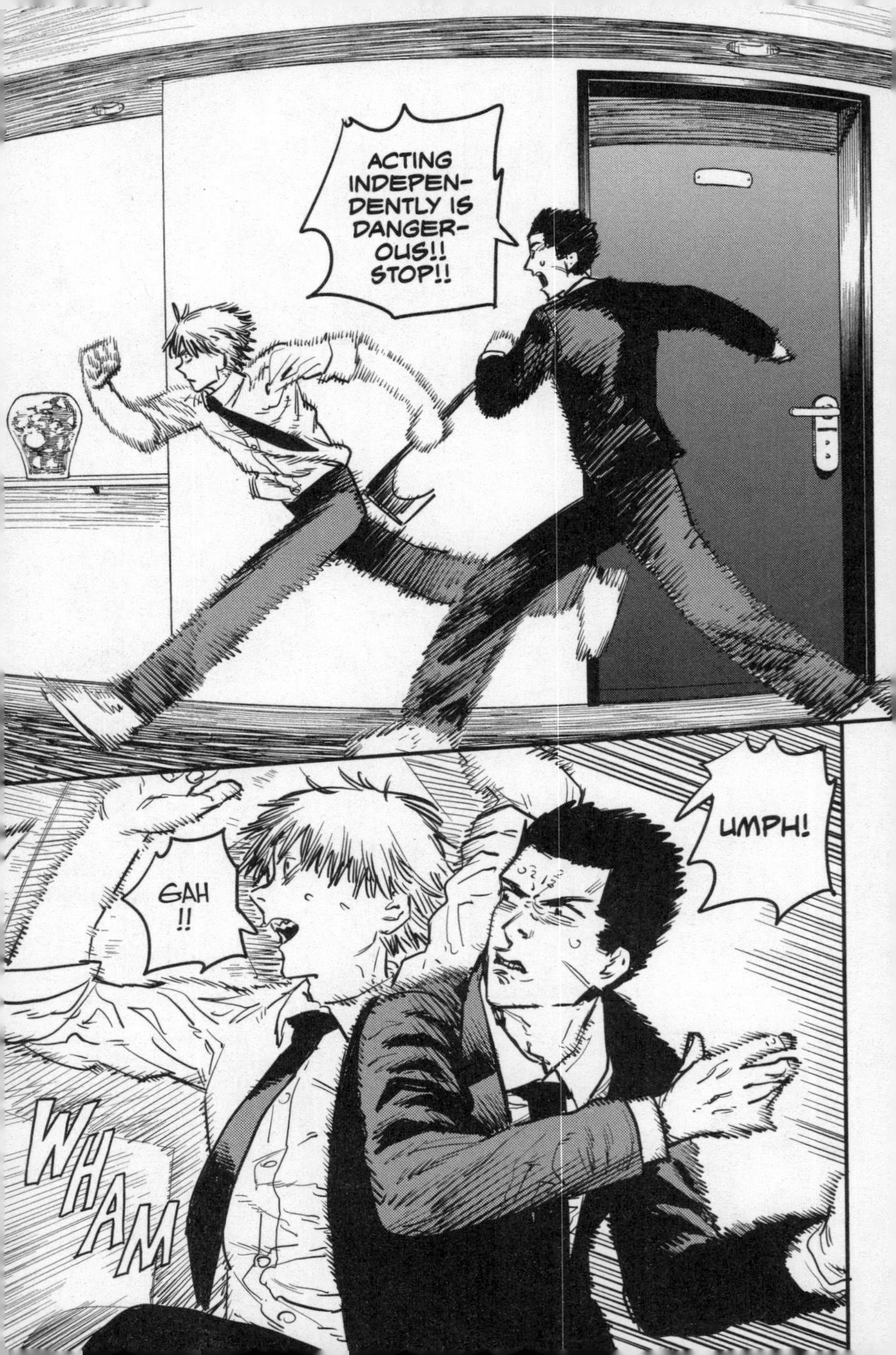
ACTING INDEPENDENTLY IS DANGEROUS!! STOP!!
UMPH!
GAH !!
WHAM

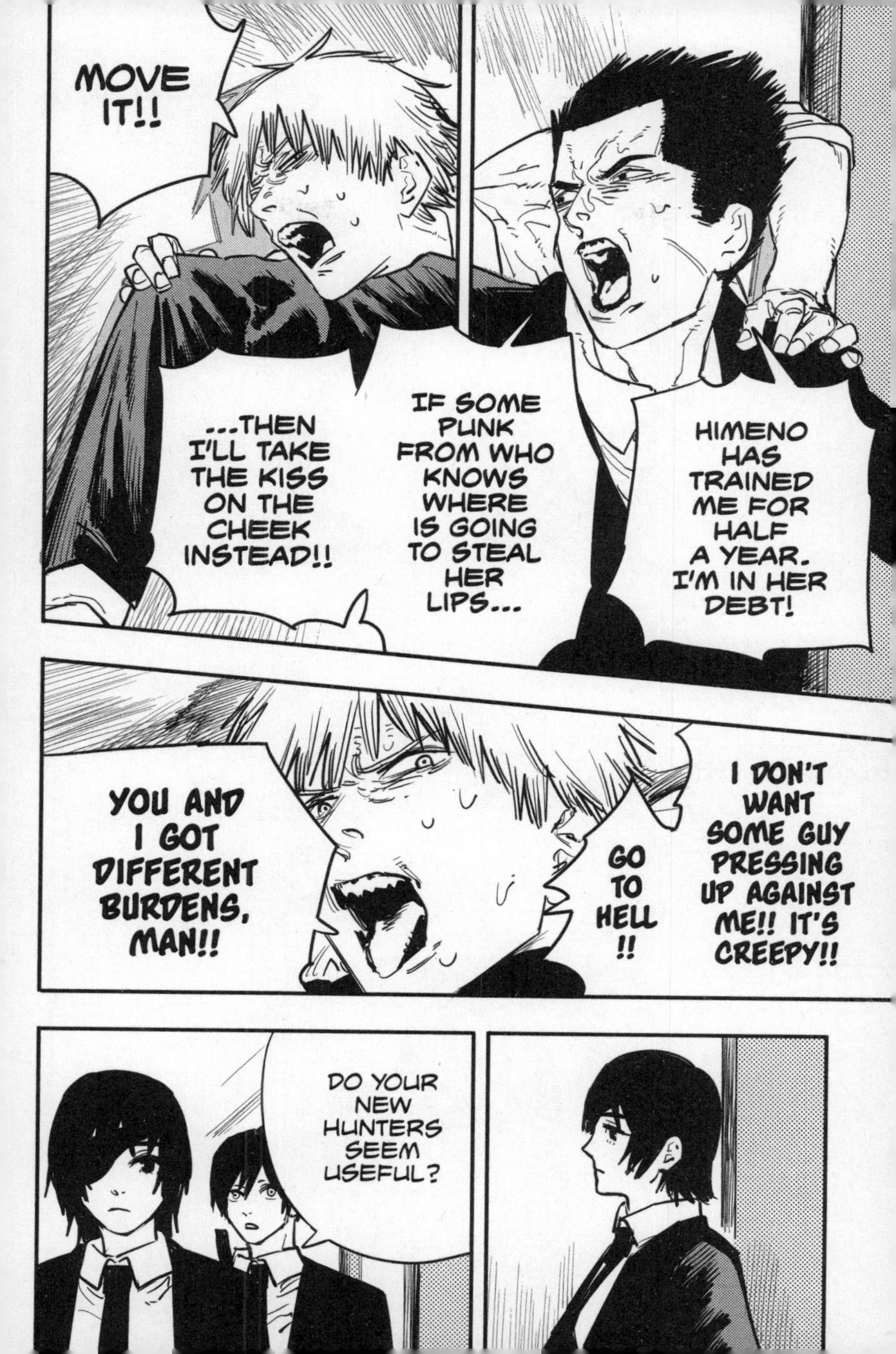
HIMENO HAS TRAINED ME FOR HALF A YEAR. I'M IN HER DEBT!
IF SOME PUNK FROM WHO KNOWS WHERE IS GOING TO STEAL HER LIPS...
...THEN I'LL TAKE THE KISS ON THE CHEEK INSTEAD!!
MOVE IT!!
I DON'T WANT SOME GUY PRESSING UP AGAINST ME!! IT'S CREEPY!!
GO TO HELL !!
YOU AND I GOT DIFFERENT BURDENS, MAN!!
DO YOUR NEW HUNTERS SEEM USEFUL?

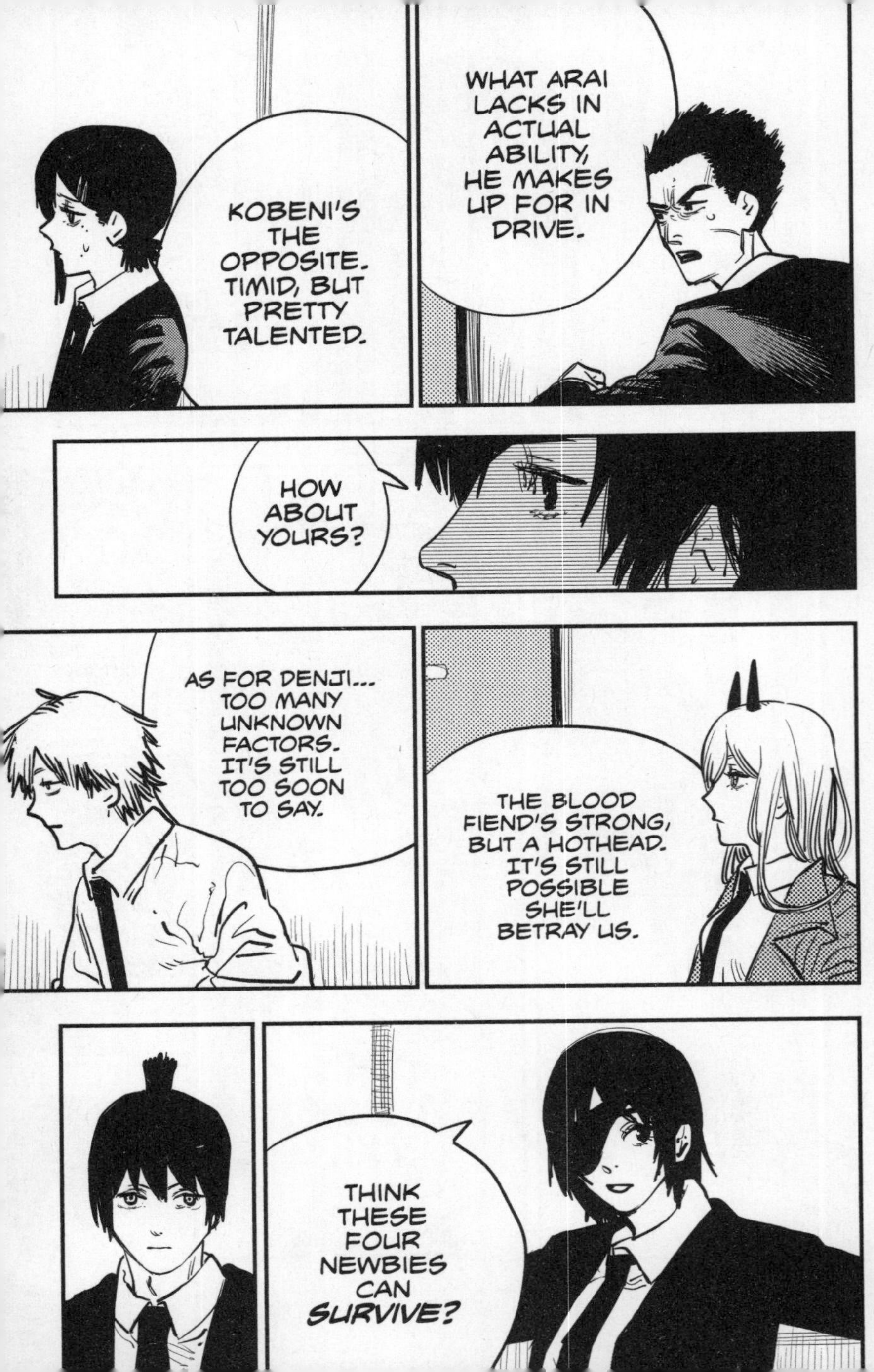
WHAT ARAI LACKS IN ACTUAL ABILITY, HE MAKES UP FOR IN DRIVE.
KOBENI'S THE OPPOSITE. TIMID, BUT PRETTY TALENTED.
HOW ABOUT YOURS?
THE BLOOD FIEND'S STRONG, BUT A HOTHEAD. IT'S STILL POSSIBLE SHE'LL BETRAY US.
AS FOR DENJI... TOO MANY UNKNOWN FACTORS. IT'S STILL TOO SOON TO SAY.
THINK THESE FOUR NEWBIES CAN *SURVIVE?*

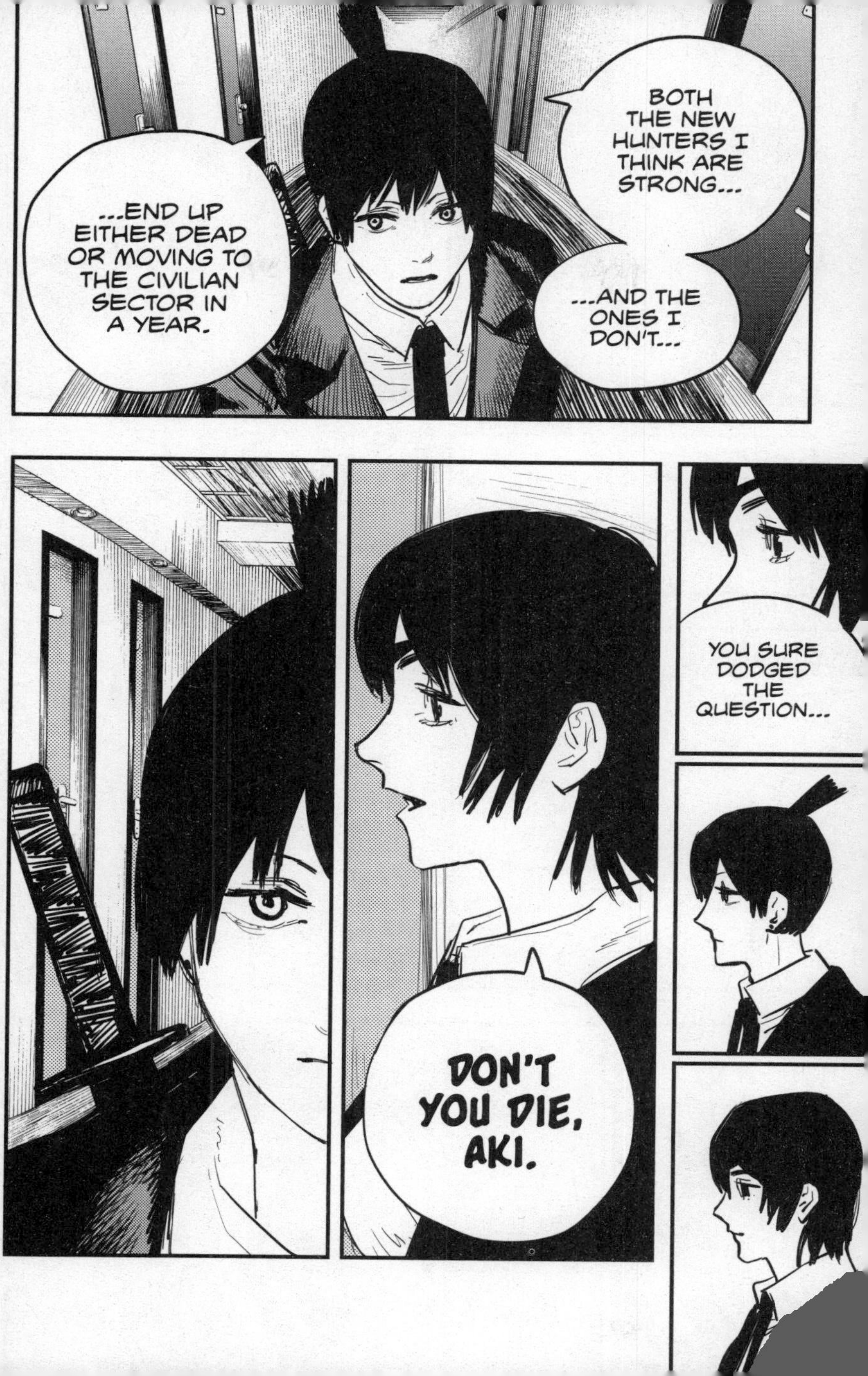
BOTH THE NEW HUNTERS I THINK ARE STRONG...
...AND THE ONES I DON'T...
...END UP EITHER DEAD OR MOVING TO THE CIVILIAN SECTOR IN A YEAR.
YOU SURE DODGED THE QUESTION...
DON'T YOU DIE, AKI.

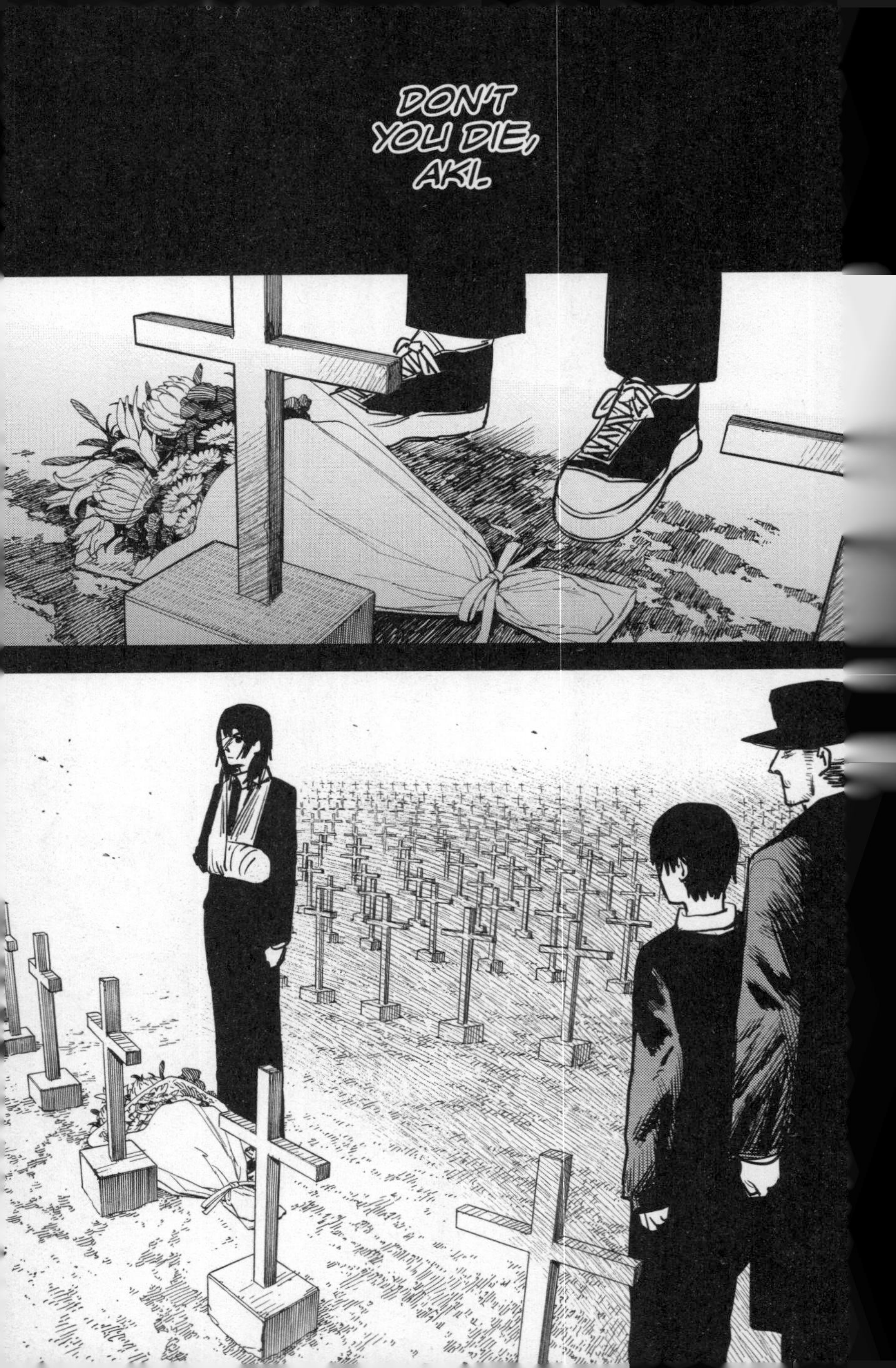
DON'T YOU DIE, AKI.

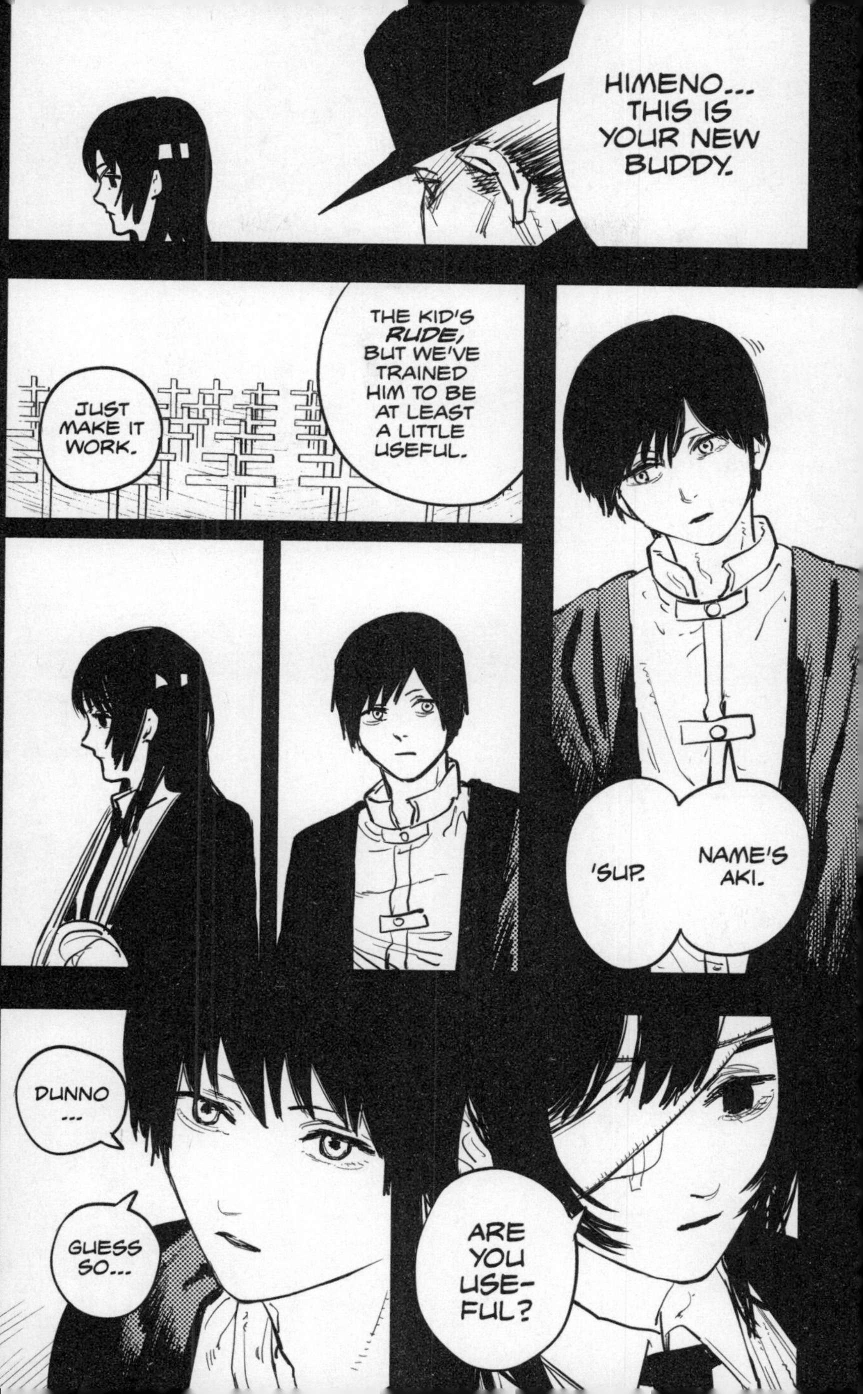
HIMENO... THIS IS YOUR NEW BUDDY.
THE KID'S *RUDE,* BUT WE'VE TRAINED HIM TO BE AT LEAST A LITTLE USEFUL.
JUST MAKE IT WORK.
'SUP. NAME'S AKI.
ARE YOU USE-FUL?
DUNNO...
GUESS SO...

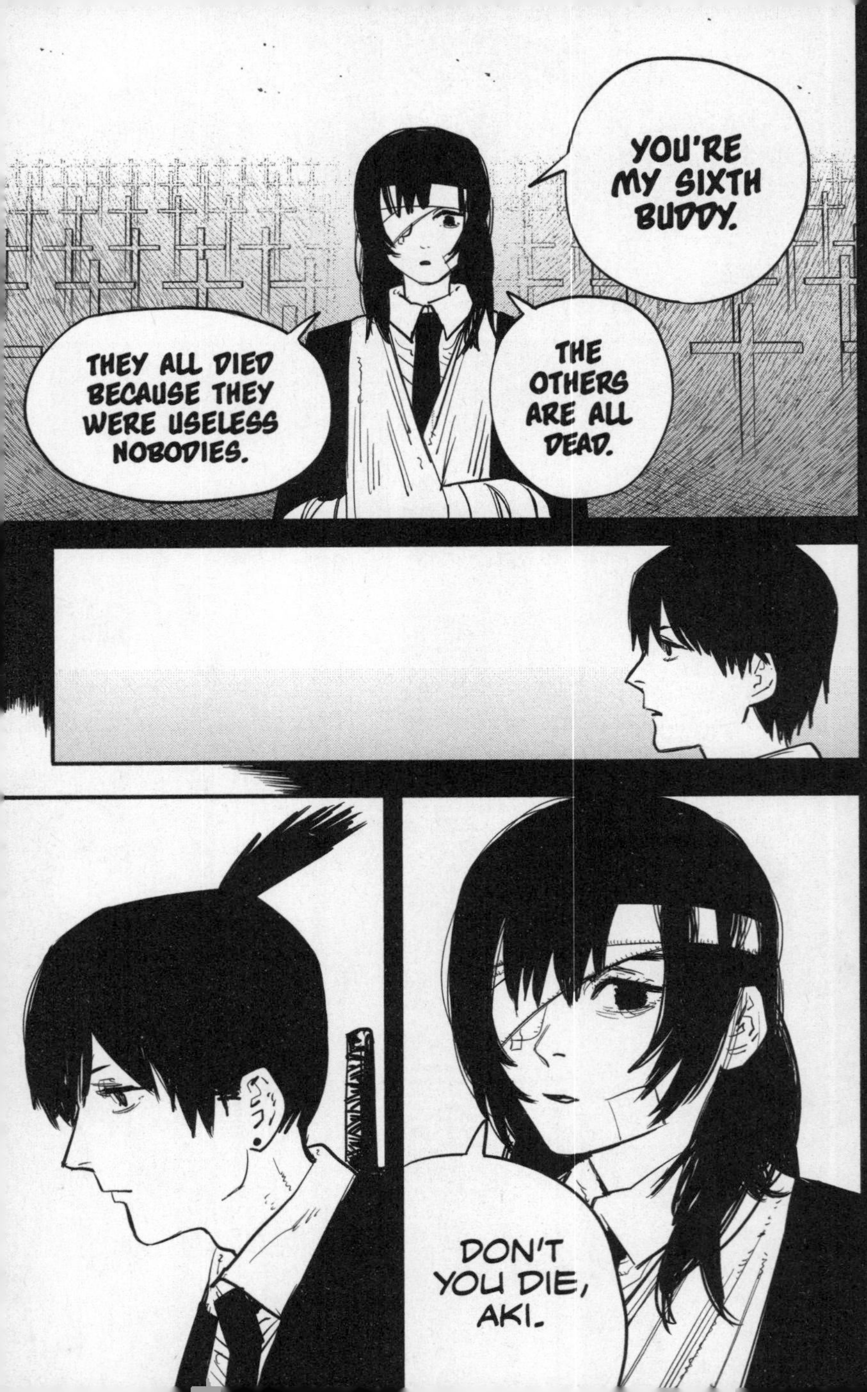
YOU'RE MY SIXTH BUDDY.
THE OTHERS ARE ALL DEAD.
THEY ALL DIED BECAUSE THEY WERE USELESS NOBODIES.
DON'T YOU DIE, AKI.

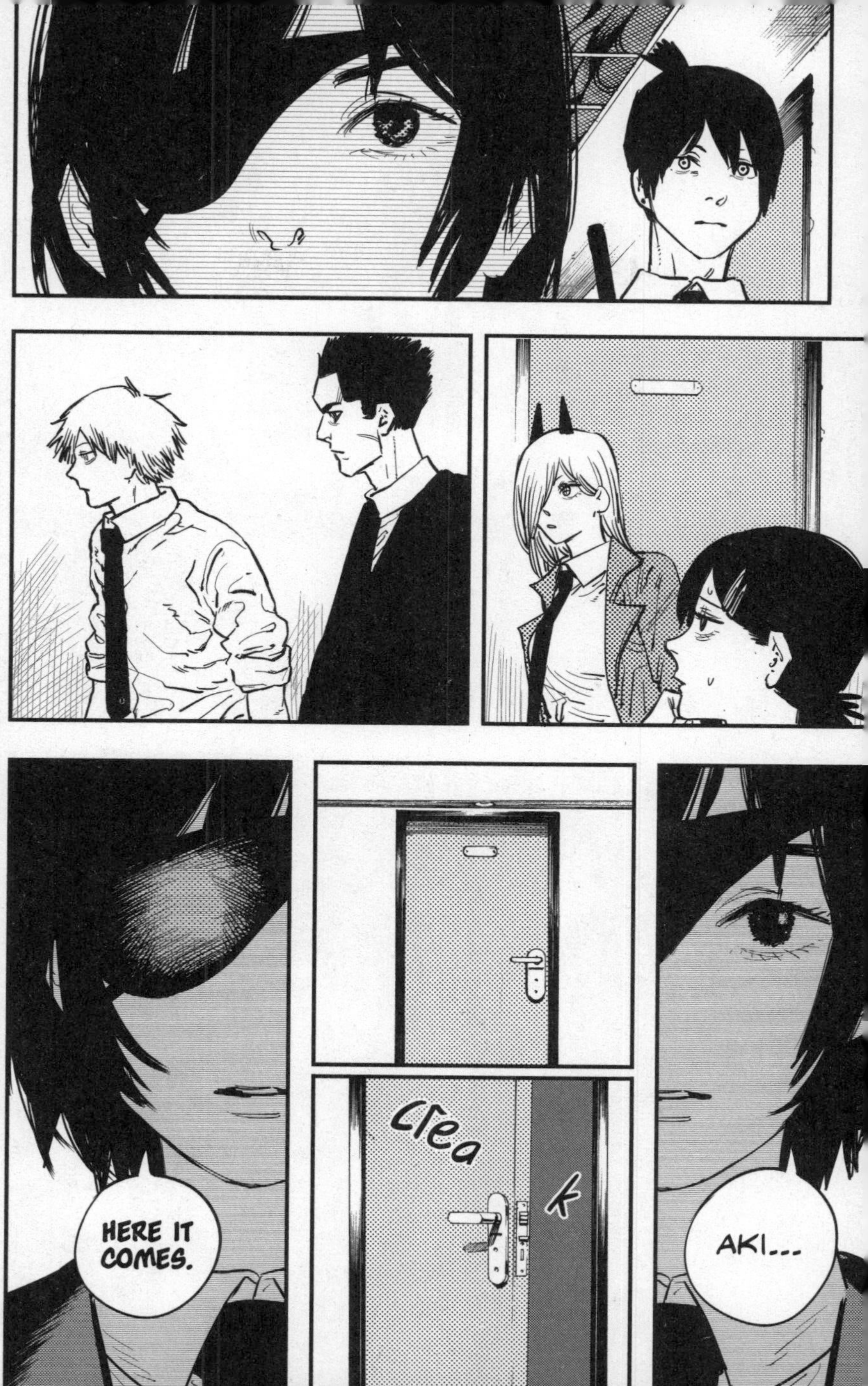
AKI...
Creak
HERE IT COMES.

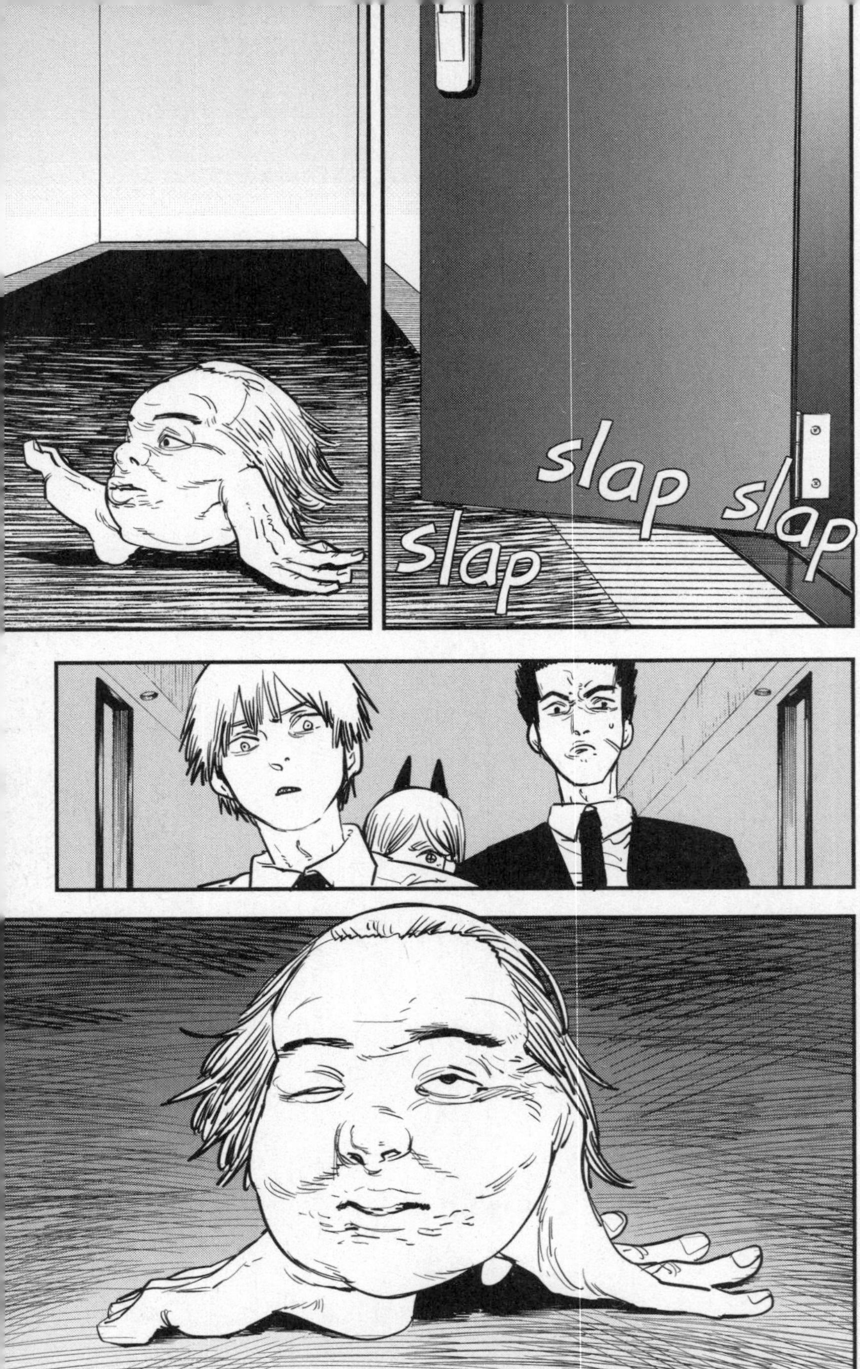
slap slap slap

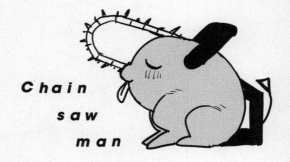

Chain
saw
man

# Chapter 15: Endless 8th Floor

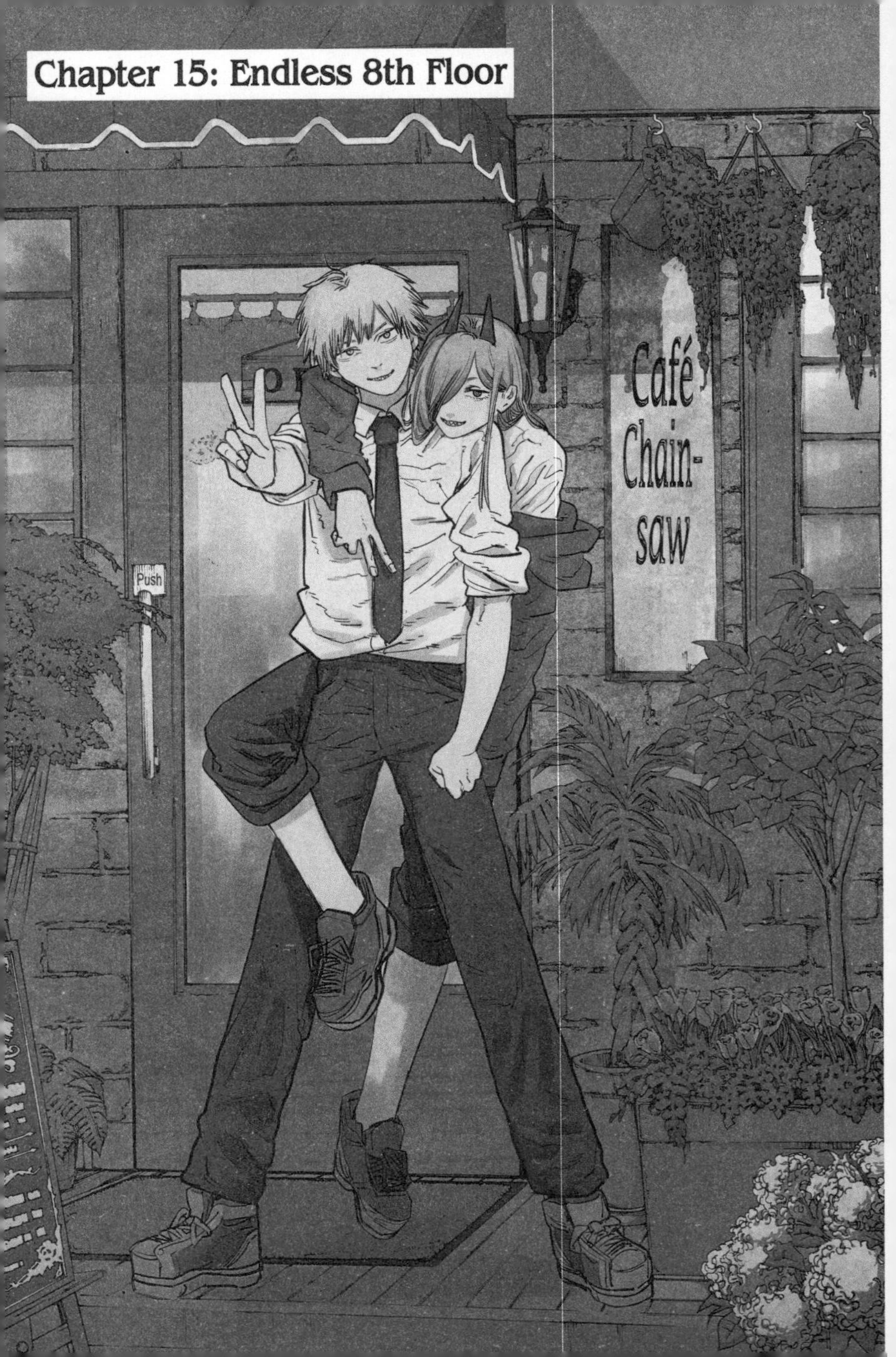

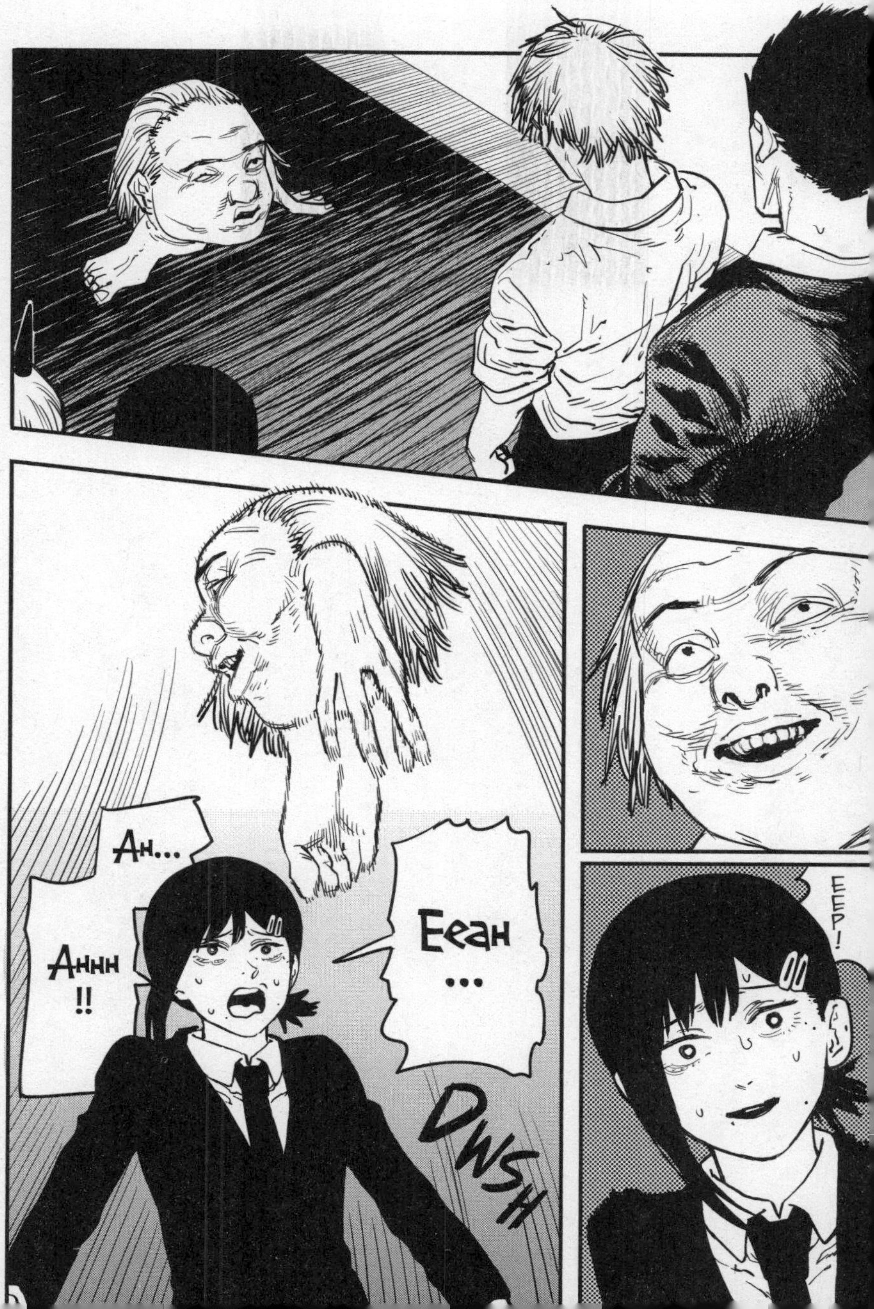
EEEP!
Eeah ...
Ah...
Ahhh !!
DWSH

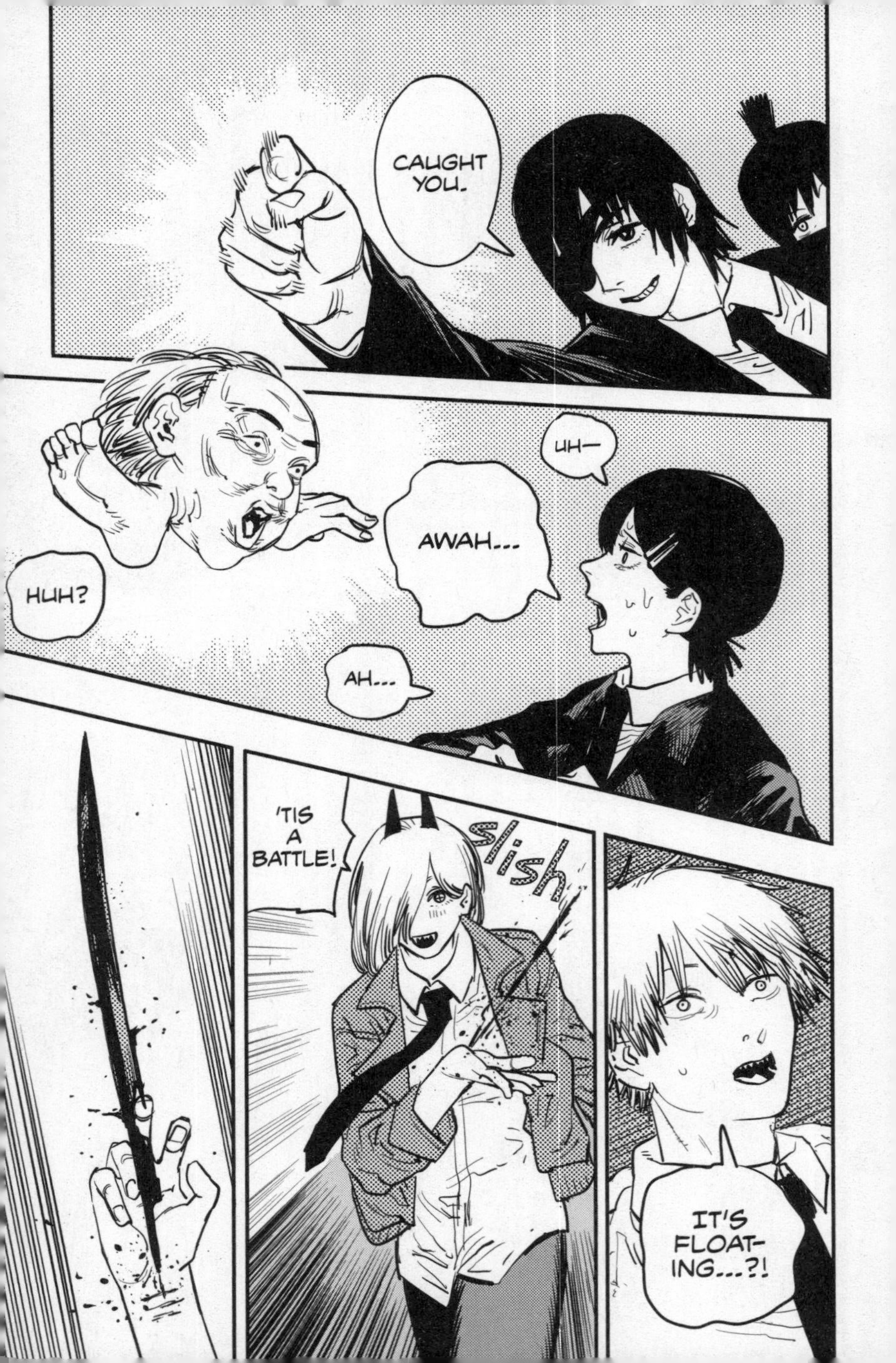
CAUGHT YOU.
UH—
AWAH...
HUH?
AH...
IT'S FLOATING...?!
'TIS A BATTLE!
slish

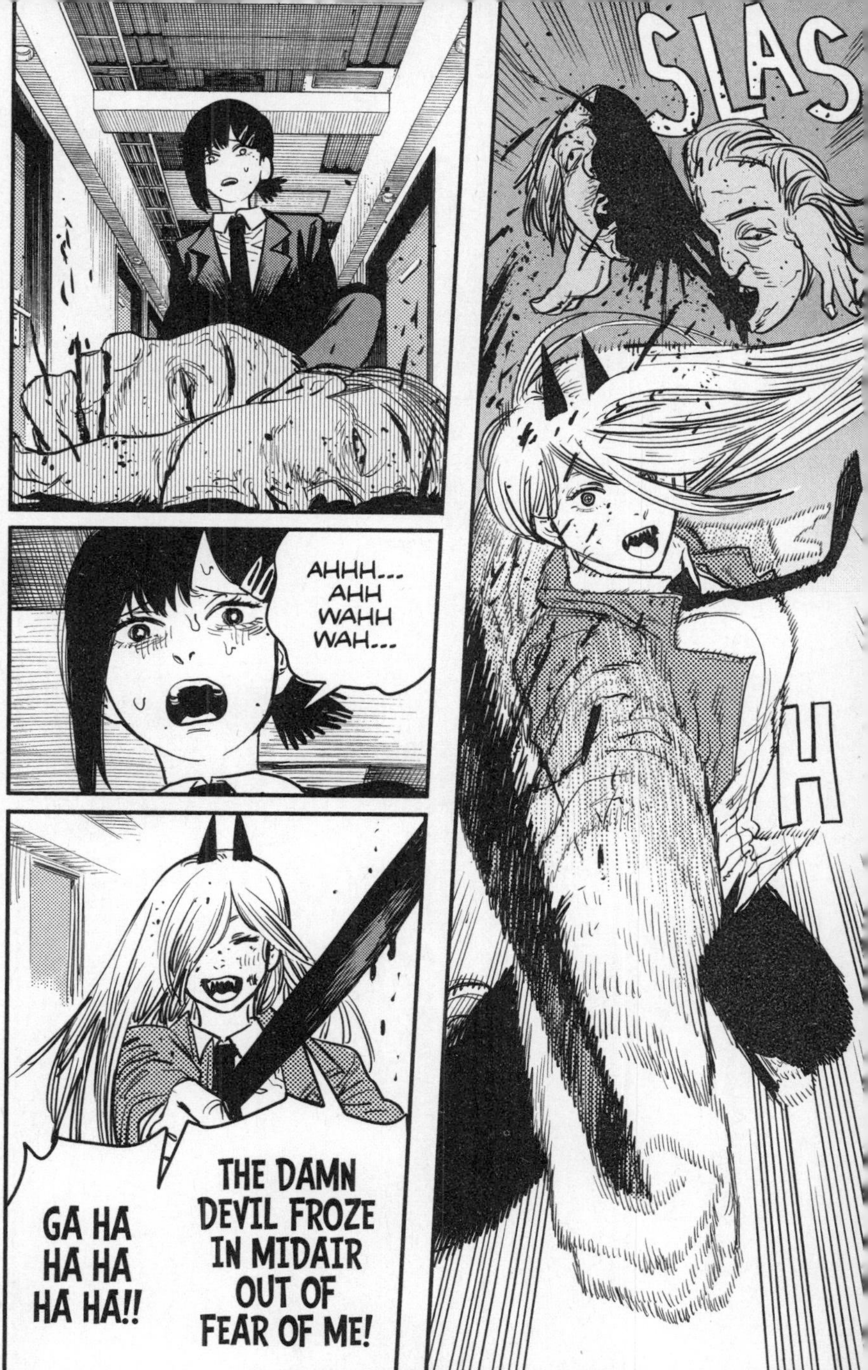
SLASH
AHHH... AHH WAHH WAH...
THE DAMN DEVIL FROZE IN MIDAIR OUT OF FEAR OF ME!
GA HA HA HA HA HA!!

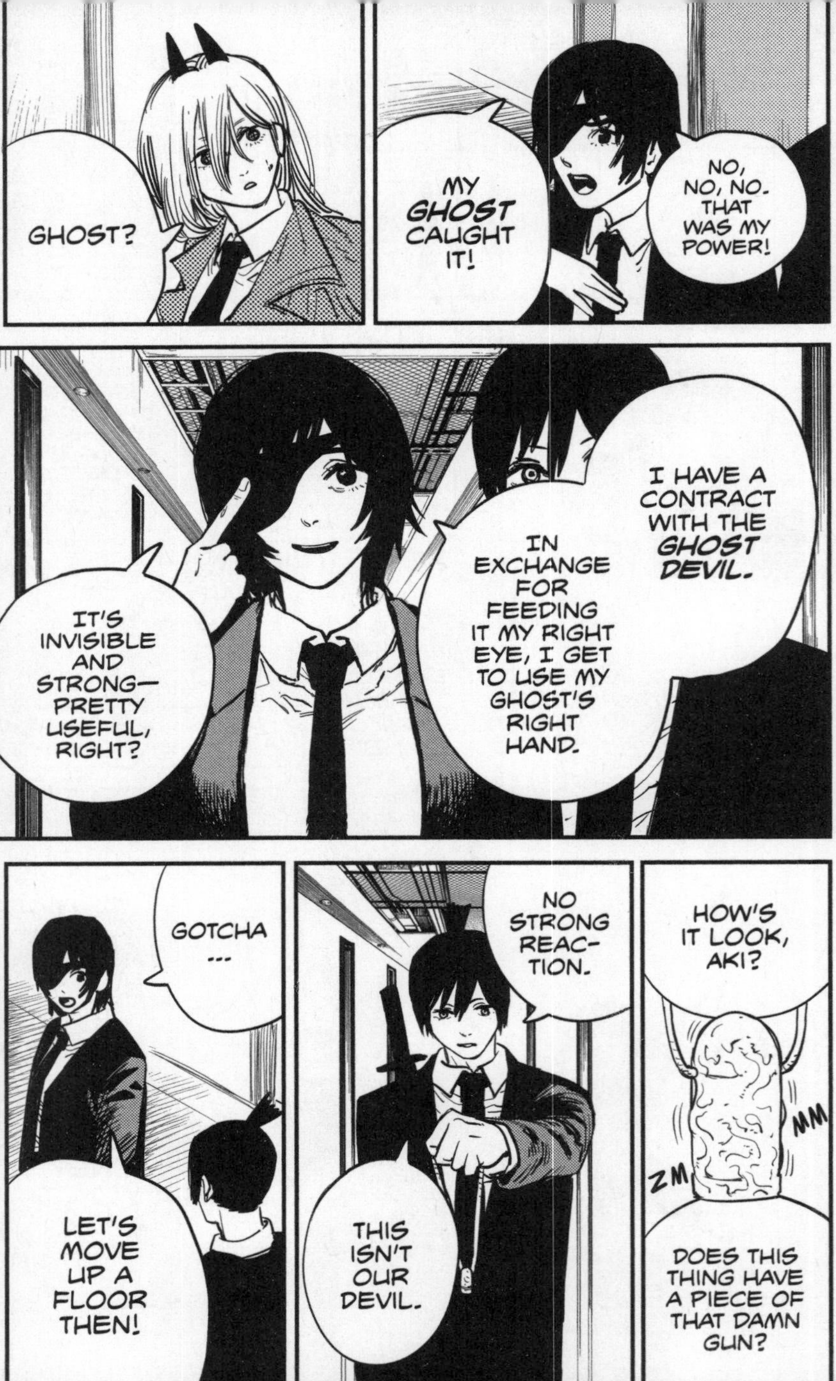
NO, NO, NO. THAT WAS MY POWER!
MY GHOST CAUGHT IT!
GHOST?
I HAVE A CONTRACT WITH THE GHOST DEVIL.
IN EXCHANGE FOR FEEDING IT MY RIGHT EYE, I GET TO USE MY GHOST'S RIGHT HAND.
IT'S INVISIBLE AND STRONG—PRETTY USEFUL, RIGHT?
HOW'S IT LOOK, AKI?
MM
ZM
DOES THIS THING HAVE A PIECE OF THAT DAMN GUN?
NO STRONG REAC-TION.
THIS ISN'T OUR DEVIL.
GOTCHA ...
LET'S MOVE UP A FLOOR THEN!

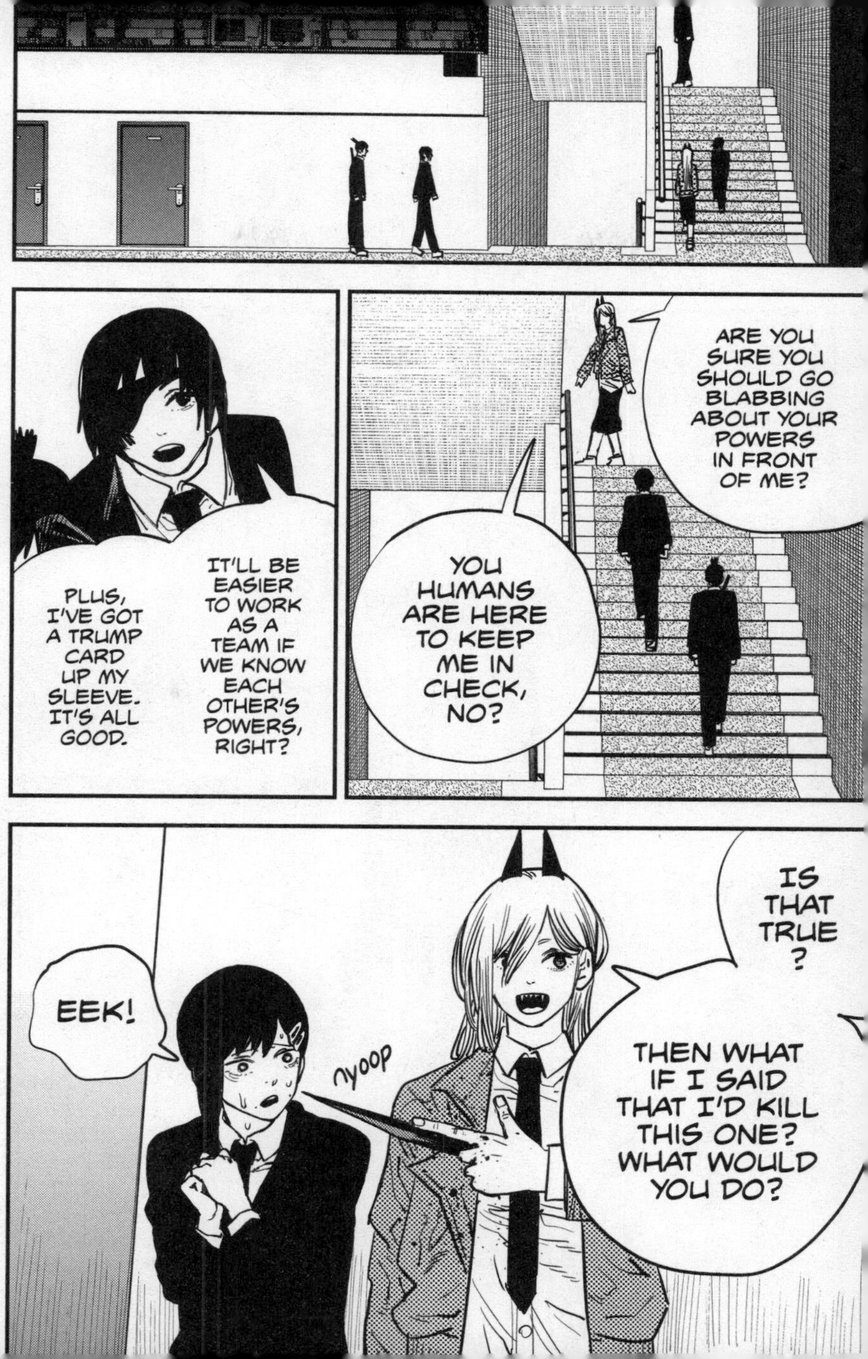
ARE YOU SURE YOU SHOULD GO BLABBING ABOUT YOUR POWERS IN FRONT OF ME?
YOU HUMANS ARE HERE TO KEEP ME IN CHECK, NO?
IT'LL BE EASIER TO WORK AS A TEAM IF WE KNOW EACH OTHER'S POWERS, RIGHT?
PLUS, I'VE GOT A TRUMP CARD UP MY SLEEVE. IT'S ALL GOOD.
IS THAT TRUE?
THEN WHAT IF I SAID THAT I'D KILL THIS ONE? WHAT WOULD YOU DO?
nyoop
EEK!

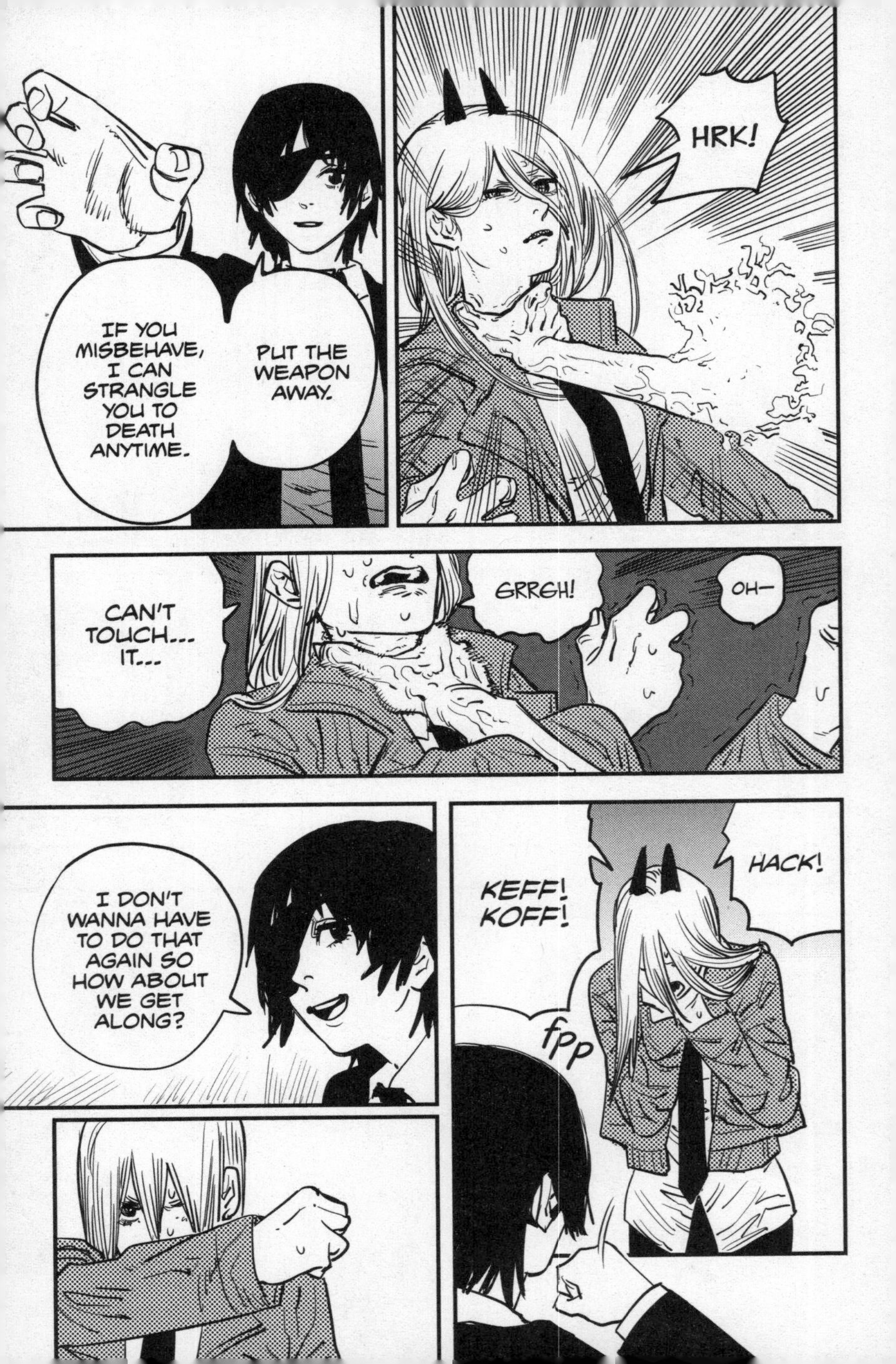
HRK!
PUT THE WEAPON AWAY.
IF YOU MISBEHAVE, I CAN STRANGLE YOU TO DEATH ANYTIME.
OH—
GRRGH!
CAN'T TOUCH... IT...
HACK!
KEFF! KOFF!
fpp
I DON'T WANNA HAVE TO DO THAT AGAIN SO HOW ABOUT WE GET ALONG?

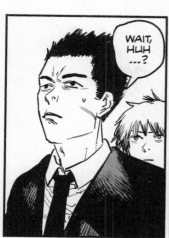

WAIT, HUH ---?

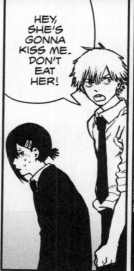

HEY, SHE'S GONNA KISS ME. DON'T EAT HER!

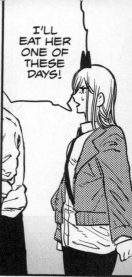

I'LL EAT HER ONE OF THESE DAYS!

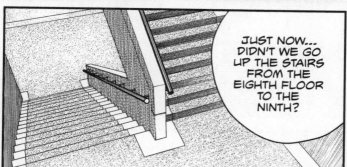

JUST NOW... DIDN'T WE GO UP THE STAIRS FROM THE EIGHTH FLOOR TO THE NINTH?

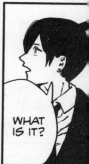

WHAT IS IT?

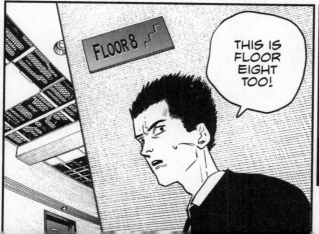

FLOOR 8

THIS IS FLOOR EIGHT TOO!

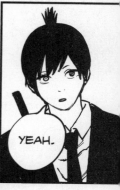

YEAH.

154

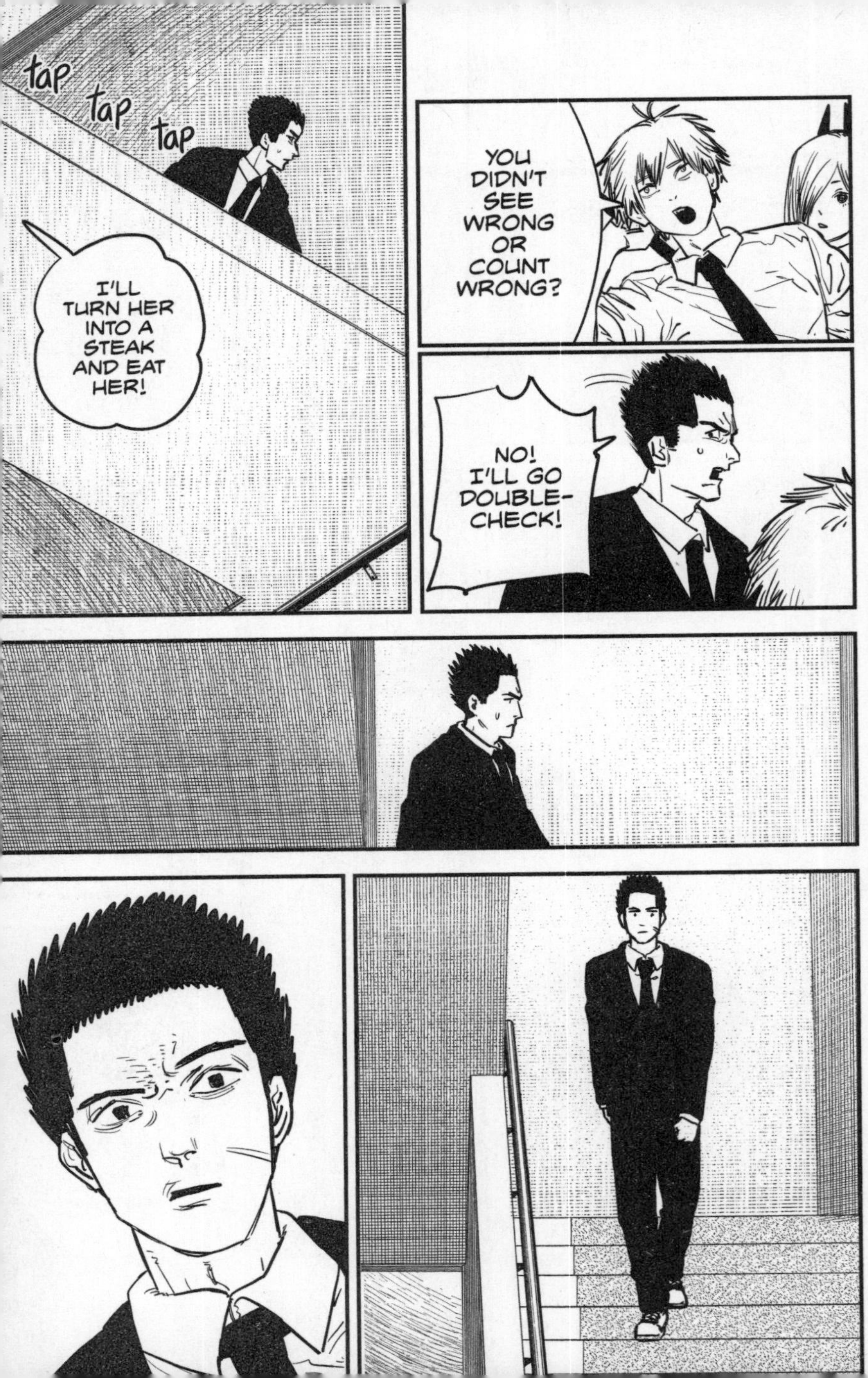
YOU DIDN'T SEE WRONG OR COUNT WRONG?
NO! I'LL GO DOUBLE-CHECK!
tap tap tap
I'LL TURN HER INTO A STEAK AND EAT HER!

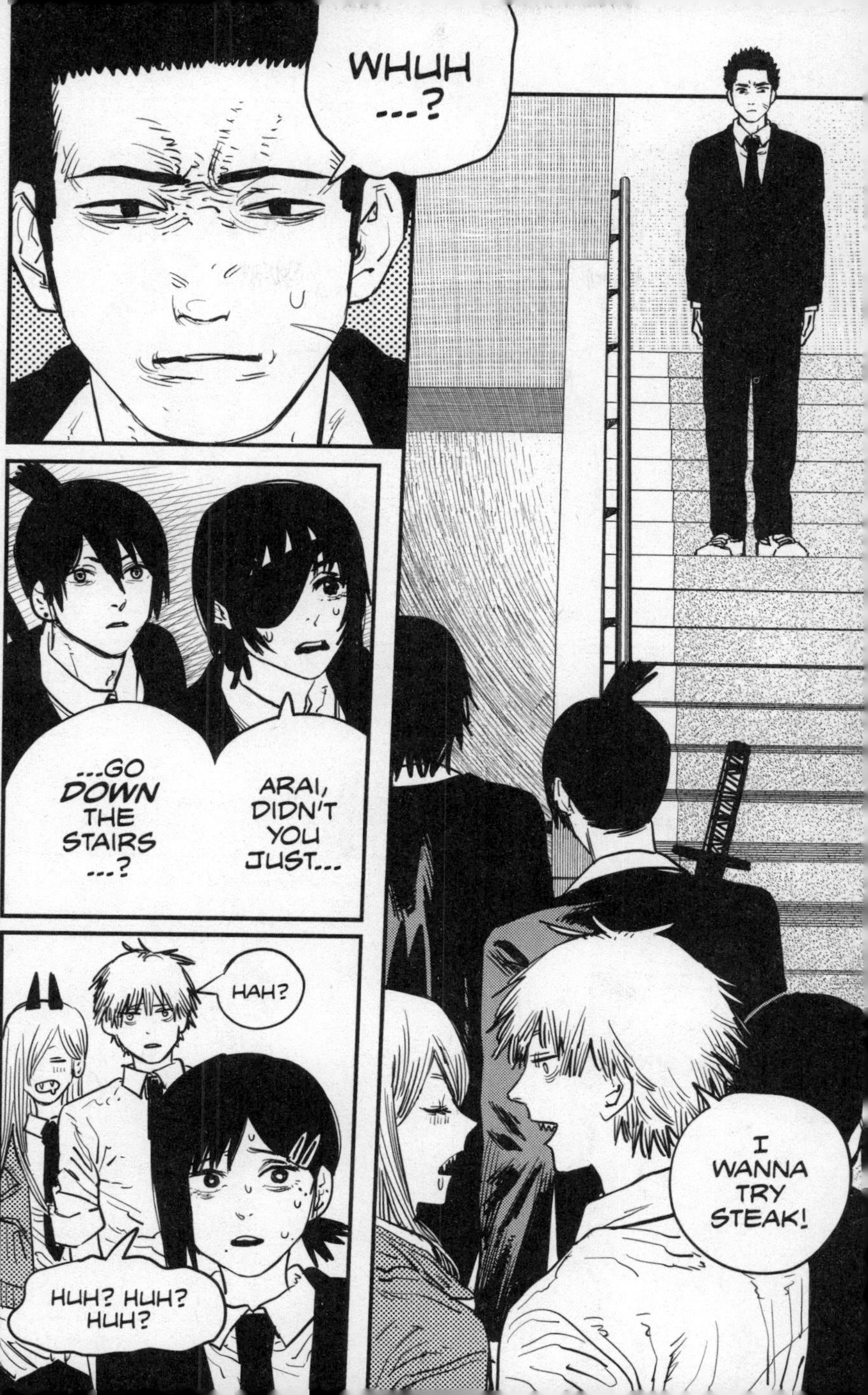
I WANNA TRY STEAK!
WHUH ---?
ARAI, DIDN'T YOU JUST...
...GO DOWN THE STAIRS ---?
HAH?
HUH? HUH? HUH?

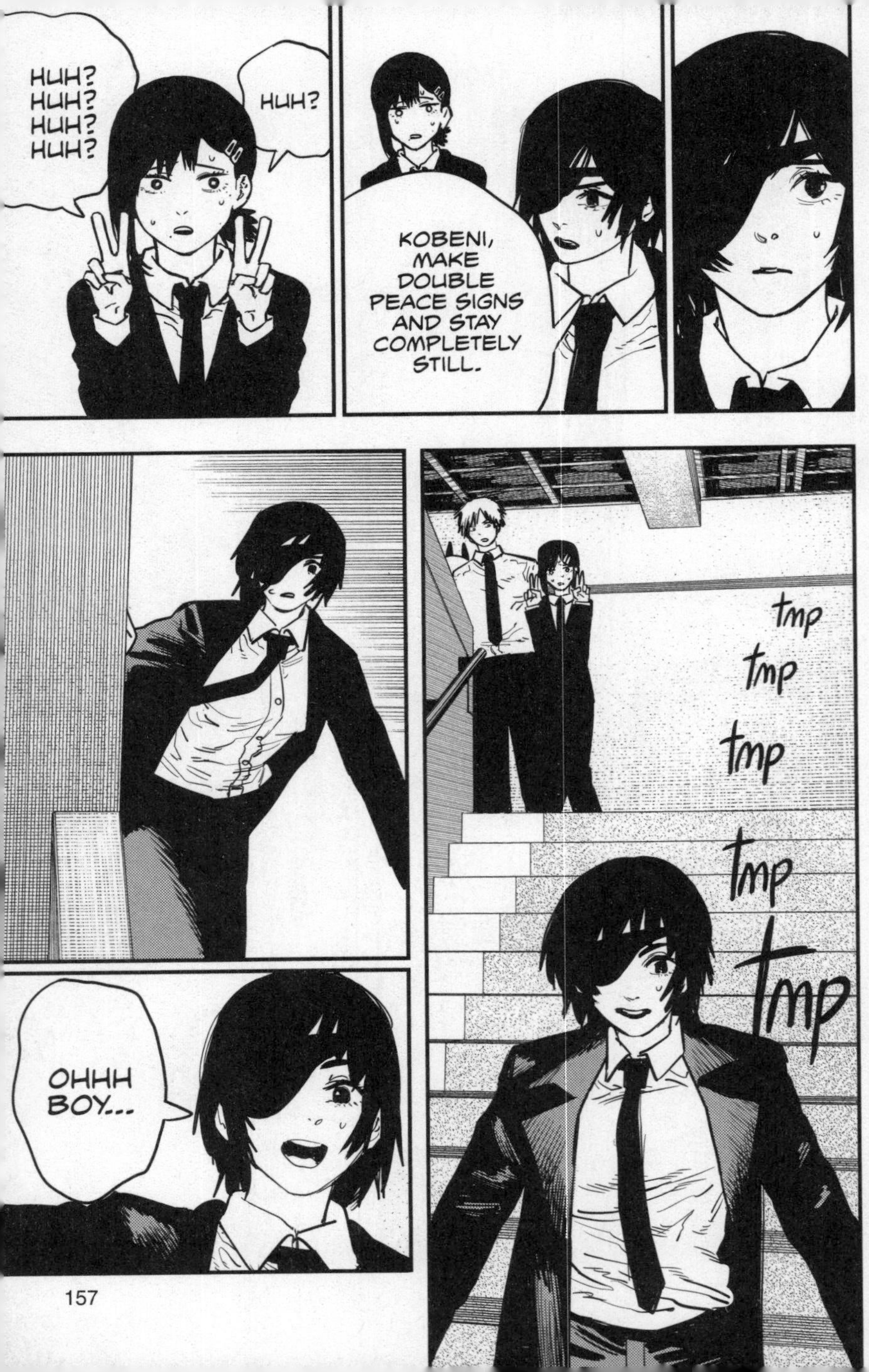
KOBENI, MAKE DOUBLE PEACE SIGNS AND STAY COMPLETELY STILL.
HUH?
HUH? HUH? HUH? HUH?
tmp tmp tmp tmp tmp
OHHH BOY...

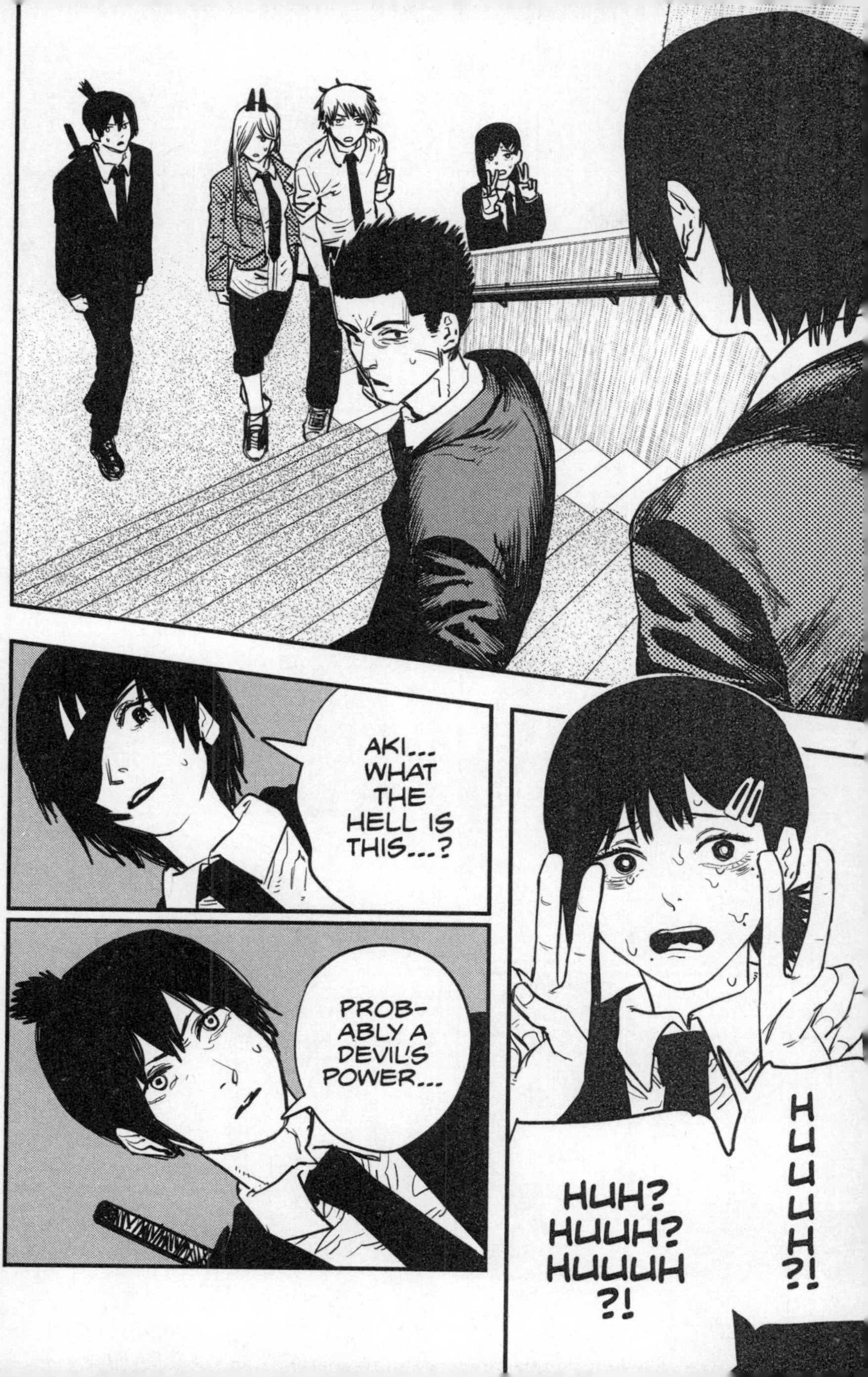
HUUUUH?!
HUH? HUUH? HUUUUH ?!
AKI... WHAT THE HELL IS THIS...?
PROB-ABLY A DEVIL'S POWER...

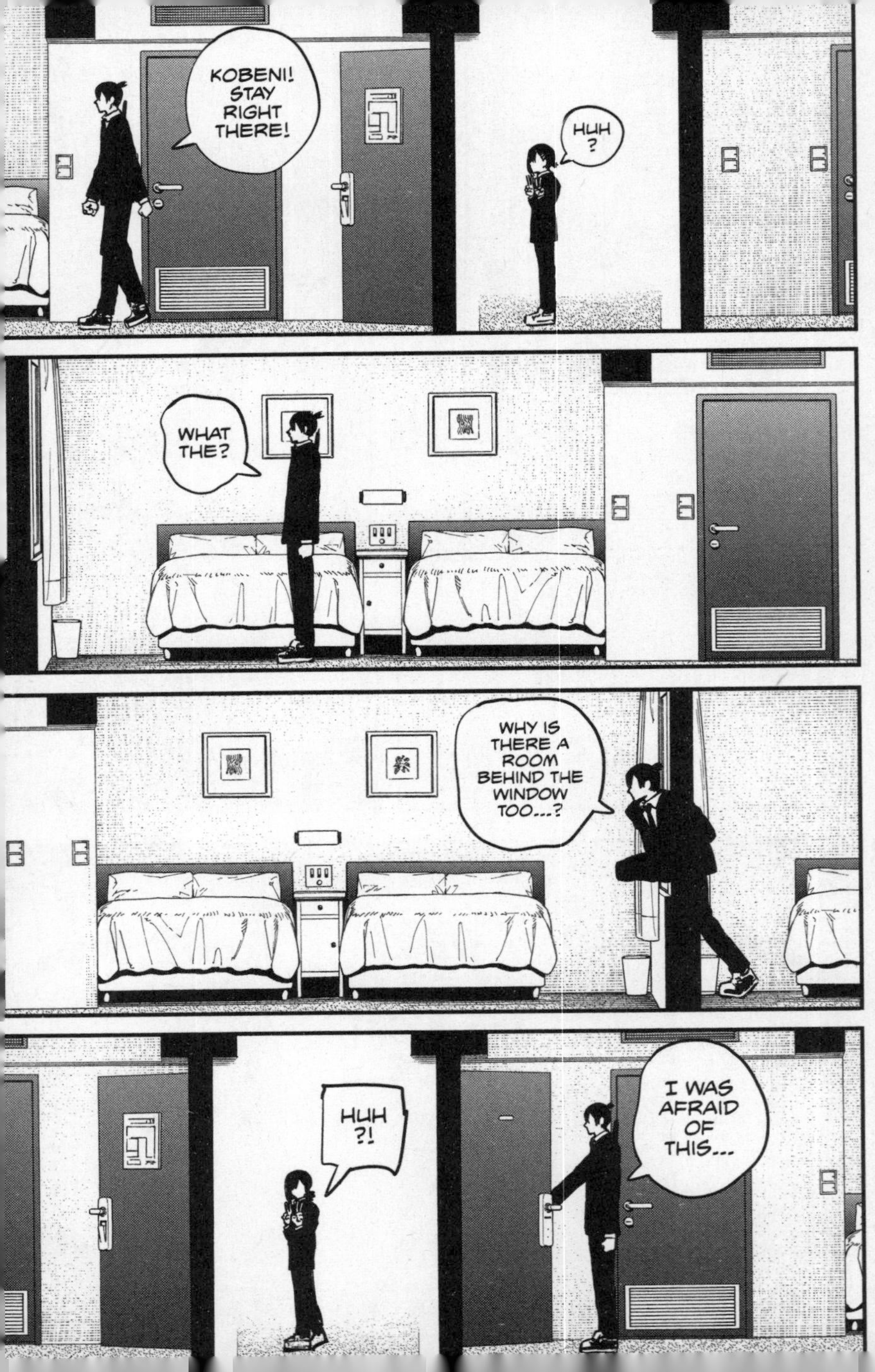
KOBENI! STAY RIGHT THERE!
HUH?
WHAT THE?
WHY IS THERE A ROOM BEHIND THE WINDOW TOO...?
HUH?!
I WAS AFRAID OF THIS...

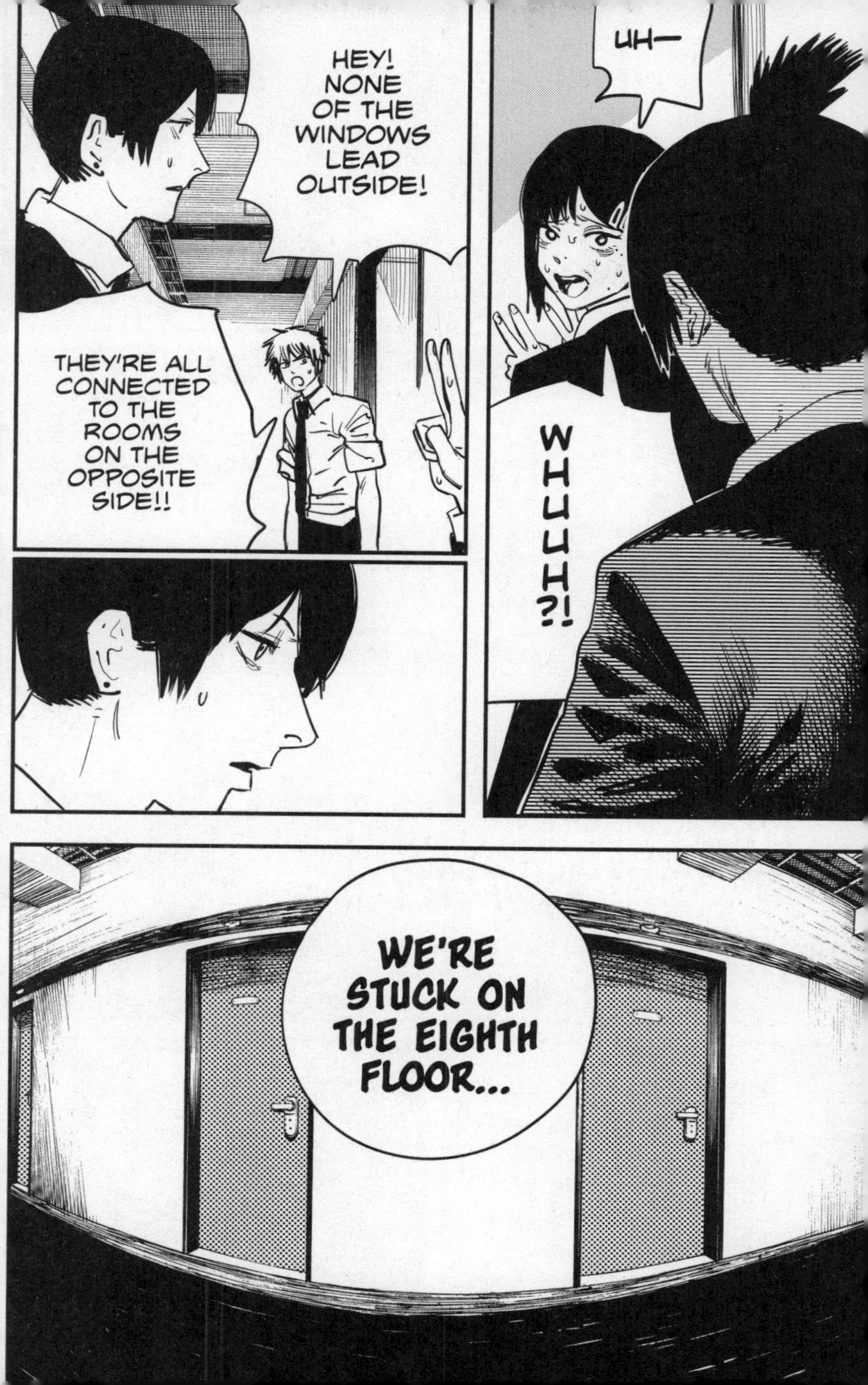
UH—
WHUUUH?!
HEY! NONE OF THE WINDOWS LEAD OUTSIDE!
THEY'RE ALL CONNECTED TO THE ROOMS ON THE OPPOSITE SIDE!!
WE'RE STUCK ON THE EIGHTH FLOOR...

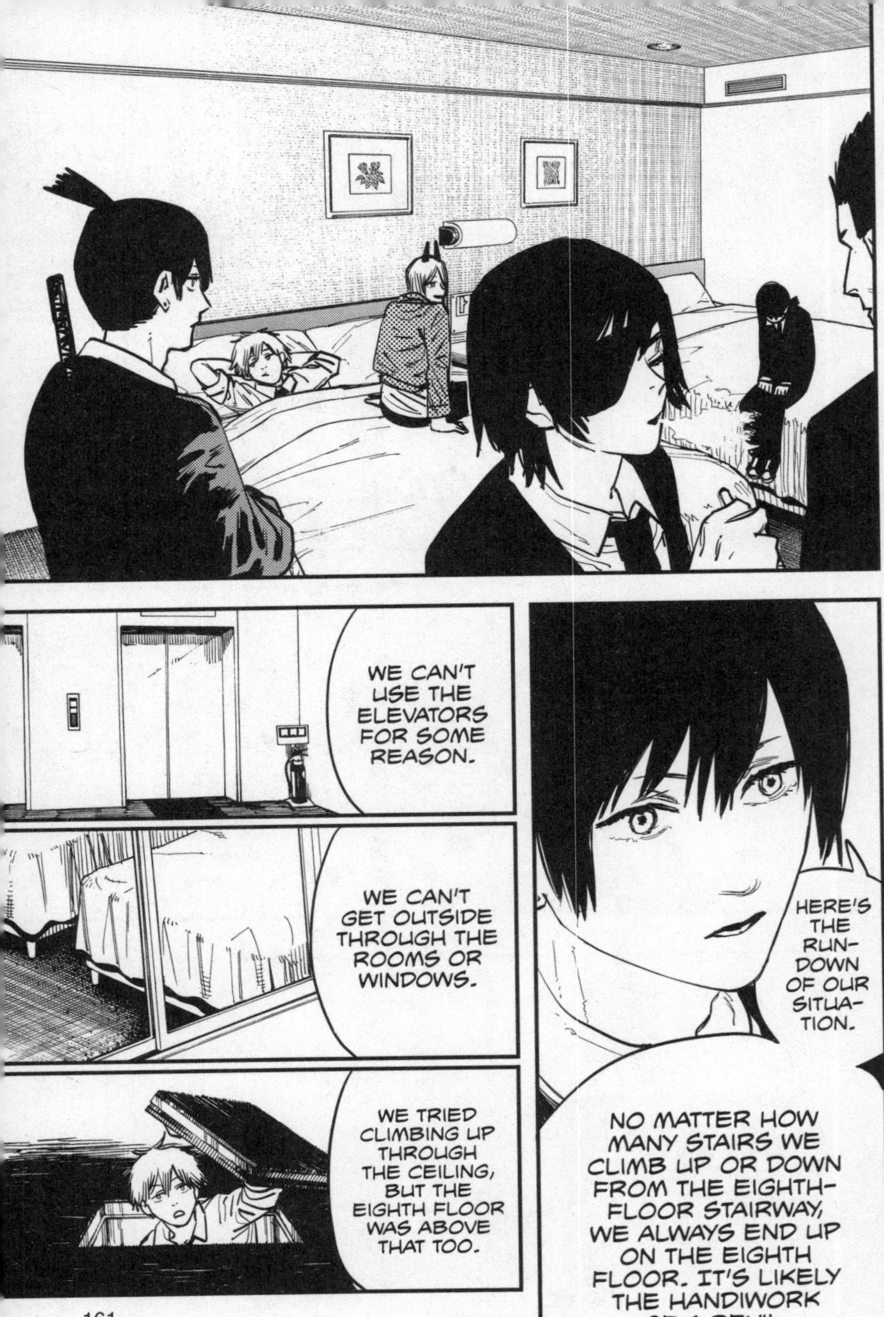
HERE'S THE RUN-DOWN OF OUR SITUATION.
NO MATTER HOW MANY STAIRS WE CLIMB UP OR DOWN FROM THE EIGHTH-FLOOR STAIRWAY, WE ALWAYS END UP ON THE EIGHTH FLOOR. IT'S LIKELY THE HANDIWORK OF A DEVIL.
WE CAN'T USE THE ELEVATORS FOR SOME REASON.
WE CAN'T GET OUTSIDE THROUGH THE ROOMS OR WINDOWS.
WE TRIED CLIMBING UP THROUGH THE CEILING, BUT THE EIGHTH FLOOR WAS ABOVE THAT TOO.

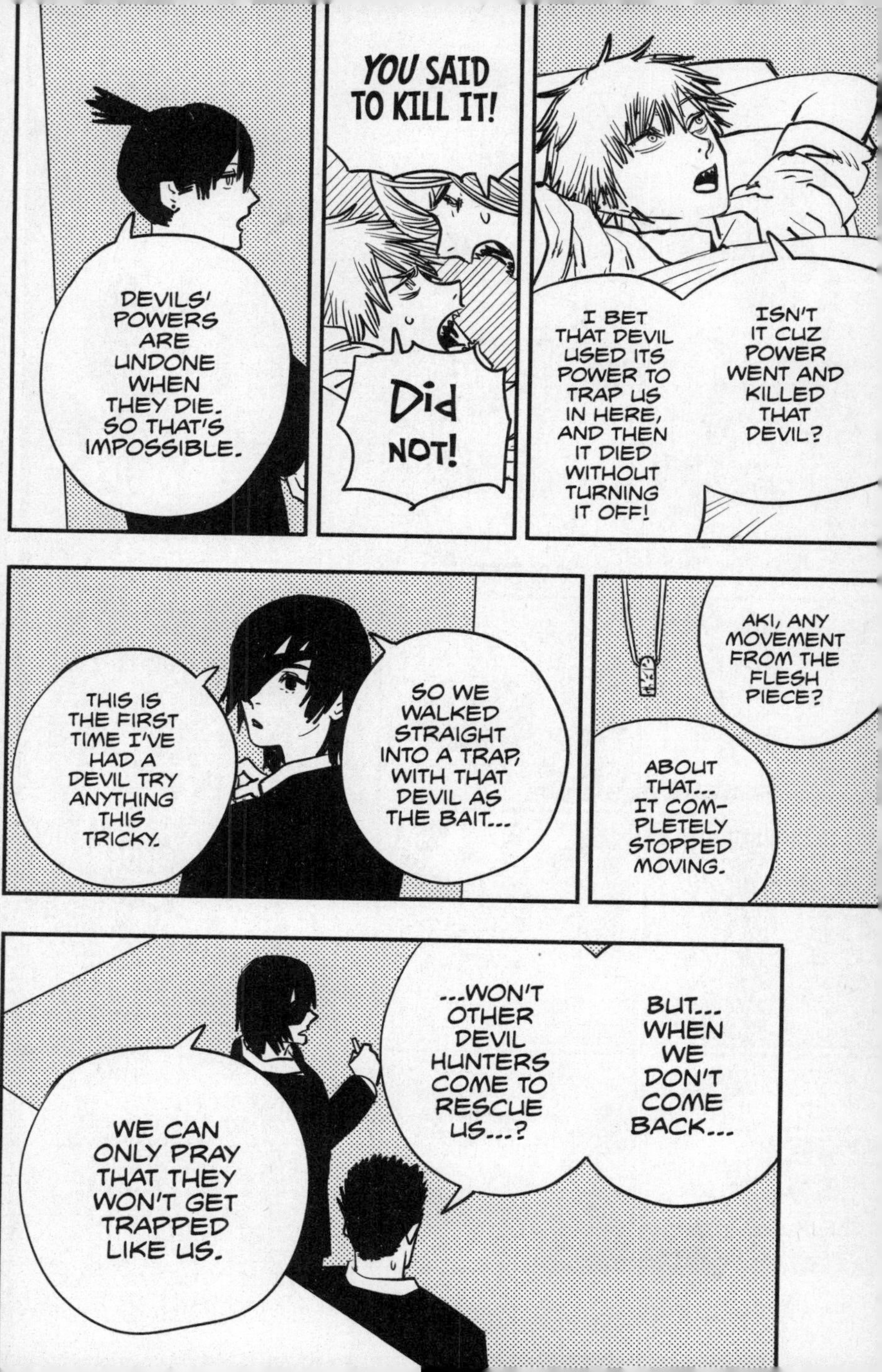
ISN'T IT CUZ POWER WENT AND KILLED THAT DEVIL?
I BET THAT DEVIL USED ITS POWER TO TRAP US IN HERE, AND THEN IT DIED WITHOUT TURNING IT OFF!
Did NOT!
YOU SAID TO KILL IT!
DEVILS' POWERS ARE UNDONE WHEN THEY DIE. SO THAT'S IMPOSSIBLE.
AKI, ANY MOVEMENT FROM THE FLESH PIECE?
ABOUT THAT... IT COM-PLETELY STOPPED MOVING.
SO WE WALKED STRAIGHT INTO A TRAP, WITH THAT DEVIL AS THE BAIT...
THIS IS THE FIRST TIME I'VE HAD A DEVIL TRY ANYTHING THIS TRICKY.
BUT... WHEN WE DON'T COME BACK...
...WON'T OTHER DEVIL HUNTERS COME TO RESCUE US...?
WE CAN ONLY PRAY THAT THEY WON'T GET TRAPPED LIKE US.

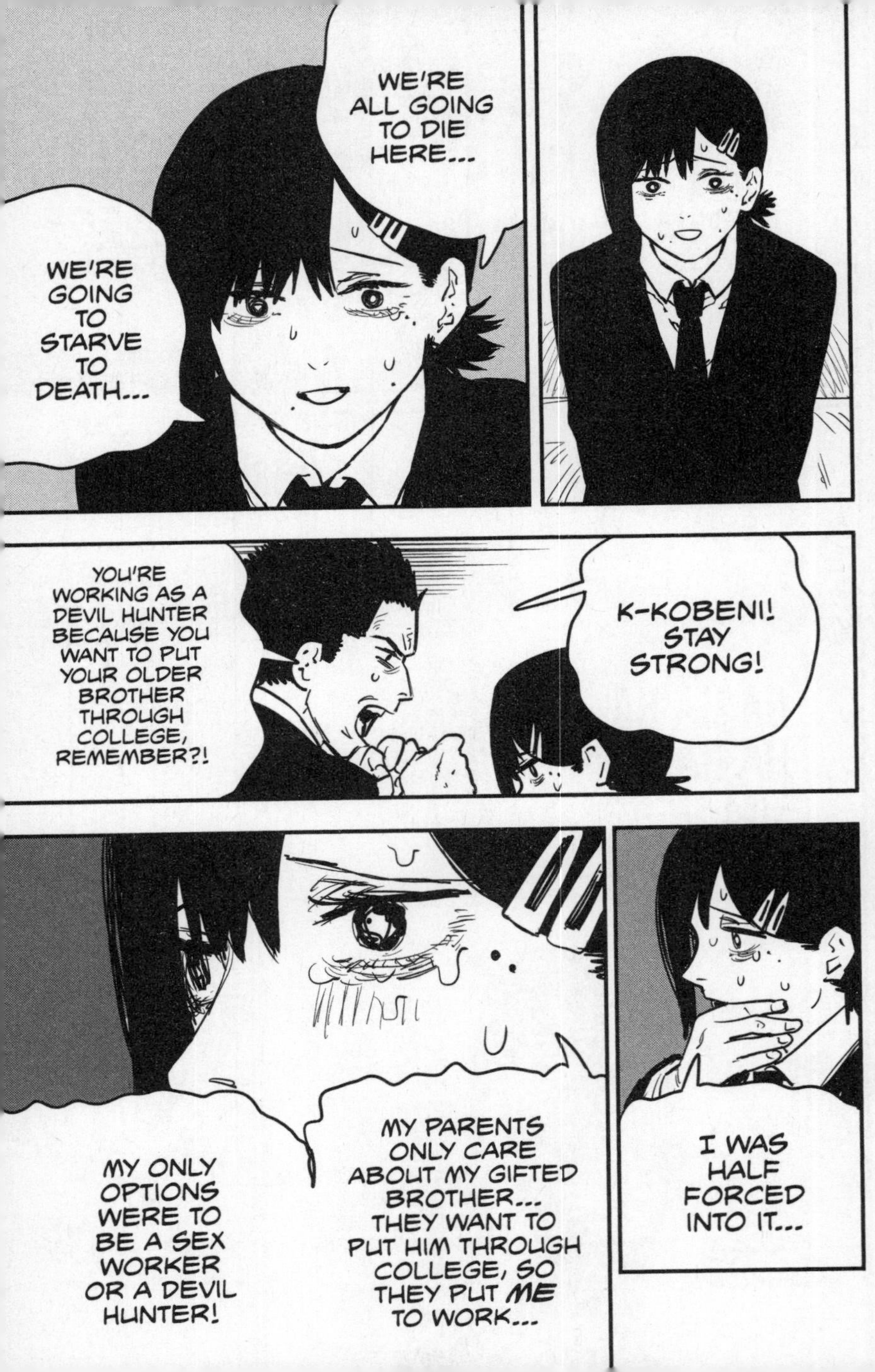
WE'RE ALL GOING TO DIE HERE...
WE'RE GOING TO STARVE TO DEATH...
K-KOBENI! STAY STRONG!
YOU'RE WORKING AS A DEVIL HUNTER BECAUSE YOU WANT TO PUT YOUR OLDER BROTHER THROUGH COLLEGE, REMEMBER?!
I WAS HALF FORCED INTO IT...
MY PARENTS ONLY CARE ABOUT MY GIFTED BROTHER... THEY WANT TO PUT HIM THROUGH COLLEGE, SO THEY PUT *ME* TO WORK...
MY ONLY OPTIONS WERE TO BE A SEX WORKER OR A DEVIL HUNTER!

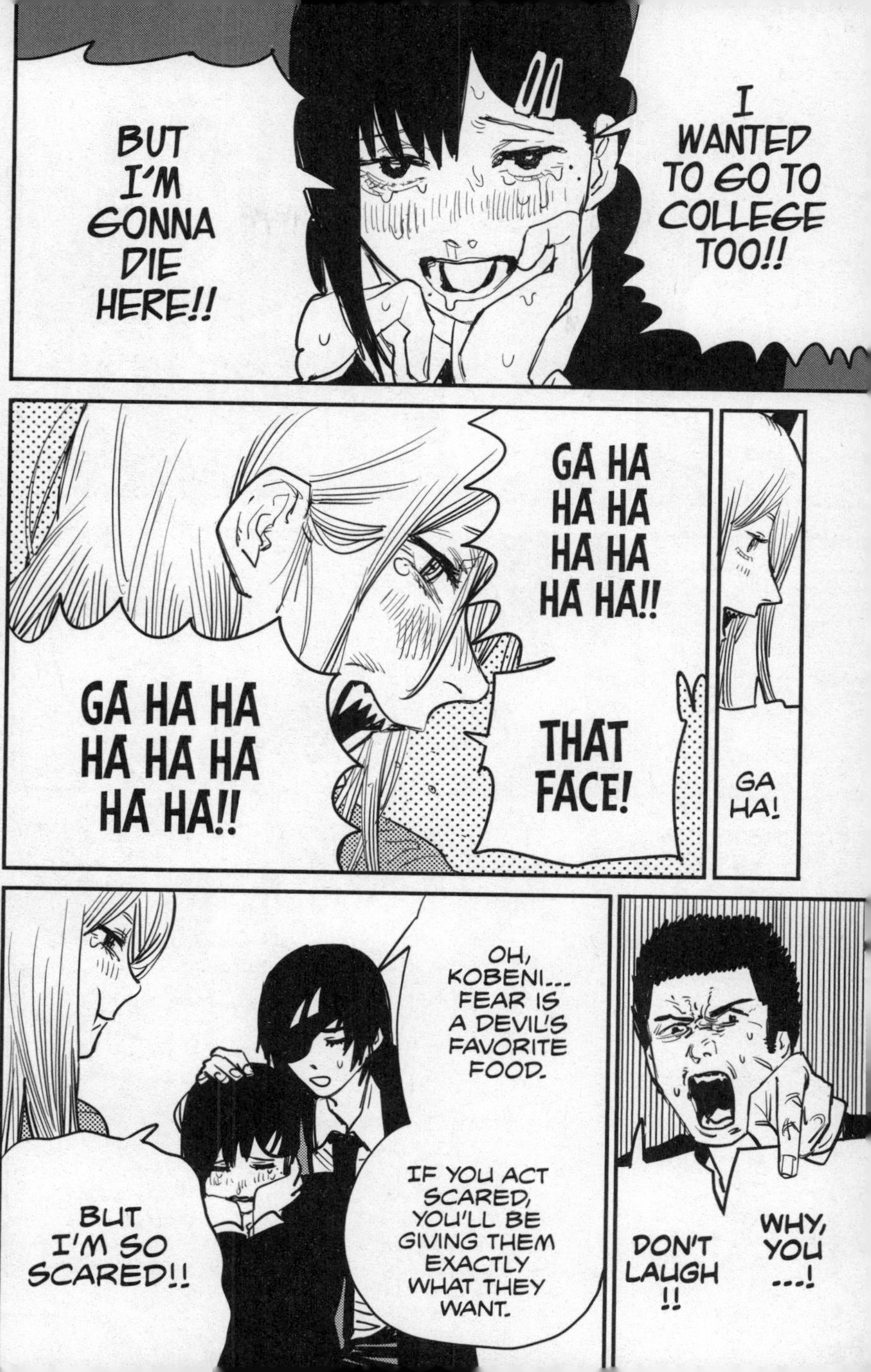
I WANTED TO GO TO COLLEGE TOO!!
BUT I'M GONNA DIE HERE!!
GA HA!
GA HA HA HA HA HA HA HA!!
THAT FACE!
GA HA HA HA HA HA HA HA!!
WHY, YOU ...!
DON'T LAUGH !!
OH, KOBENI... FEAR IS A DEVIL'S FAVORITE FOOD.
IF YOU ACT SCARED, YOU'LL BE GIVING THEM EXACTLY WHAT THEY WANT.
BUT I'M SO SCARED!!

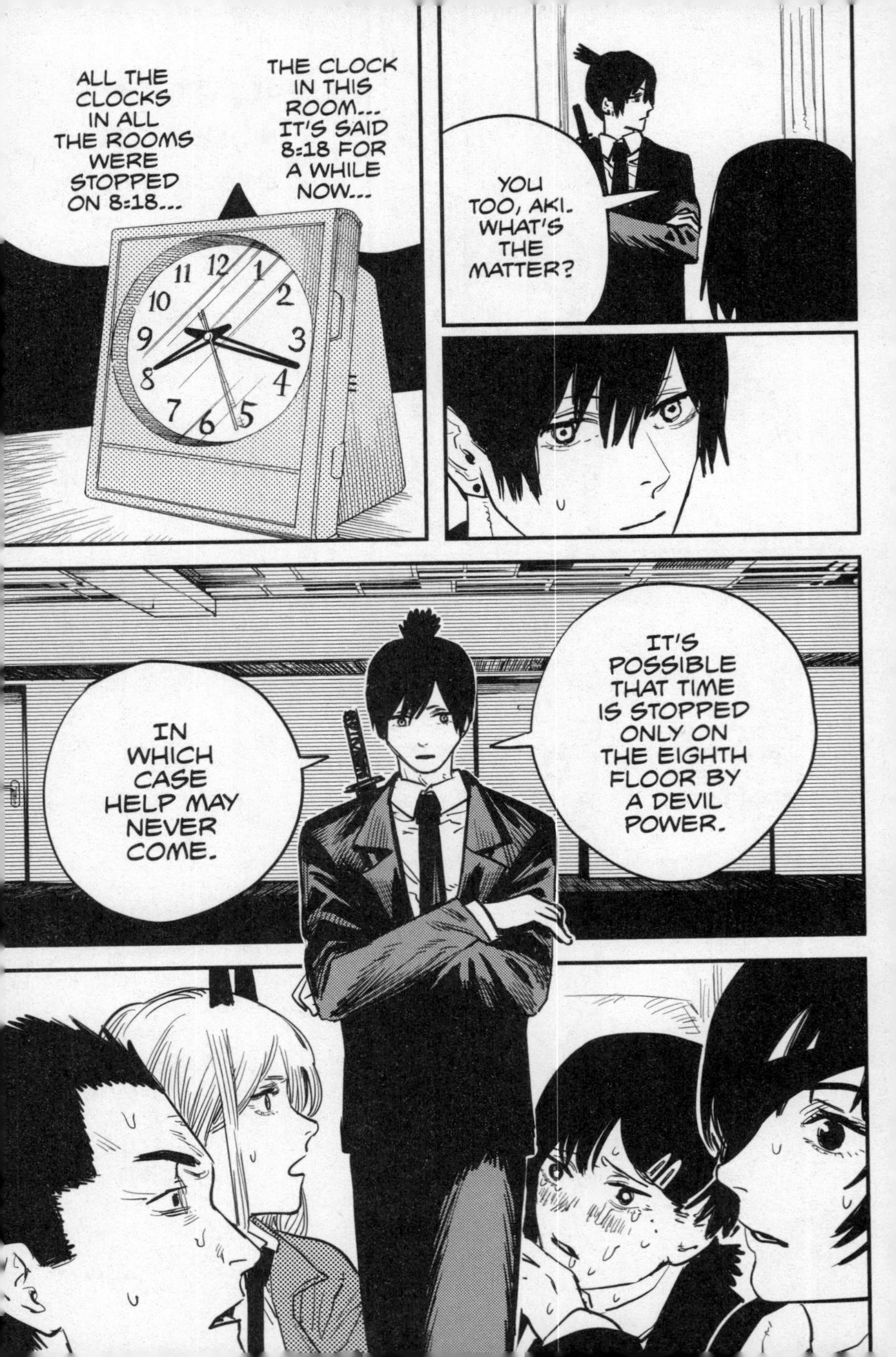
YOU TOO, AKI. WHAT'S THE MATTER?
THE CLOCK IN THIS ROOM... IT'S SAID 8:18 FOR A WHILE NOW...
ALL THE CLOCKS IN ALL THE ROOMS WERE STOPPED ON 8:18...
IT'S POSSIBLE THAT TIME IS STOPPED ONLY ON THE EIGHTH FLOOR BY A DEVIL POWER.
IN WHICH CASE HELP MAY NEVER COME.

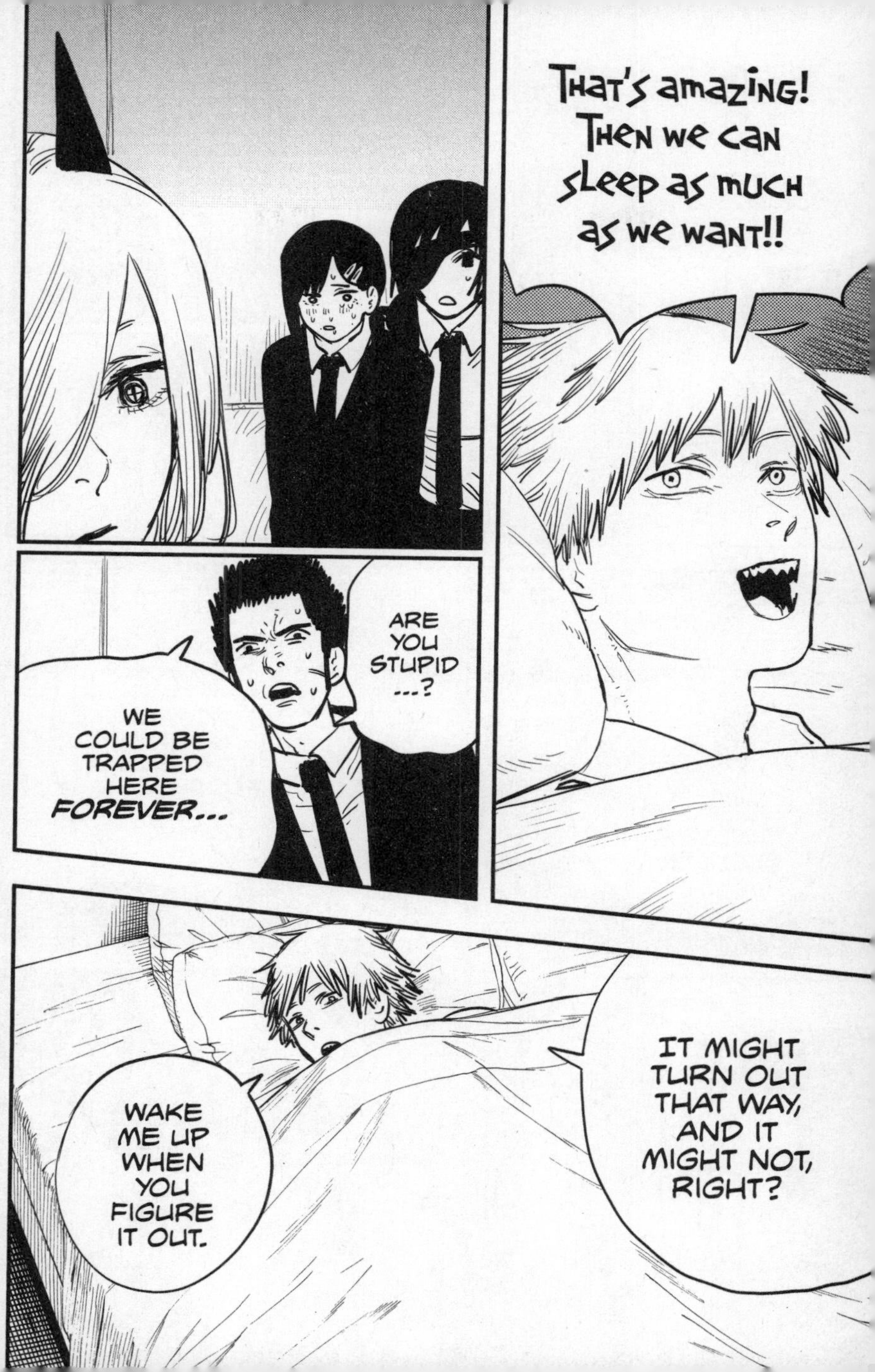
That's amazing! Then we can sleep as much as we want!!
ARE YOU STUPID...?
WE COULD BE TRAPPED HERE FOREVER...
IT MIGHT TURN OUT THAT WAY, AND IT MIGHT NOT, RIGHT?
WAKE ME UP WHEN YOU FIGURE IT OUT.

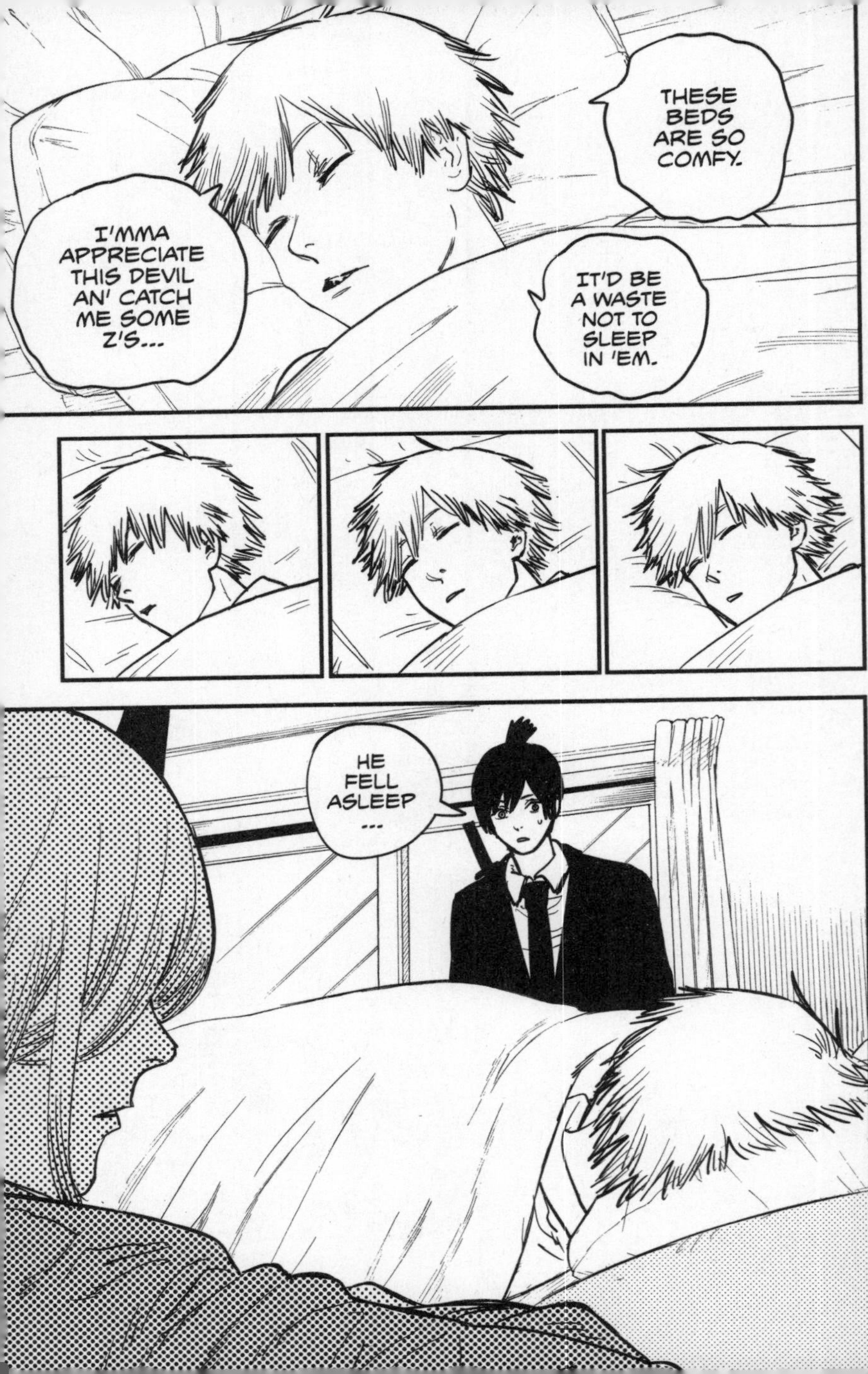
THESE BEDS ARE SO COMFY.
IT'D BE A WASTE NOT TO SLEEP IN 'EM.
I'MMA APPRECIATE THIS DEVIL AN' CATCH ME SOME Z'S...
HE FELL ASLEEP ...

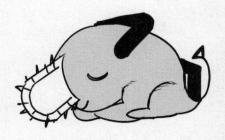

*Chain saw man*

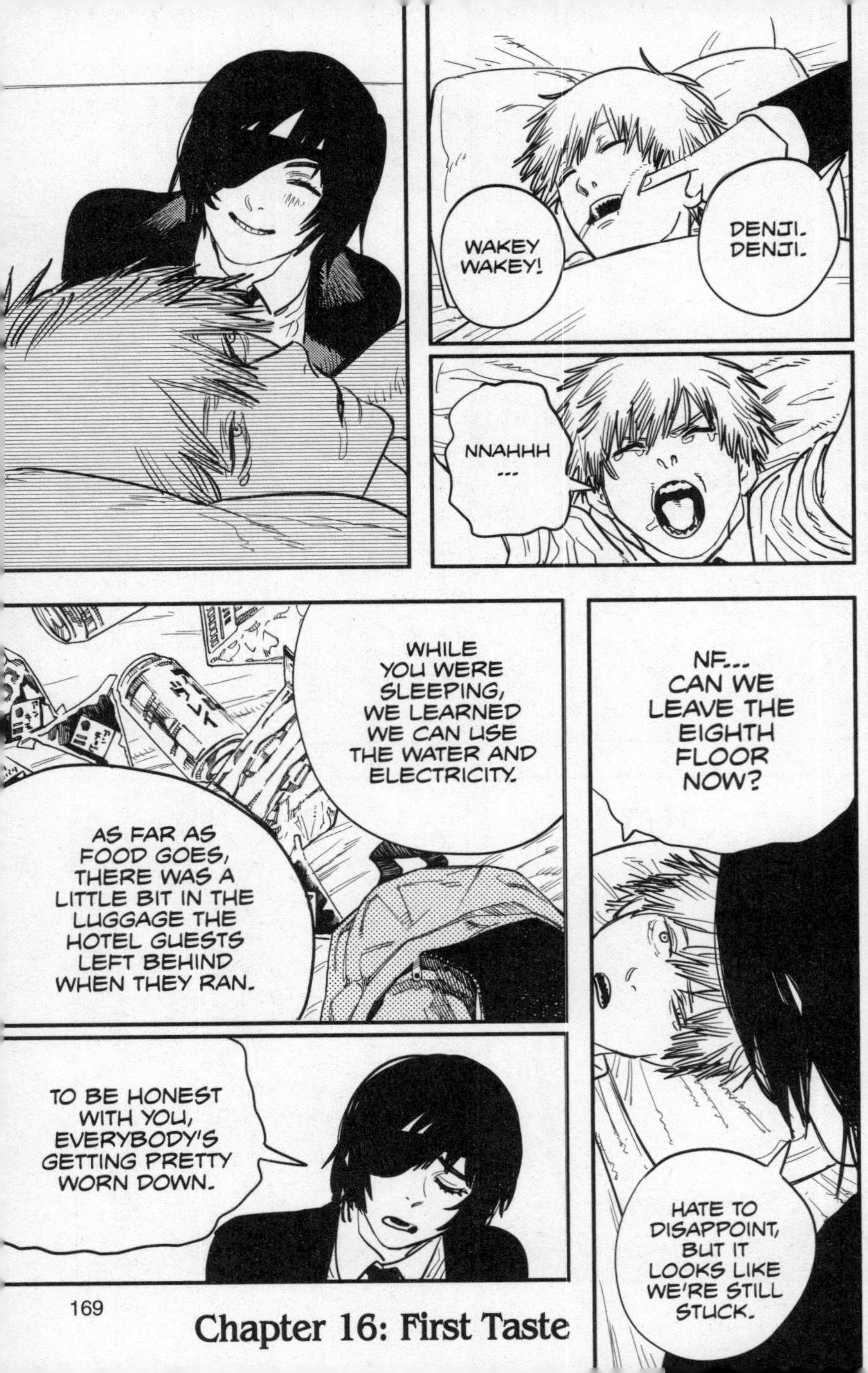
DENJI. DENJI.
WAKEY WAKEY!
NNAHHH ...
NF... CAN WE LEAVE THE EIGHTH FLOOR NOW?
HATE TO DISAPPOINT, BUT IT LOOKS LIKE WE'RE STILL STUCK.
WHILE YOU WERE SLEEPING, WE LEARNED WE CAN USE THE WATER AND ELECTRICITY.
AS FAR AS FOOD GOES, THERE WAS A LITTLE BIT IN THE LUGGAGE THE HOTEL GUESTS LEFT BEHIND WHEN THEY RAN.
TO BE HONEST WITH YOU, EVERYBODY'S GETTING PRETTY WORN DOWN.



# Chapter 16: First Taste

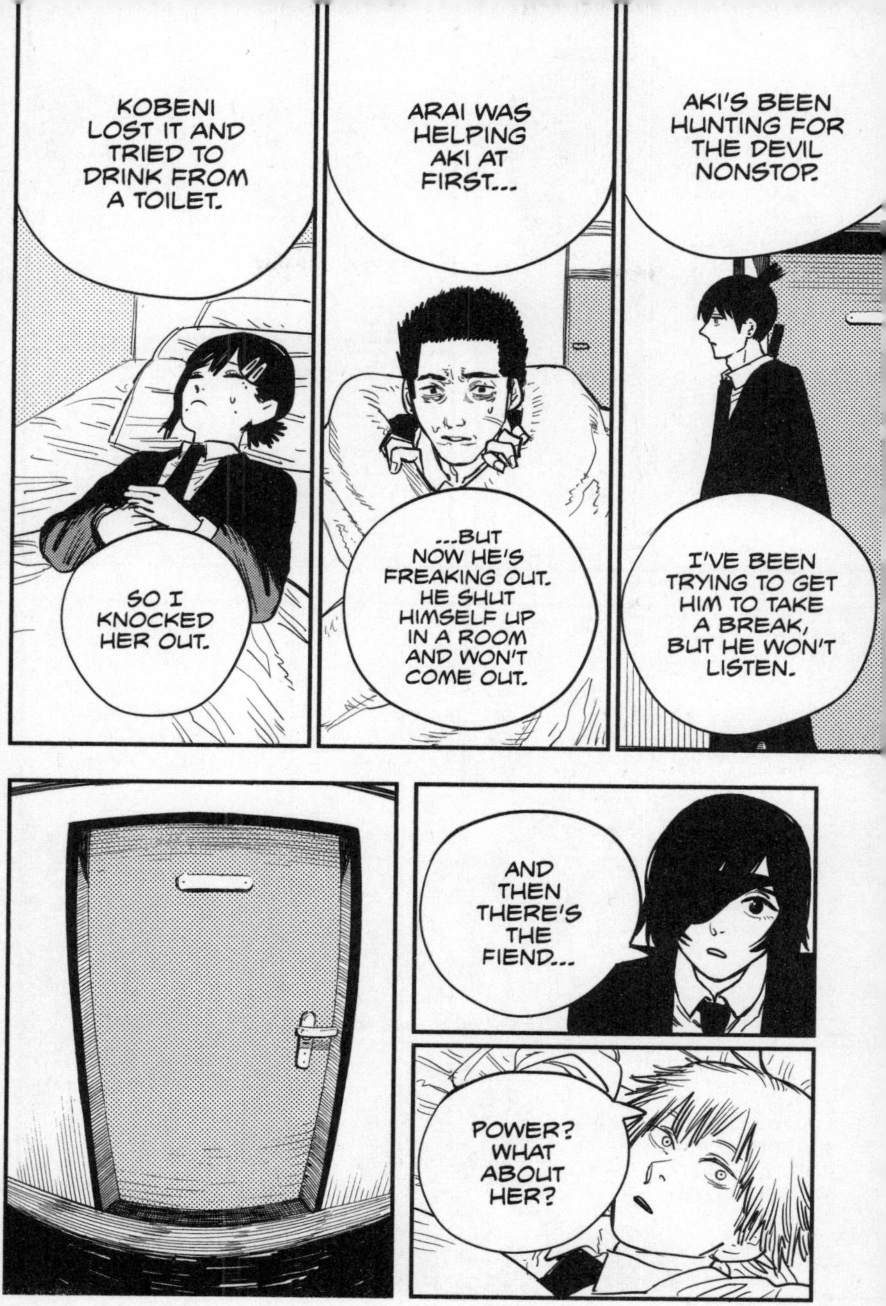
AKI'S BEEN HUNTING FOR THE DEVIL NONSTOP.
I'VE BEEN TRYING TO GET HIM TO TAKE A BREAK, BUT HE WON'T LISTEN.
ARAI WAS HELPING AKI AT FIRST...
...BUT NOW HE'S FREAKING OUT. HE SHUT HIMSELF UP IN A ROOM AND WON'T COME OUT.
KOBENI LOST IT AND TRIED TO DRINK FROM A TOILET.
SO I KNOCKED HER OUT.
AND THEN THERE'S THE FIEND...
POWER? WHAT ABOUT HER?

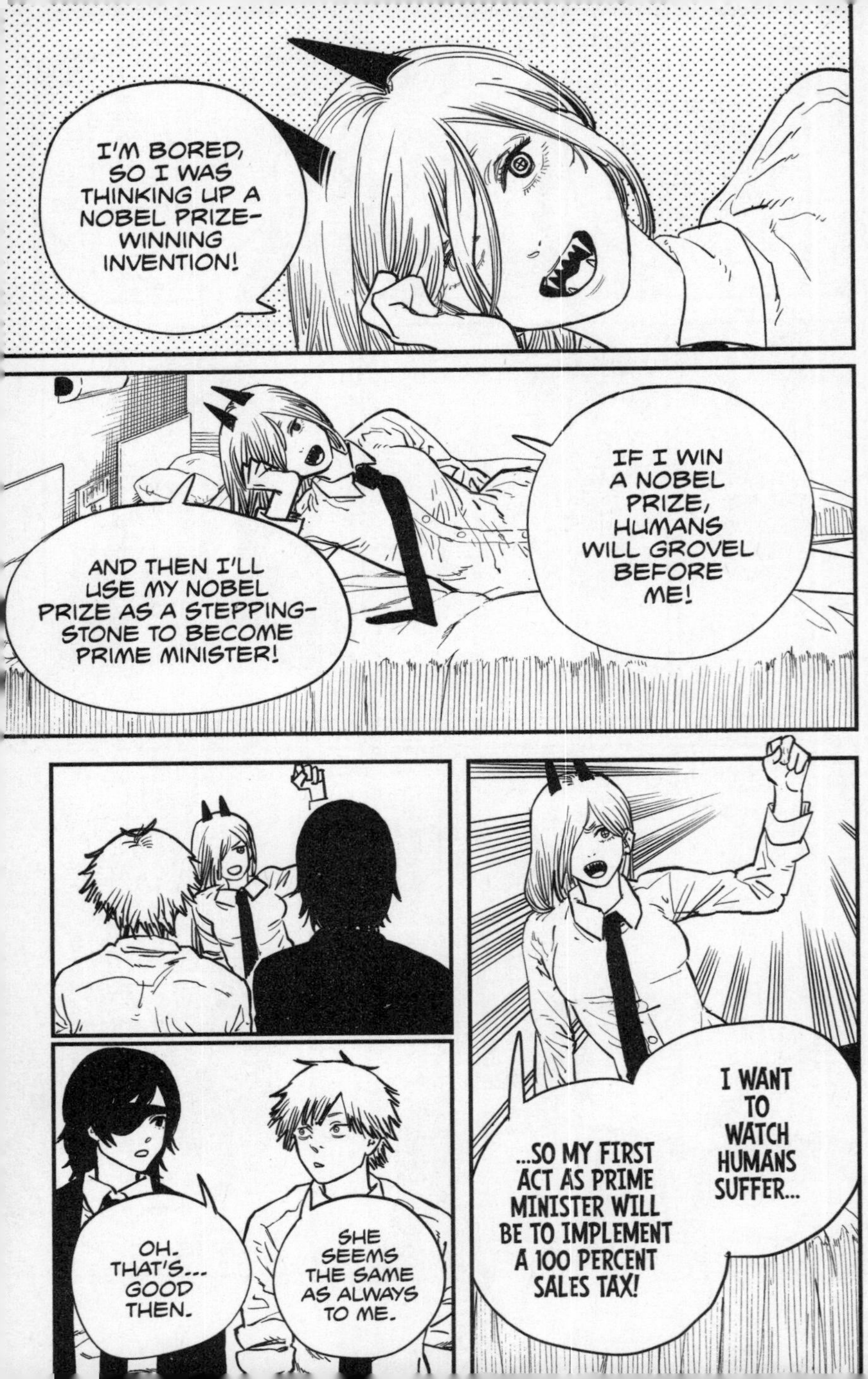
I'M BORED, SO I WAS THINKING UP A NOBEL PRIZE-WINNING INVENTION!
IF I WIN A NOBEL PRIZE, HUMANS WILL GROVEL BEFORE ME!
AND THEN I'LL USE MY NOBEL PRIZE AS A STEPPING-STONE TO BECOME PRIME MINISTER!
I WANT TO WATCH HUMANS SUFFER...
...SO MY FIRST ACT AS PRIME MINISTER WILL BE TO IMPLEMENT A 100 PERCENT SALES TAX!
SHE SEEMS THE SAME AS ALWAYS TO ME.
OH. THAT'S... GOOD THEN.

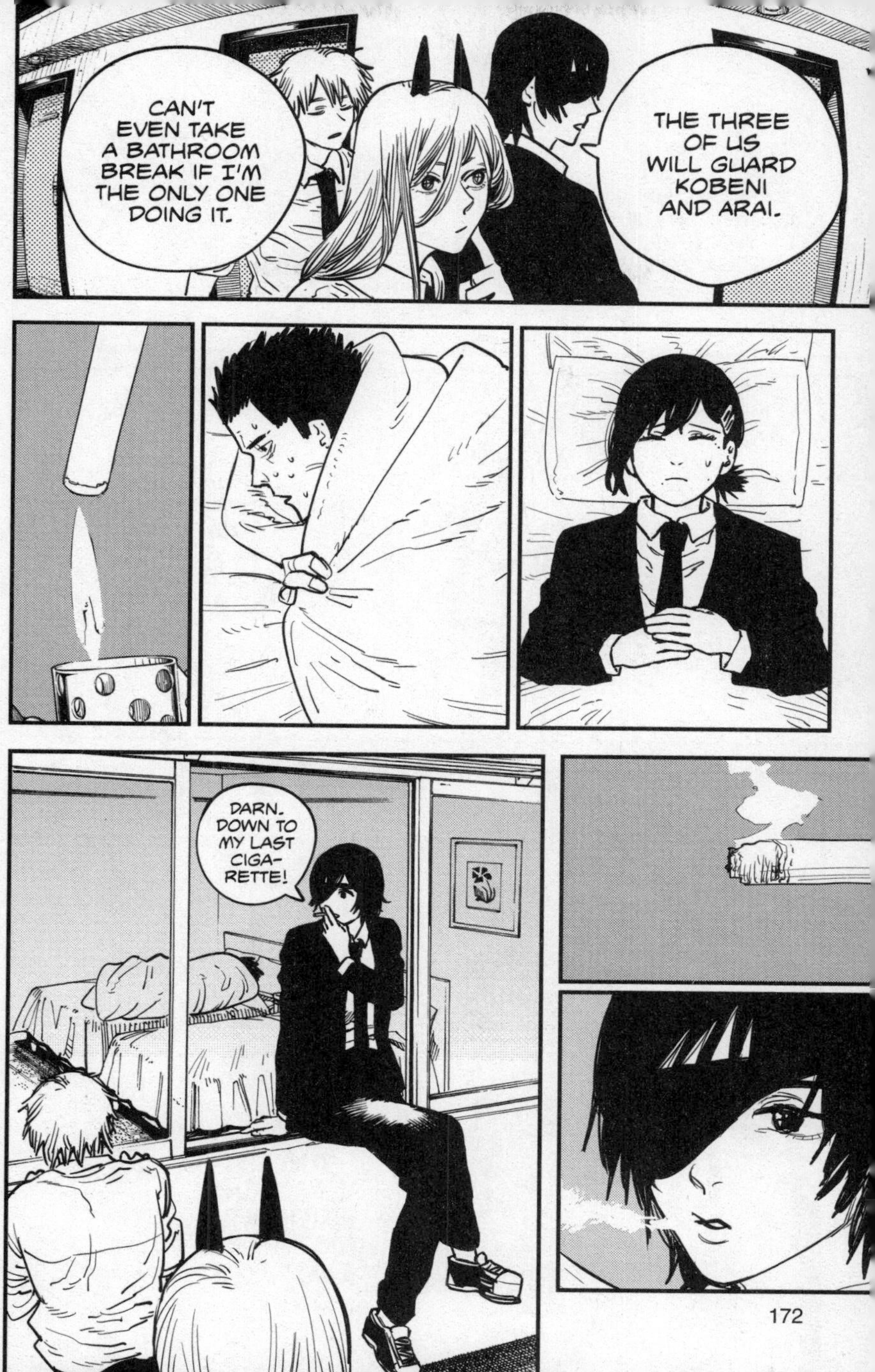
THE THREE OF US WILL GUARD KOBENI AND ARAI.
CAN'T EVEN TAKE A BATHROOM BREAK IF I'M THE ONLY ONE DOING IT.
DARN. DOWN TO MY LAST CIGA-RETTE!

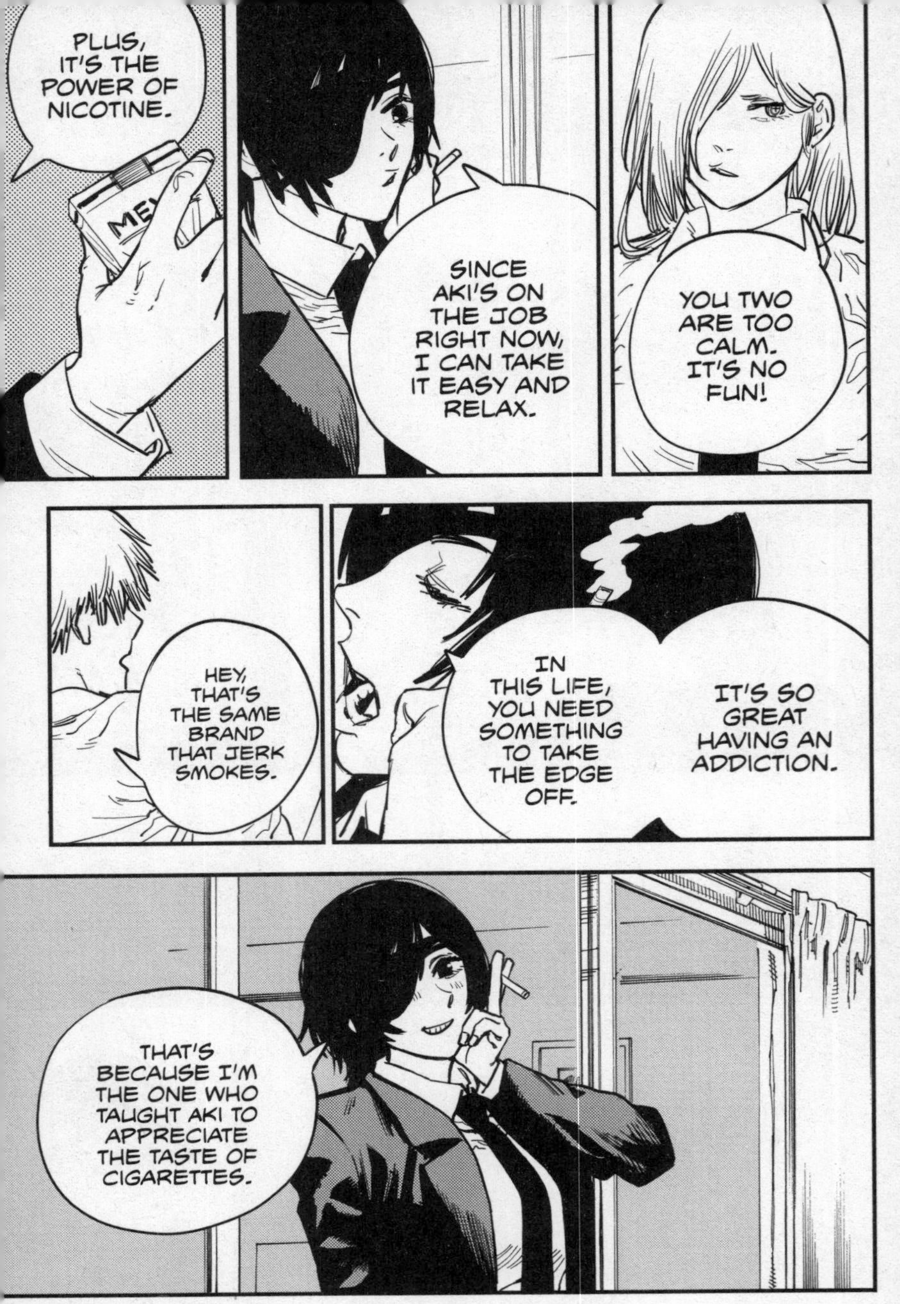
YOU TWO ARE TOO CALM. IT'S NO FUN!
SINCE AKI'S ON THE JOB RIGHT NOW, I CAN TAKE IT EASY AND RELAX.
PLUS, IT'S THE POWER OF NICOTINE.
IT'S SO GREAT HAVING AN ADDICTION.
IN THIS LIFE, YOU NEED SOMETHING TO TAKE THE EDGE OFF.
HEY, THAT'S THE SAME BRAND THAT JERK SMOKES.
THAT'S BECAUSE I'M THE ONE WHO TAUGHT AKI TO APPRECIATE THE TASTE OF CIGARETTES.

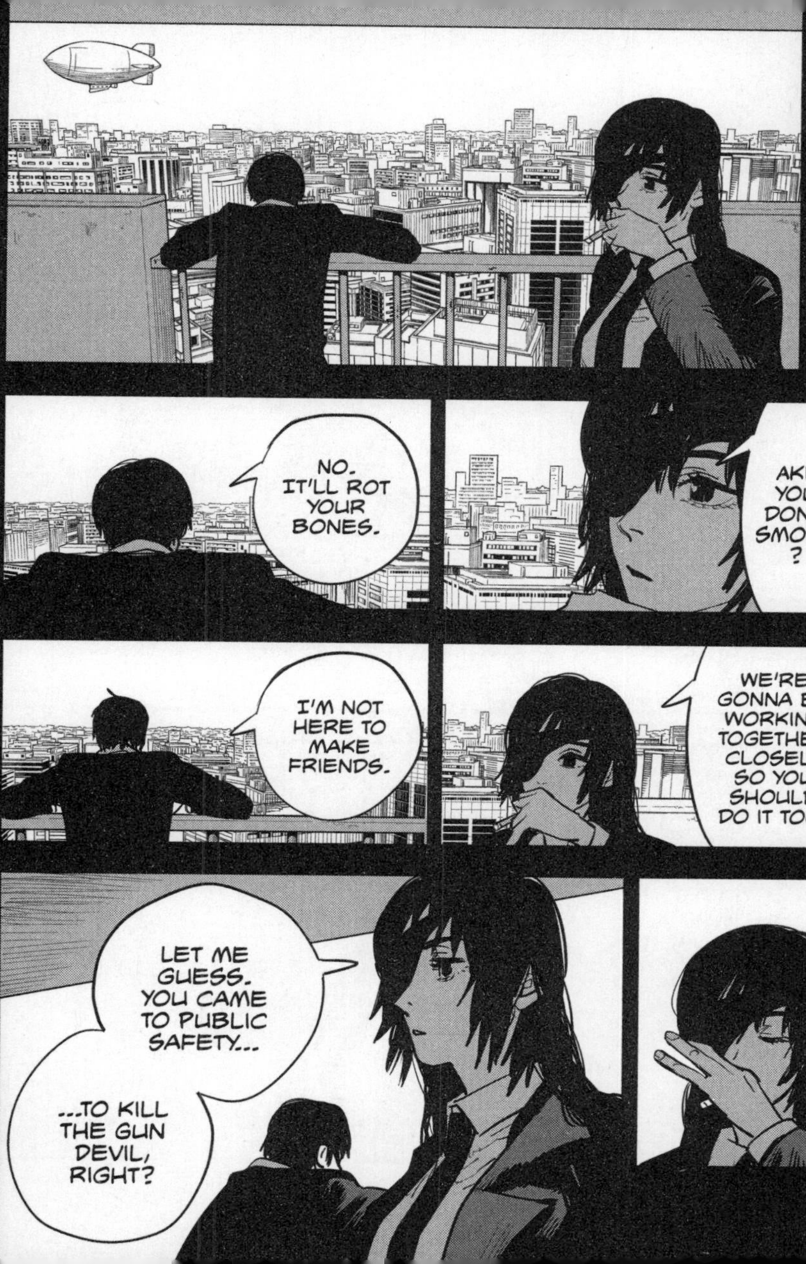
AKI, YOU DON'T SMOKE ?
NO. IT'LL ROT YOUR BONES.
WE'RE GONNA BE WORKING TOGETHER CLOSELY, SO YOU SHOULD DO IT TOO.
I'M NOT HERE TO MAKE FRIENDS.
LET ME GUESS. YOU CAME TO PUBLIC SAFETY...
...TO KILL THE GUN DEVIL, RIGHT?

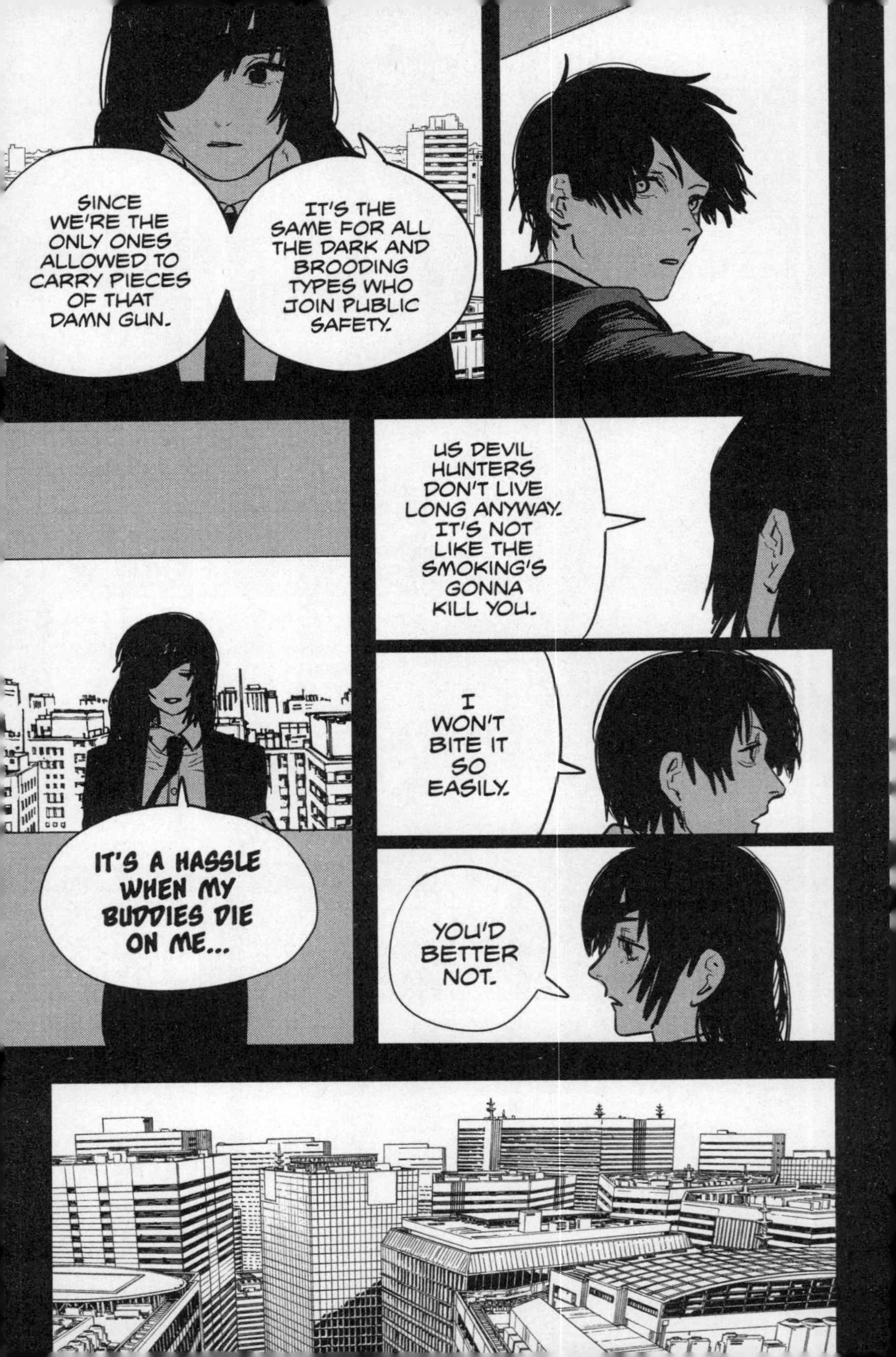
IT'S THE SAME FOR ALL THE DARK AND BROODING TYPES WHO JOIN PUBLIC SAFETY.
SINCE WE'RE THE ONLY ONES ALLOWED TO CARRY PIECES OF THAT DAMN GUN.
US DEVIL HUNTERS DON'T LIVE LONG ANYWAY. IT'S NOT LIKE THE SMOKING'S GONNA KILL YOU.
IT'S A HASSLE WHEN MY BUDDIES DIE ON ME...
I WON'T BITE IT SO EASILY.
YOU'D BETTER NOT.

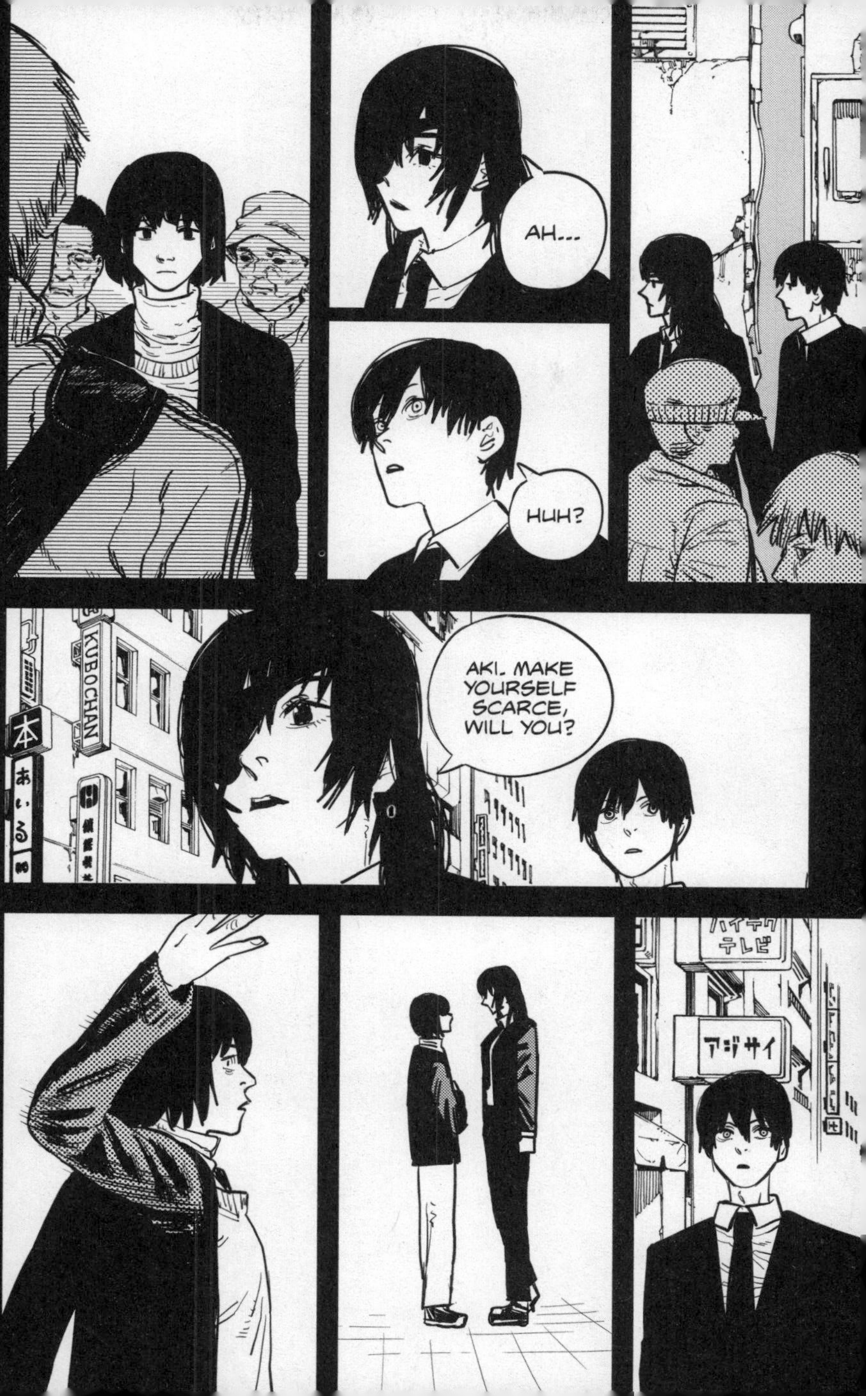
AH...
HUH?
KUBOCHAN
本
AKI. MAKE YOURSELF SCARCE, WILL YOU?
ハイテク
テレビ
アジサイ

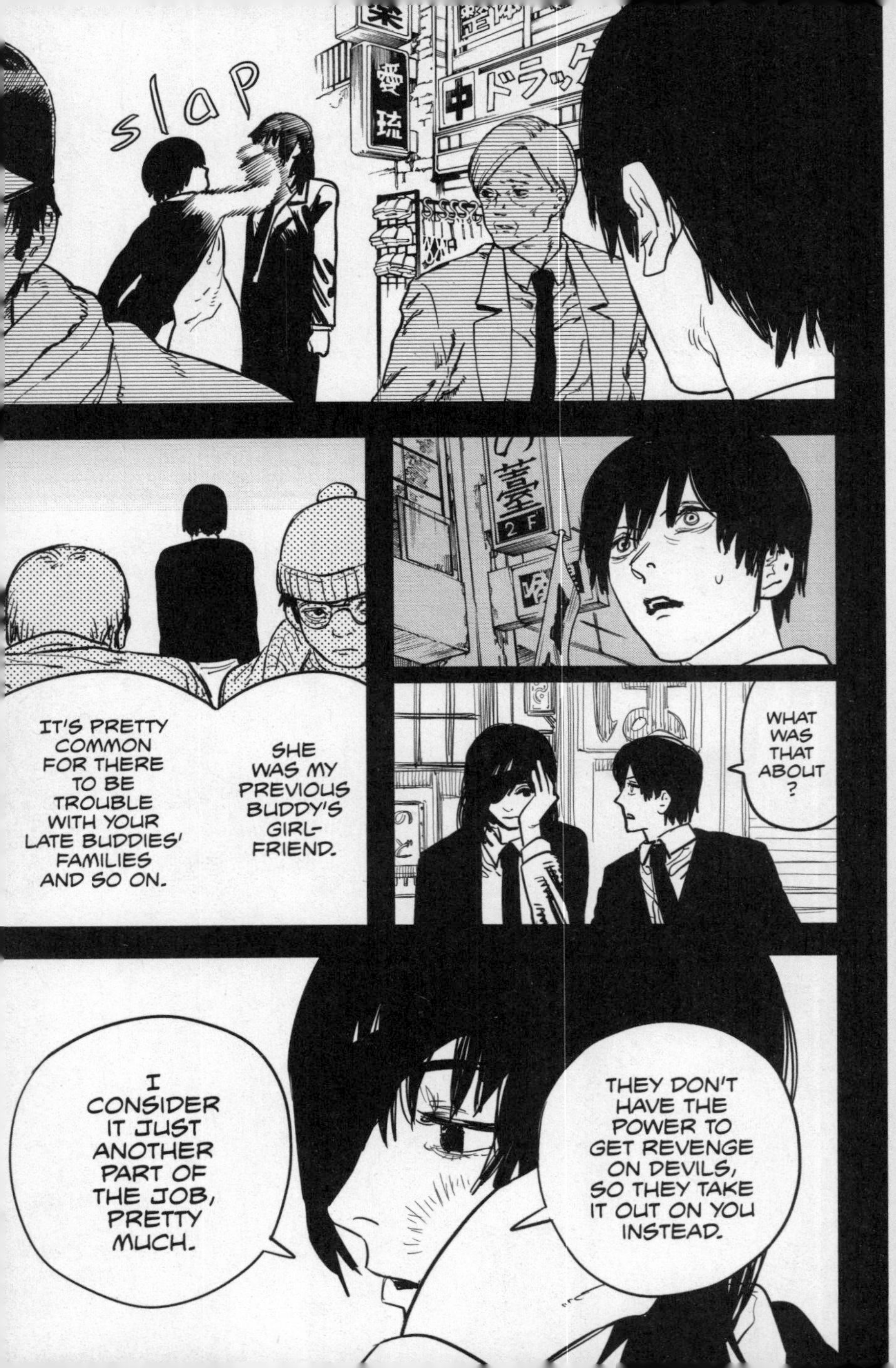
slap
WHAT WAS THAT ABOUT?
SHE WAS MY PREVIOUS BUDDY'S GIRL-FRIEND.
IT'S PRETTY COMMON FOR THERE TO BE TROUBLE WITH YOUR LATE BUDDIES' FAMILIES AND SO ON.
THEY DON'T HAVE THE POWER TO GET REVENGE ON DEVILS, SO THEY TAKE IT OUT ON YOU INSTEAD.
I CONSIDER IT JUST ANOTHER PART OF THE JOB, PRETTY MUCH.

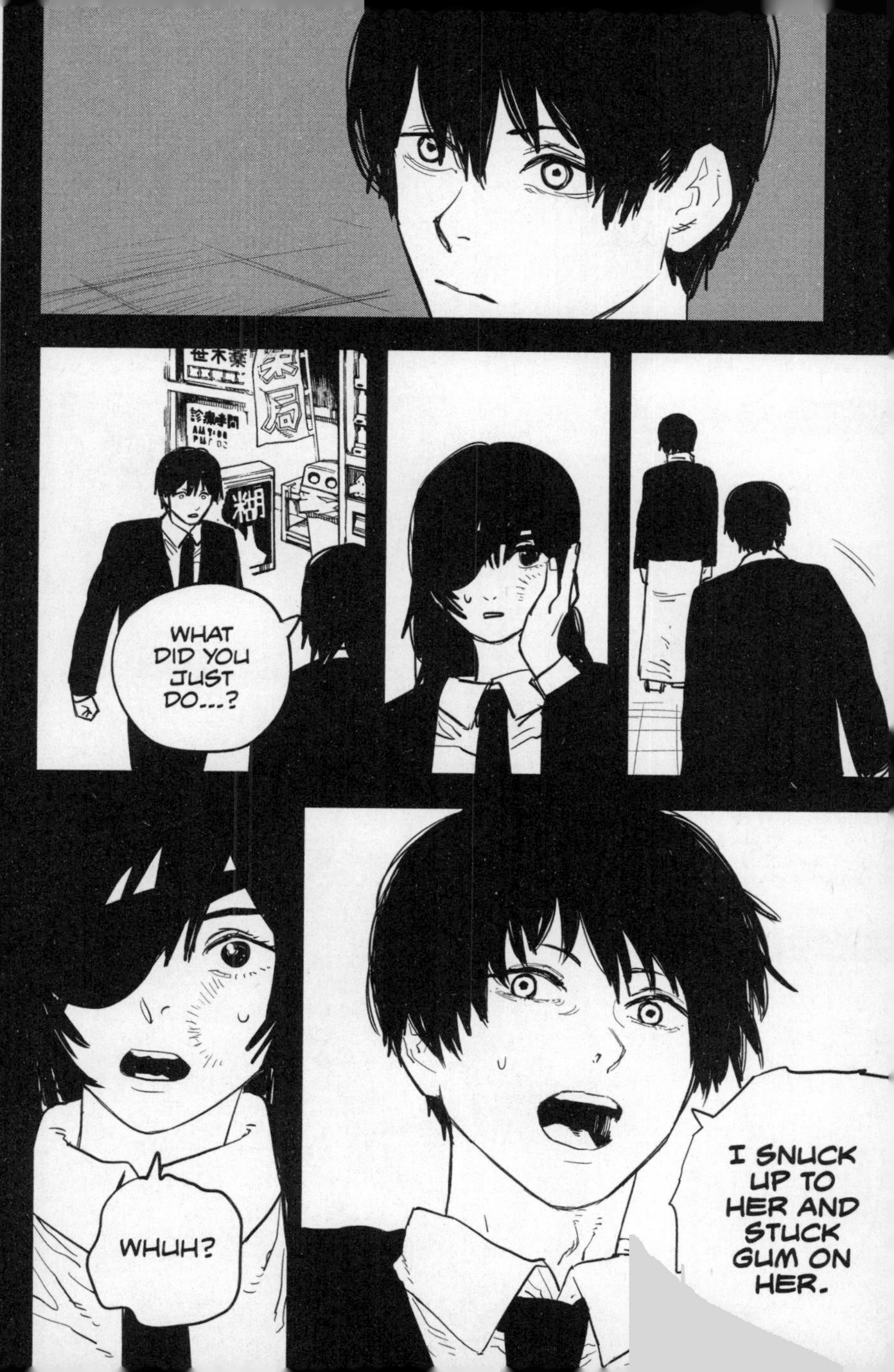
WHAT DID YOU JUST DO...?
I SNUCK UP TO HER AND STUCK GUM ON HER.
WHUH?

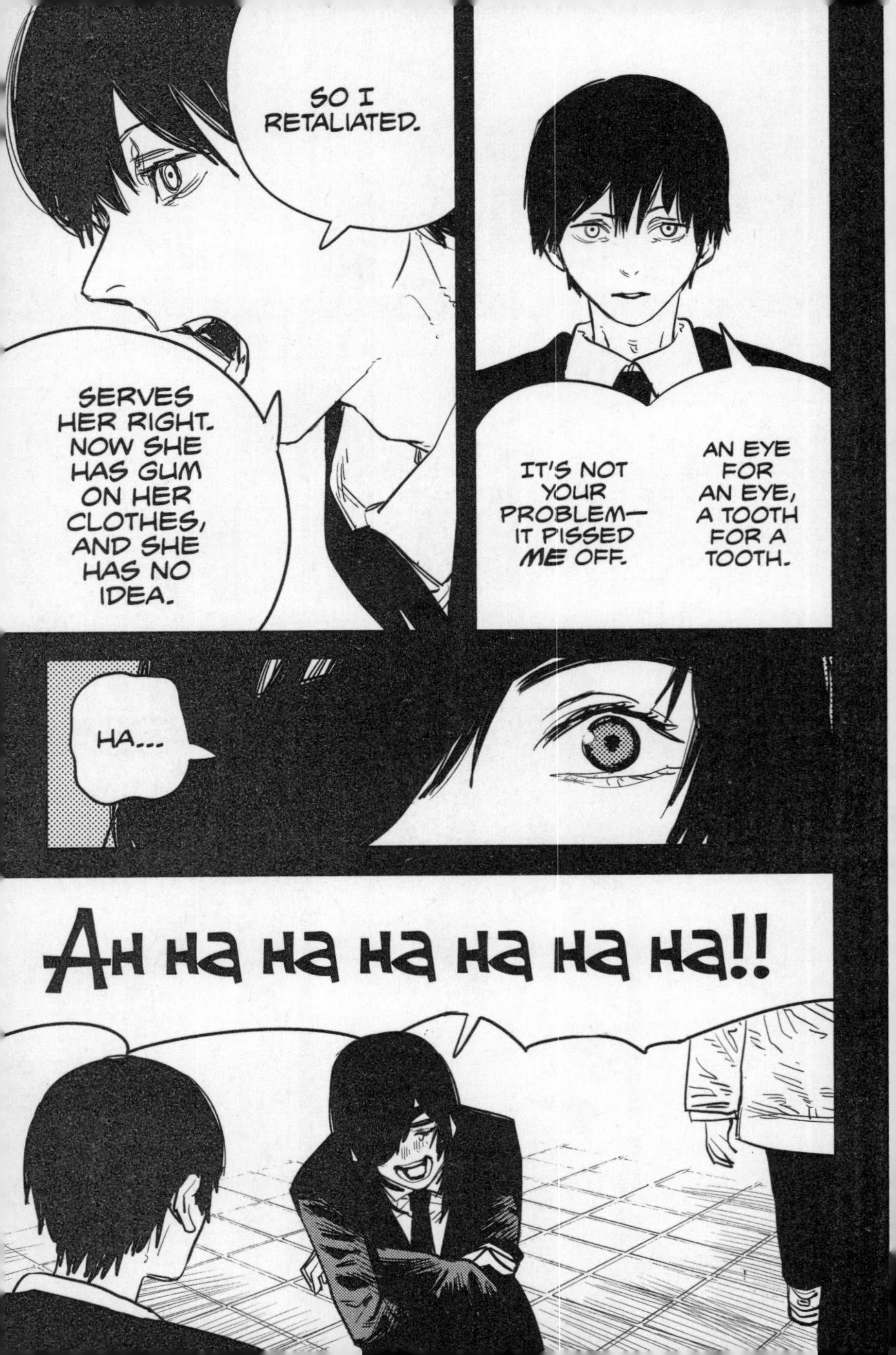
AN EYE FOR AN EYE, A TOOTH FOR A TOOTH.
IT'S NOT YOUR PROBLEM— IT PISSED *ME* OFF.
SO I RETALIATED.
SERVES HER RIGHT. NOW SHE HAS GUM ON HER CLOTHES, AND SHE HAS NO IDEA.
HA...
AH HA HA HA HA HA HA HA!!

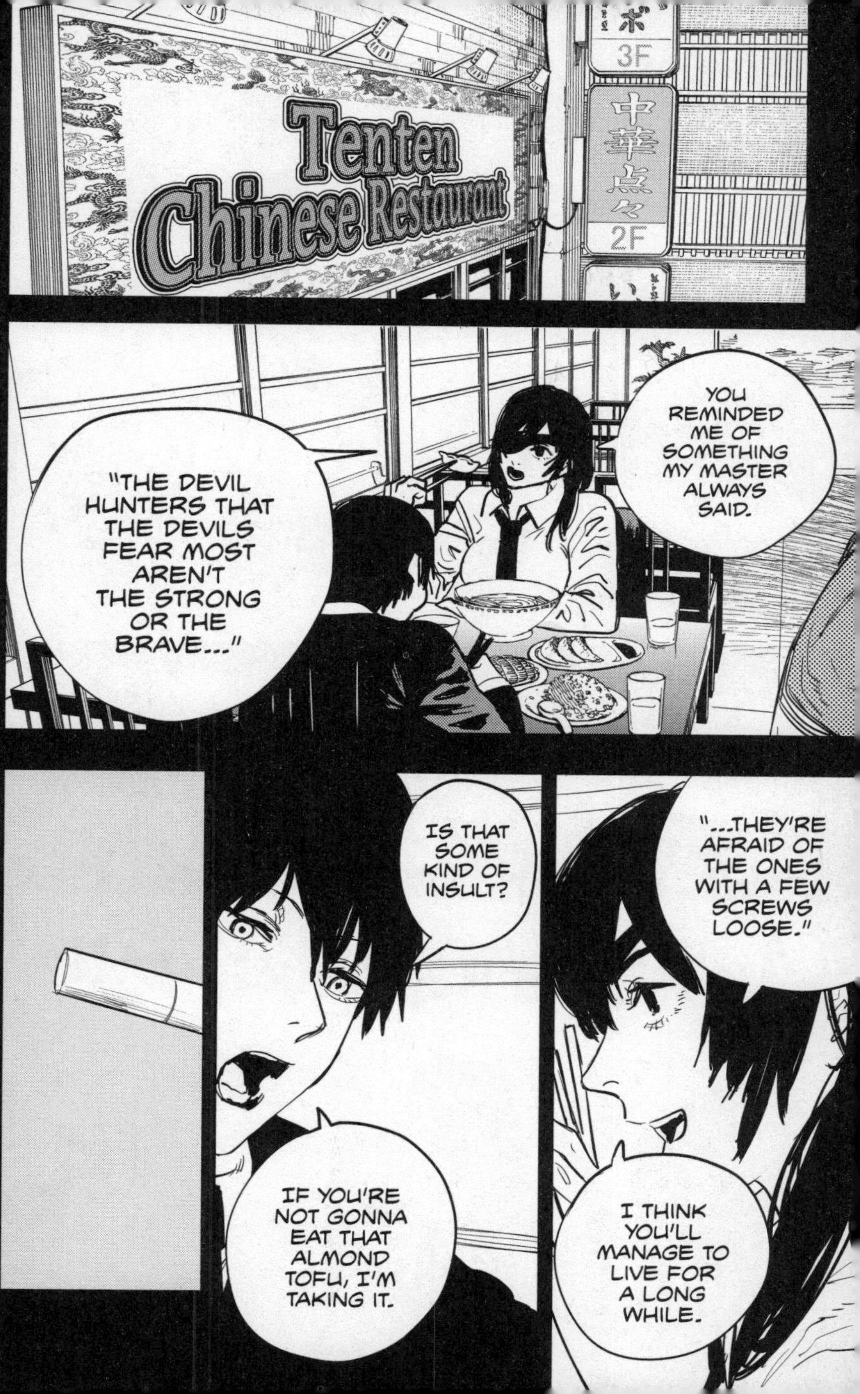

3F
中華点々
2F
Tenten Chinese Restaurant
YOU REMINDED ME OF SOMETHING MY MASTER ALWAYS SAID.
"THE DEVIL HUNTERS THAT THE DEVILS FEAR MOST AREN'T THE STRONG OR THE BRAVE..."
"...THEY'RE AFRAID OF THE ONES WITH A FEW SCREWS LOOSE."
I THINK YOU'LL MANAGE TO LIVE FOR A LONG WHILE.
IS THAT SOME KIND OF INSULT?
IF YOU'RE NOT GONNA EAT THAT ALMOND TOFU, I'M TAKING IT.

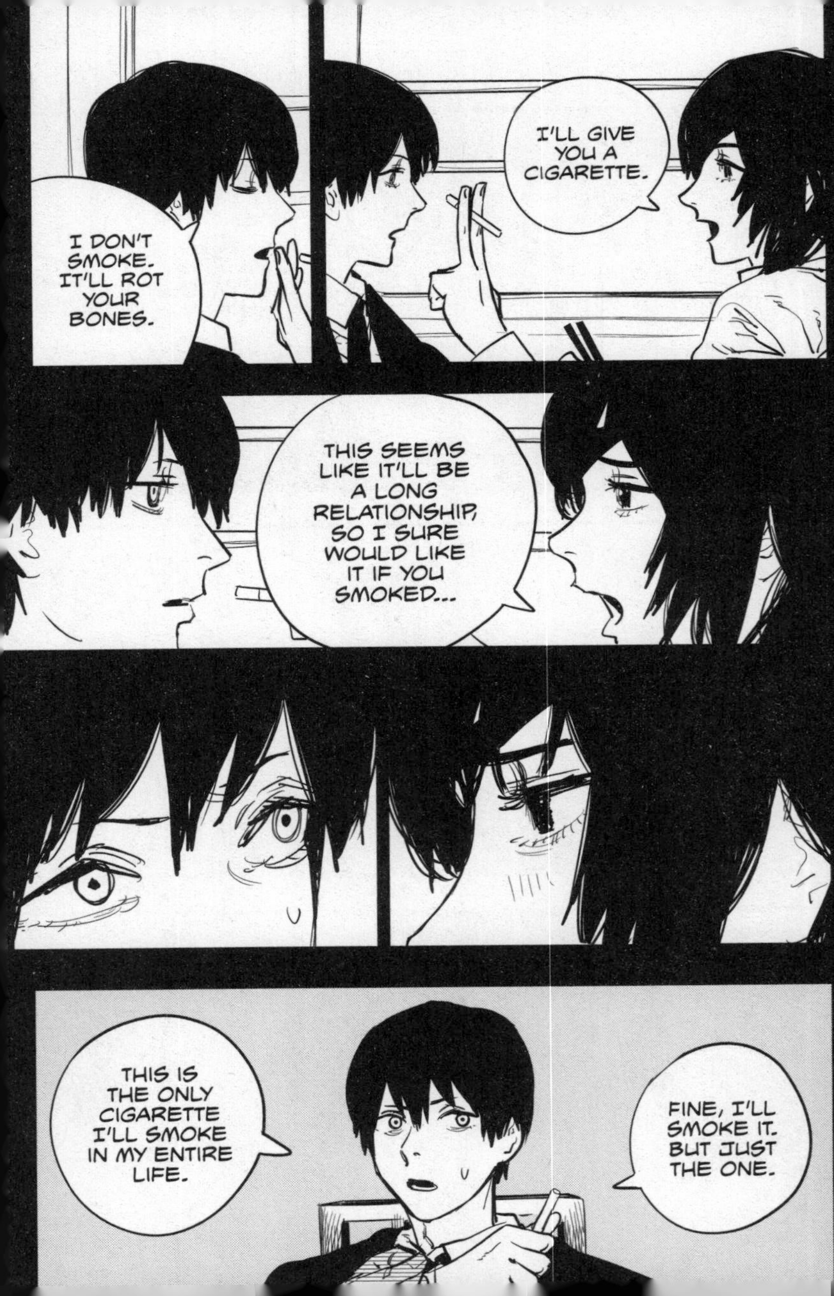
I'LL GIVE YOU A CIGARETTE.
I DON'T SMOKE. IT'LL ROT YOUR BONES.
THIS SEEMS LIKE IT'LL BE A LONG RELATIONSHIP, SO I SURE WOULD LIKE IT IF YOU SMOKED...
FINE, I'LL SMOKE IT. BUT JUST THE ONE.
THIS IS THE ONLY CIGARETTE I'LL SMOKE IN MY ENTIRE LIFE.

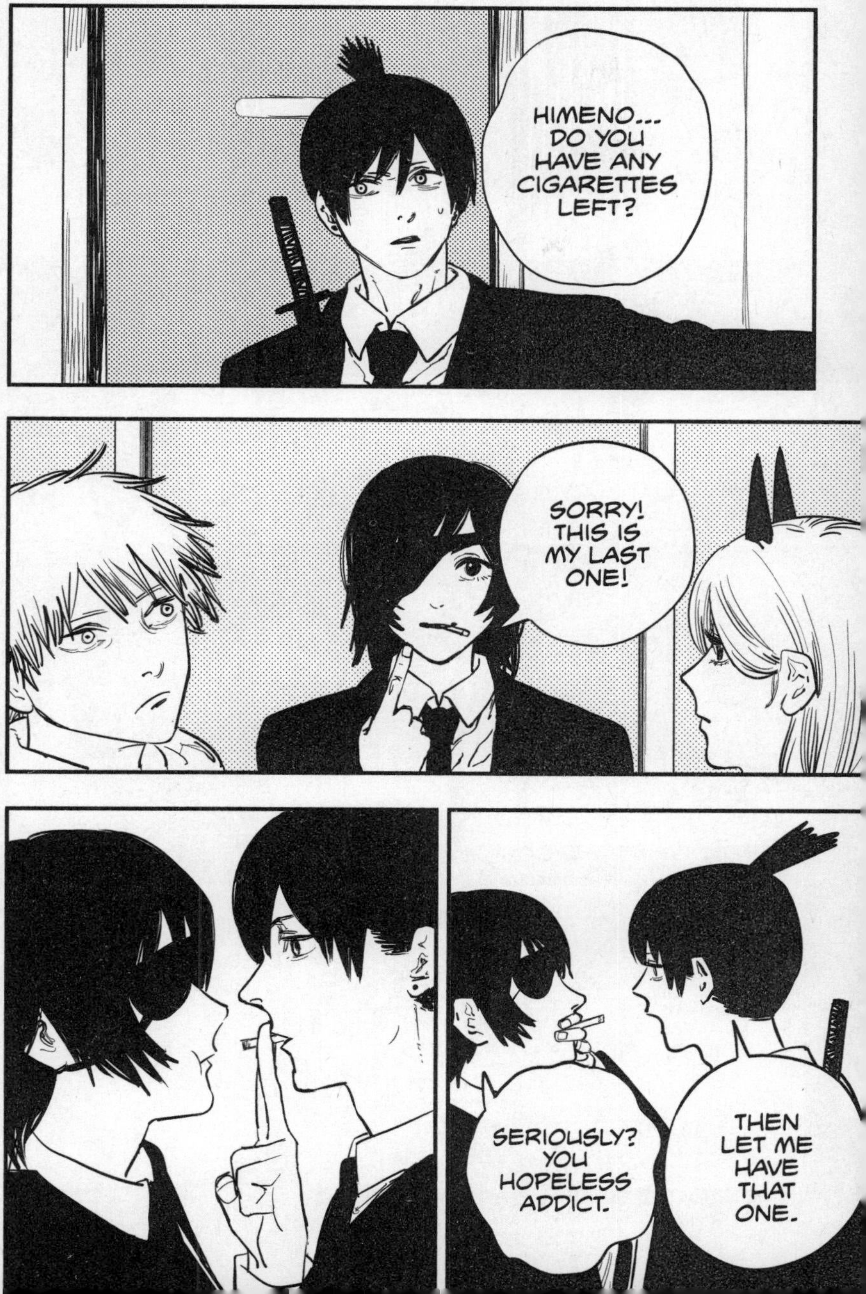
HIMENO... DO YOU HAVE ANY CIGARETTES LEFT?
SORRY! THIS IS MY LAST ONE!
SERIOUSLY? YOU HOPELESS ADDICT.
THEN LET ME HAVE THAT ONE.

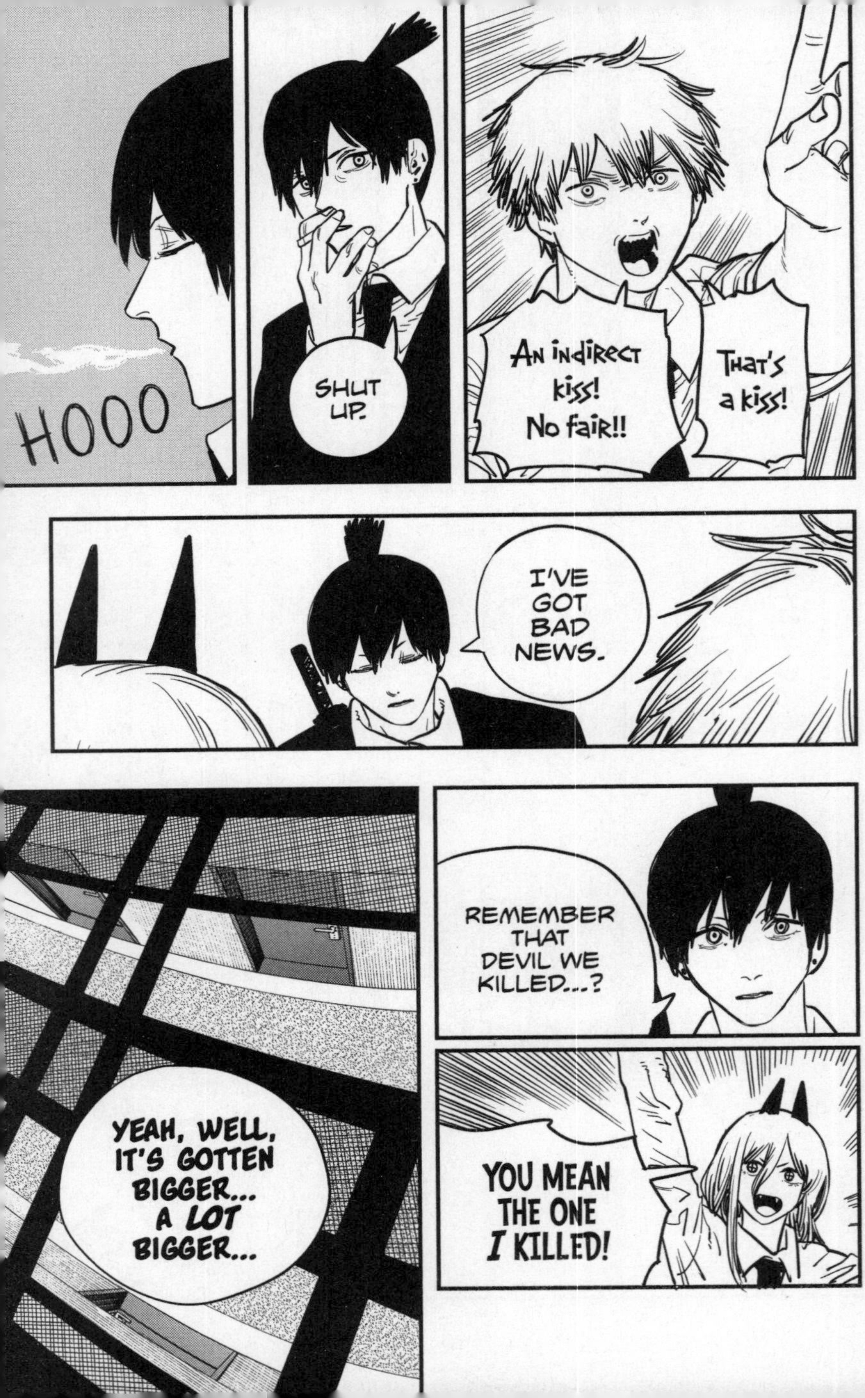
That's a kiss!
An indirect kiss! No fair!!
SHUT UP.
HOOO
I'VE GOT BAD NEWS.
REMEMBER THAT DEVIL WE KILLED...?
YOU MEAN THE ONE *I* KILLED!
YEAH, WELL, IT'S GOTTEN BIGGER... A *LOT* BIGGER...

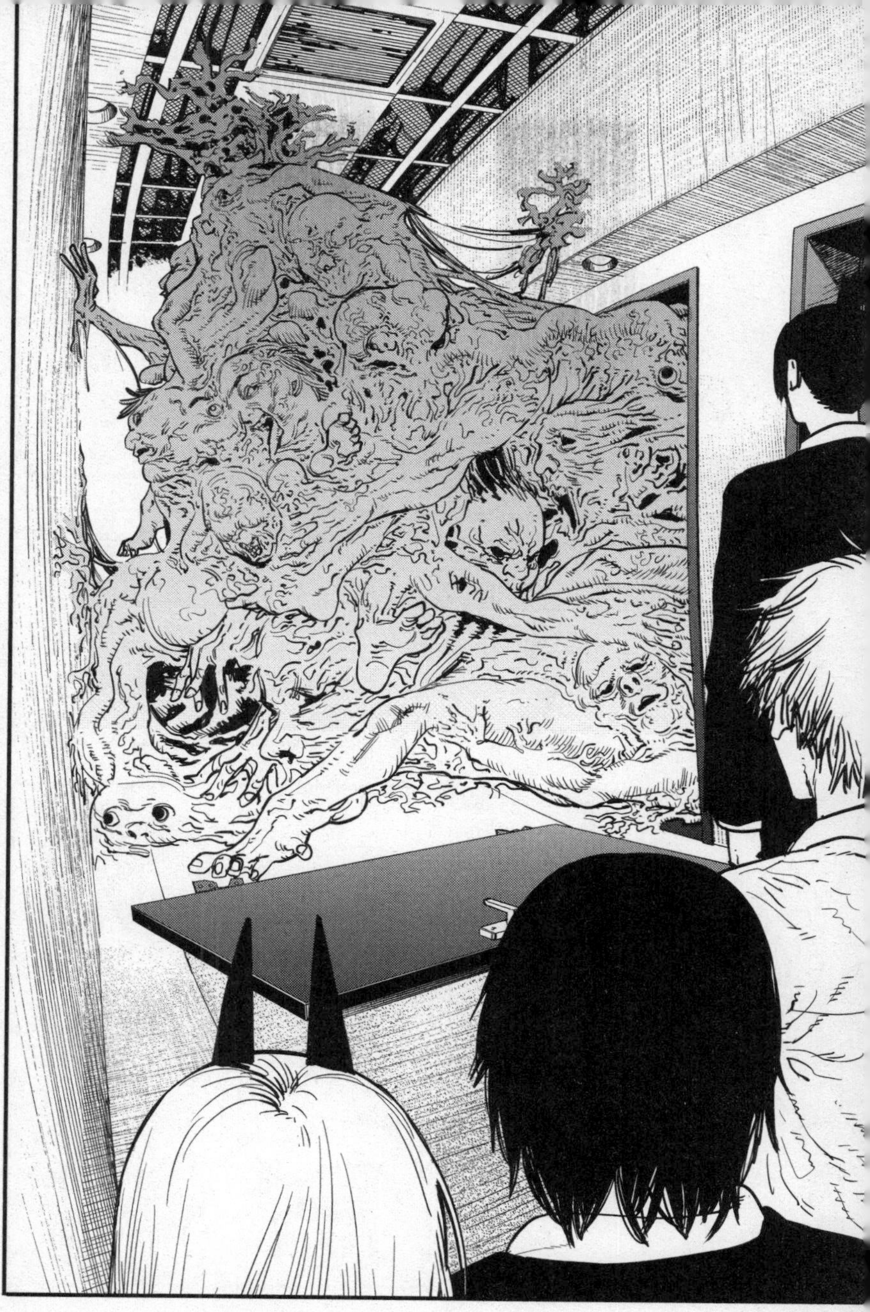

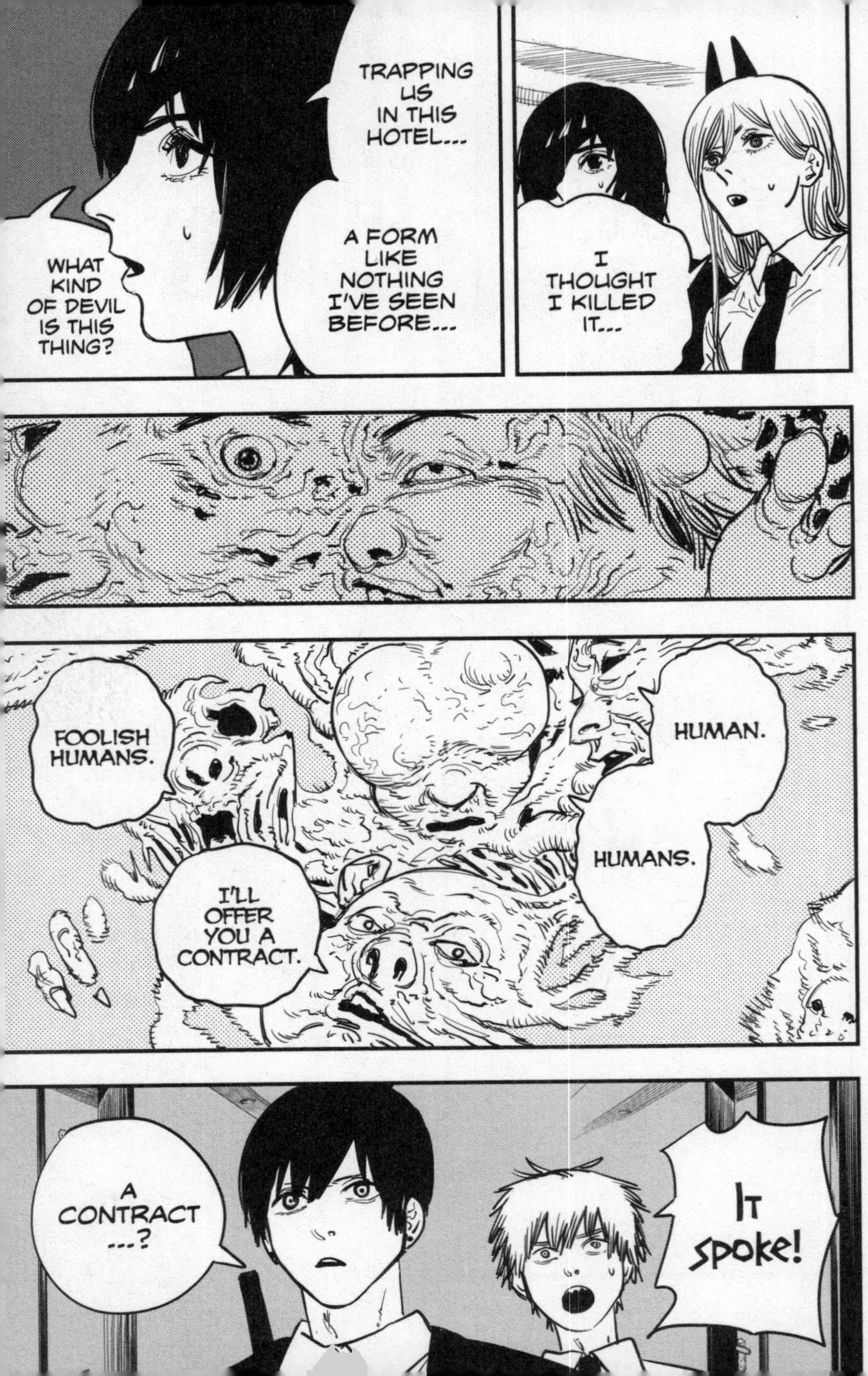
I THOUGHT I KILLED IT...
TRAPPING US IN THIS HOTEL...
A FORM LIKE NOTHING I'VE SEEN BEFORE...
WHAT KIND OF DEVIL IS THIS THING?
HUMAN.
FOOLISH HUMANS.
HUMANS.
I'LL OFFER YOU A CONTRACT.
It spoke!
A CONTRACT ...?

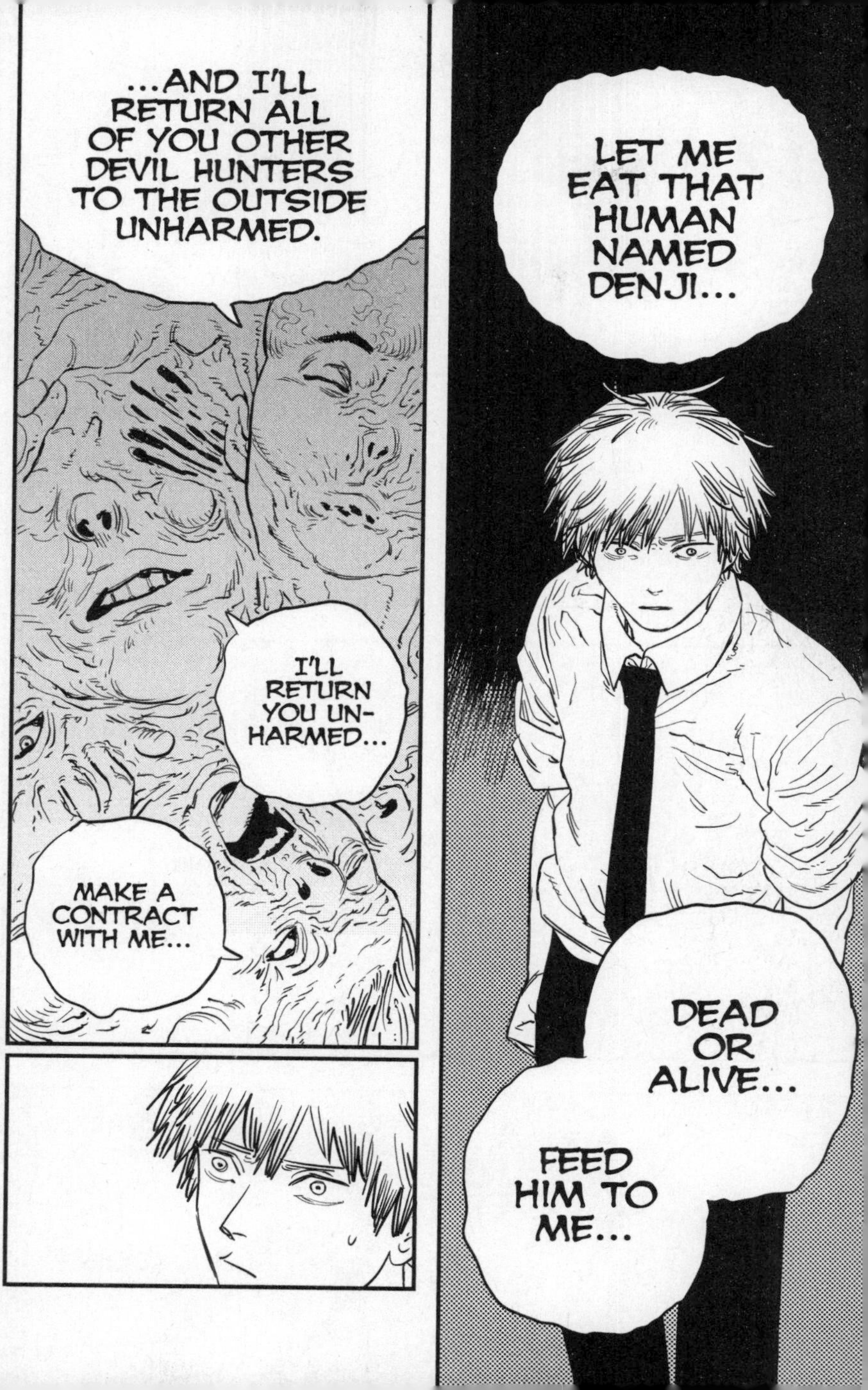
LET ME EAT THAT HUMAN NAMED DENJI...
DEAD OR ALIVE...
FEED HIM TO ME...
...AND I'LL RETURN ALL OF YOU OTHER DEVIL HUNTERS TO THE OUTSIDE UNHARMED.
I'LL RETURN YOU UN-HARMED...
MAKE A CONTRACT WITH ME...

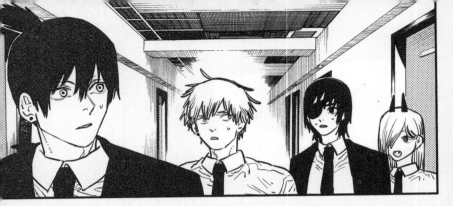

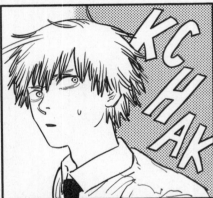

DENJI...

LET IT EAT YOU...

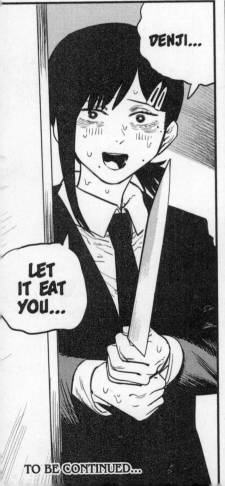

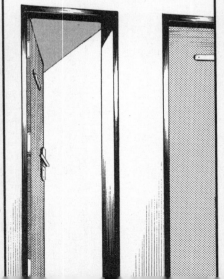

TO BE CONTINUED...

Chainsaw man

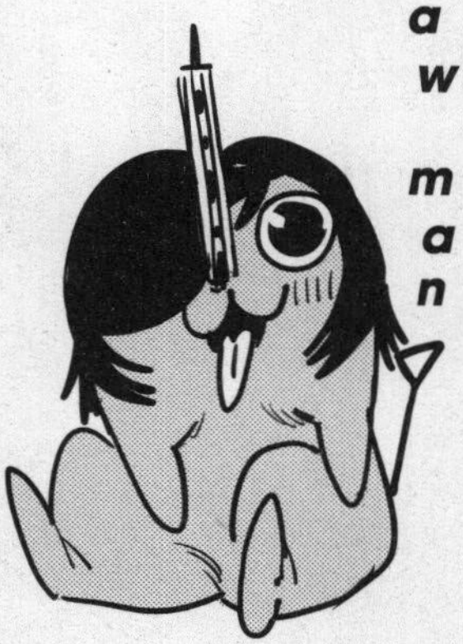